The Wallace Book

The Wallace Book

EDITED BY EDWARD J. COWAN

JOHN DONALD

First published in 2007 by John Donald, an imprint of Birlinn Ltd
West Newington House
10 Newington Road
Edinburgh EH9 1QS

www.birlinn.co.uk

ISBN 13: 978 1 906566 24 1

British Library Cataloguing-in-Publication Data
A catalogue record for this book is available from the British Library

Type design by Clare Crawford

Printed in Great Britain by The Cromwell Press Group, Trowbridge

Contents

Illustrations

1

William Wallace: 'The Choice of the Estates'

Edward J. Cowan

> At Wallace name what Scottish blood
> But boils up in a spring-tide flood!
> Oft have our fearless fathers strode
> By Wallace' side,
> Still pressed onward, red-wat shod [ankle deep in blood],
> Or glorious dy'd.
> *Robert Burns*

For 700 years William Wallace has been revered as the consummate, incomparable Scottish hero yet, remarkably for such a paragon, almost all that is known about him contemporaneously derives from enemy sources.[1] In English accounts he was public enemy or thief, 'a bloody man who was chief of brigands in Scotland',[2] but this was a man who was to initiate resistance against foreign occupation and who would lead the Scottish army to astonishing victory against the odds at Stirling Bridge. Following the battle, the supposed outlaw demonstrated his commercial acumen by informing German cities in the Hanseatic League that Scotland was once again open for business. As Guardian of the kingdom, he exhibited his not inconsiderable abilities in governance. It cannot be denied that bloodlust and hatred shaped his achievements as a warrior, but he was also a multilingual diplomat who was sent on embassies to France and Rome. In the anguish and painful hell of his brutal execution at Smithfield on 23 August 1305 he met his epiphany. Having lived, struggled and died, he entered the ranks of the immortals to become the stuff of legend and the greatest hero in all Scottish history.

The earliest Scottish narrative to cover the period of Wallace's career was *Gesta Annalia*,[3] incorporated in John of Fordun's Latin *Chronicle* compiled around 1370. Therein William rose from his 'den' to slay the English sheriff of Lanark; although the nobility regarded him as lowborn his father rejoiced in a knighthood. The hero won the great battle at Stirling Bridge, occupied the north of England and returned to defeat at Falkirk.[4] That disastrous outcome was allegedly attributable to none other than Robert Bruce, who attacked the Scots in the rear. 'It is remarkable that we seldom read of the Scots being overcome by the English, unless through the envy of lords, or the treachery and defeat of the natives.' It is also noteworthy that Fordun, who lived through the reign of Bruce's son, David II, should have incorporated such a claim, which lost nothing through repetition from generation to generation, and which would become absolutely central to the entire Wallace debate. William chose to resign as Guardian, preferring 'rather to serve with the crowd, than to be set over them to their ruin, and the grievous wasting of the people'. All Scotland, except Wallace, eventually submitted to Edward I.[5] Surrendered, or as many insist, 'betrayed', by Sir John Menteith, he was taken south to be torn limb from limb. It has recently been perceptively and convincingly suggested that part of the motivation for Edward's unseemly haste in the vicious despatch of Wallace was occasioned by the date, for 23 August was the eve of St Bartholomew's Fair at Smithfield to which, in 1305, his execution was a spectacular, and doubtless welcome, curtain-raiser,[6] made more poignant by the likelihood that St Bartholomew's Church was probably the last thing he saw on this earth.

The first vernacular account of the hero's exploits was presented in Andrew of Wyntoun's *Original Chronicle of Scotland* composed about 1420, in often tedious rhyming couplets. A run-in with the English led to the sheriff of Lanark killing Wallace's 'lemman', or mistress, whose death was duly avenged by her lover who swiftly became leader of the resistance. As in Fordun's account, he lost Falkirk through the treachery of Bruce and the Comyn faction. Supported by the leal commons of Scotland he had to live simply as an outlaw before his tragic end. According to Wyntoun, Wallace was worthy of a great book, a task for which he himself had neither the wit nor the leisure.[7]

The full-blown legend first appears in Walter Bower's *Scotichronicon*, written in the 1440s, which describes him as a tall man with the body of a giant, pleasing in appearance but with a wild look, broad in the hips, with strong arms and legs, a most spirited fighting man. 'God had distinguished him and his changing features with a certain good humour, had so blessed his words and deeds with a certain heavenly gift, that by his appearance alone he won over to himself the grace and favour of the hearts of all loyal Scots. And this is not surprising, for he was most liberal in his gifts, very fair in his judgments, most compassionate in comforting the sad, a most skilful counsellor, very patient when suffering, a distinguished speaker, who above all hunted down falsehood and deceit and detested treachery.'[8] He was, in short, a man successful in everything.

After Stirling Bridge he brought the English to heel, mounting devastating raids on Northumbria. 'Intoxicated by a stream of envy', however, the great ones of the kingdom plotted against Wallace's cause and the freedom of the country, although he retained the support of 'the ordinary folk and populace' and those nobles devoted to the public interest. Bower was emphatic that Wallace did not insinuate himself into a position of authority; rather (in a striking phrase) 'by the choice of the estates, he was raised up to be ruler, *eleccione statuum erigitur ad rectorem*, after the previously nominated guardians had been removed'. Bower was of course guilty of anachronism in this passage since the idea of the Three Estates, which comprised the Scottish parliament, was familiar to the fifteenth century but unknown to the thirteenth, yet what he was suggesting was that Wallace was the only man who was acceptable across a broad range of the social spectrum. For those who did not support Wallace, Bower had nothing but contempt tinged with regret. 'Why is covetous envy so much in control in Scotland?' asked the chronicler. 'How sad that it is natural for Scots to detest not only the happiness of other people, but also the happiness of their own countrymen.'[9] Complicity between Bruce and the Comyns led to Scottish defeat at Falkirk, after which Wallace abdicated as Guardian, choosing to throw in his lot with the common people. He stood for the liberty of his kingdom and would obey none but the king of Scots or his lieutenant. Indeed, he always consistently claimed to be acting in the name of the deposed King John (Balliol 1292–95), 'by God's grace illustrious king of Scotland, by the consent of the community of the realm'. Wallace was a committed monarchist; radical although he undoubtedly was, by no stretch of the imagination could he be described as a democrat or a republican. It is, however, remarkable, as well as diagnostic, that Bower, who strove to produce the 'page written in a firm fashion and unadorned, not bound with the knots of flowery eloquence', should have abandoned his own rules and objectives when confronted by the towering figure of Wallace. The latter's legend was as much a product of the chroniclers as it was of the poets. Three of the contributors to this volume explore the sources for Wallace's career in great detail. Fiona Watson, who has studied this period in considerable depth, lays out what historically is actually known about the hero. Archie Duncan, who has pondered these matters much longer than anyone else in the volume, presents an important analysis of the few surviving documents with which Wallace had a personal connection. Alexander Grant minutely and revealingly explores Wallace's career in a medieval context, while Michael Prestwich sagely examines Wallace's greatest victory from an English perspective.

The Wallace story acquired as much obfuscation as it did elaboration with the appearance, around 1478, of Hary's *Wallace*, pronounced by a recent editor 'the greatest single work of imagination in early Scots poetry'.[10] 'Imagination' is the key word here. Wallace as we now think of him is largely the creation of the writer popularly known as Blind Hary who, to judge from his colourful poetic descriptions, certainly did not suffer from lifelong blindness and whose first name may not even have been Hary. Furthermore, he purported to base his effusion upon a Latin work by Master Blair, a supposed contemporary of, and chaplain to, the hero, although in all probability neither Blair nor his book ever existed. Stirling Bridge does not occur until Book 7 of the twelve books that comprise the poem, the first six being occupied with various fights and battles with the English, climaxing in the slaughter of Wallace's wife, said to have been a daughter of Hew Braidfute of Lamington in Lanarkshire. In general, Wallace's activities were greatly elaborated by Hary, who also inserted additional battles (such as that at Biggar) for his hero to win, or English atrocities (such as the Barns of Ayr episode) for Wallace to revenge. Neither Hary nor any of the other medieval commentators made any bones about the fact that Wallace was utterly ruthless in his treatment of the English and recalcitrant Scots. No one pretended that he was other than a man of blood and, indeed, they were rather impressed by that side of his character. Felicity Riddy considers the poem in the context of, and as part of, late fifteenth-century Scottish medieval literary production, which manifests something of a renaissance, but she also asks why Hary's work remained so central to the Scottish popular tradition for so long. A book about Wallace may not be the obvious place to expect a contribution on philosophy, but Alexander Broadie, with characteristic learning, explores the search for independence which tantalisingly, if tenuously, links the careers of Duns Scotus and Wallace.

The later fifteenth century was apparently a period when the search for heroes was widespread. In England William Caxton published Malory's *Le Morte D'Arthur* (1485), a prose work that, notably in the extended passages about warfare, recalls *The Wallace*. Malory's Blaise resembles Hary's Blair. It is possible that Wallace was conceived, at least in part, as a sort of Scottish answer to Arthur. It is also of interest that the legend of William Tell was being concocted during the same decade in which Hary wrote. Scotland in the 1470s clearly needed a hero in common with other places in Europe. Hary obliged, placing not only his contemporaries, but posterity, in his debt. Many critics and pundits over the centuries have desperately, but erroneously, wanted to believe that *The Wallace* preserves historically verifiable material. While he undoubtedly drew on traditional materials such as ballads and folk tales, Hary's achievement was to create an unhistorical character who has survived intact into the twenty-first century as a man of destiny.

Meanwhile, historians continued to discover Wallace, his exploits inspiring even the least inspired of them to heights of rhetoric of which perhaps they did not suspect themselves to be capable. John Mair was a great admirer but because of his innate Latinate superiority and snobbery he was less enthusiastic about Henry the (blind) minstrel who, he claimed, 'used to recite his tales in the households of nobles, and thereby got the food and clothing he deserved'. However, he regarded Wallace as wise, prudent and possessed of a loftiness of aim that allowed him to win over some of the nobility and gained the 'universal acclamation of the common people'.[11] George Buchanan, another great humanist, regarded Wallace as one who could be compared to the greatest leaders of antiquity. 'In love of his country he was inferior to none of the most eminent ancient patriots, amid the general slavery he stood alone unsubdued and free, and neither could rewards induce, nor terrors force him to desert the public cause.'[12] Writing his introduction to a version of *The Wallace* in 1594, Henrie Charteris denied that the story would simply stir up remembrance of ancient hostilities, protesting that he intended only to inspire all men 'to the defence of their native realme and common welth'. He was impressed that God, in his wisdom, chose 'ane man of simple blude' rather than a prince or a nobleman for the task. He also attempted to turn Wallace into a protestant and Blair into a minister![13] In general there was in post-Reformation Scotland, at least of the sixteenth and seventeenth centuries, a certain lack of interest in medieval Scotland because of its association with the papacy. Nor did Enlightenment historians detect much of value in the Middle Ages although William Robertson, Scotland's greatest eighteenth-century historian, was somewhat smitten by Wallace, asserting that while his valour, integrity and wisdom were such as not to require 'the heightenings of fiction', yet the admiration of his countrymen ascribed many tales of his prowess.[14] David Hume considered that his deeds had been much exaggerated but nonetheless conceded that with intrepidity and perseverance Wallace had defended the liberties of his native country against an oppressive enemy.[15] In the view of John Hill Burton, Wallace was quite simply 'a man of vast political and military genius' but so profuse were the claims and descriptions of earlier romancers that 'part of their eulogy has stuck to history'; like so many nineteenth-century writers, he set himself the task of separating fact from fable,[16] a pathway that several would follow in successive years, including A. F. Murison (1898) and James Fergusson (1938).

Hary's poem was one of the first books, issued by Chepman and Myller, Scotland's first printers, between 1508 and 1510. There were 23 editions of the poem before 1707 with a further 47 being produced in the period down to 1913 although that number could now be extended. The democratic predilections of the Scots are perhaps reflected in the fact that, during the period 1508–1800, there were 37 printings of *Wallace* compared with 12 of John Barbour's *The Bruce*; twelve *Wallaces* appeared between 1700 and 1750, compared with one *Bruce*.[17] It truly was the book, next to the Bible, most frequently found in Scottish households,[18] reprinted at many of the major crisis points in Scottish history, such as the Reformation in 1560, the Union of the Crowns in 1603, the Covenanting Revolution in 1638, the Restoration in 1660, the so-called Glorious Revolution of 1689, the Union of 1707 and the Jacobite Rising in 1745. Wallace, the man and the book, was a crutch for which folk reached in times of uncertainty and strife. Copies sold far outnumbered those of *The Bruce*, upon which *The Wallace* was clearly in part modelled.

James Hogg, the Ettrick Shepherd, first encountered *The Wallace* when he was eighteen although he regretted that it was not in prose, that everybody might have understood it.[19] In fact, the problem of Hary's language had been addressed by William Hamilton of Gilbertfield, who produced at Glasgow in 1722 *The Life and Heroic Actions of Sir William Wallace*, a poetic modernisation of the text, 'wherein the Old obsolete Words are rendered more Intelligible; and adapted to the understanding of such who have not leisure to study the Meaning and Import of such Phrases without the help of a Glossary'. This was the version that, famously and self-confessedly, 'poured a Scottish prejudice' into the veins of Robert Burns, which would 'boil along there till the flood-gates of life shut in eternal rest', sentiments expressed in the letter that contained the first version of 'Scots Wha Hae'. Virtually every literate Scot was familiar with Blind Hary or a version of his work.

Many readers must have discovered Wallace through the medium of chapbooks, which sold in their hundreds of thousands, for the folk at large a source of information all too often ignored by scholars, who seem fixated upon manuscripts or expensive printed texts to which the public was hardly ever permitted access. It is instructive, in attempting to discern the flavour and tone of such chaps, to consider just one example from the extensive collection in Glasgow University Library, *History of Sir William Wallace the Renowned Scottish Champion*, printed in Glasgow (although undated) probably *c.* 1830; like the great majority of chapbooks, it attributes neither author nor publisher. This prose version is suitably patriotic in tone and makes no bones about English cruelty and oppression. So deeply inculcated was the feeling of national resentment generated by the invaders that it overcame the hero's 'scruples of a temper which was naturally humane', a convenient way of excusing Wallace's notorious, anglophobic bloodlust. As in some earlier accounts, the chap is almost two-thirds done before Wallace triumphs at Stirling Bridge.

The language does not exactly pander to the readership, for the text is liberally sprinkled with polysyllabic words that it is difficult to believe were in everyday use – insolence, contemptuous, facilitating, apprehension, sanguinary, and, 'dastardly and perfidious barons'. Hary includes a fictional incident at the magnificently situated Dunnottar Castle, high above the sea, in which the defeated are described as follows:

> Sum hang on craggis rycht dulfully to de,
> Sum lap, sum fell, sum floteryt in the se,[20]

rendered by Hamilton:

> Some hung on craigs, and loath were to die.
> Some lap, some fell, some flutter'd in the sea.[21]

The Glasgow chapbook relates that some 'threw themselves from the precipice into the sea, and swam along to the cliffs, where they hung like sea-fowl, screaming in vain for mercy and assistance'. The latter passage, which is borrowed from none other than Walter Scott,[22] is certainly an improvement on the original, but whoever composed the chapbook was not wholly dependent upon 'The Wizard of the North'.

An episode that Scott characteristically and completely ignored was the vexed question of how Wallace the great victor at Stirling Bridge could have been so overwhelmingly defeated at Falkirk. In describing the aftermath of the latter battle the chapbook is firmly in the medieval tradition:

> The rout was now becoming universal, when Wallace, collecting the shattered remains of his forces, commenced a retreat across the Carron,—a movement which, by his precaution caused little loss.—Among those who most eagerly pressed on their rear was Bruce, who on this occasion had again leagued himself with the English. Exasperated at the sight of this selfish traitor, Wallace suddenly darted forward, and with his two-handed sword dealt him a blow, which, though it missed Bruce's head, was yet aimed with such prodigious strength as to cleave his horse to the ground. With Sir Brian le Jay, a knight-templar of high military renown, the Scottish hero was more successful. With a single blow of his battleaxe he laid him dead in the midst of his followers.
>
> Wallace now retreated across the Forth. But previous to this movement, and while wandering on the banks of the Carron, Wallace was recognised by the misguided Bruce, who descried him from the opposite bank, and, with the view perhaps of justifying his own dastardly conduct, ascribed to him ambitious motives, in his opposition to the English. 'No', said Wallace, 'my thoughts never soared so high; I only mean to deliver my country from oppression and slavery, and to support a cause which you and others have abandoned. If you have but the heart, you may yet win a crown with glory, and wear it with justice. I can do neither: but will—live and die a free born subject'.[23]

In the nineteenth century the purchase of a chapbook containing such sentiments could be seen as a patriotic act, not to mention a reinforcement of political prejudice.

Walter Scott deplored the treatment of Wallace in Jane Porter's *The Scottish Chiefs* (1810) – 'It is not safe meddling with the hero of a country and of all others I cannot endure to see the character of Wallace frittered away to that of a fine gentleman'.[24] It is a matter of mystery and regret that Scott almost totally neglected the whole period of the Wars of Independence in the vast corpus of his literary production. He deplored the mighty statue of Wallace erected in 1814 at Dryburgh by the eccentric eleventh Earl of Buchan and designed by a local self-taught sculptor, John Smith. Since Buchan was a great admirer of both the American and the French revolutions it is perhaps no coincidence that Wallace's garb is somewhat reminiscent of that of old Gaul, thus further cementing the hero's reputation as a pioneer of freedom. The impressive monument still stands, twenty-one and a half feet high, mounted on top of a hill above the Tweed and 'frowning towards England'. The quotation on the plinth from James Thomson's *Seasons* is the same as that which came into Burns' mind when referring to Wallace in a letter to Anna Dunlop of 1786 – 'Great Patriot hero! ill-requited Chief'.[25] As James Coleman demonstrates in his stimulating contribution to this volume, the nineteenth century was to become the great age of monuments, that to Wallace being erected on Abbey Craig at Stirling between 1861 and 1869 on a site that, it was anticipated, would become a metaphor for Scotland itself, 'a centre of Scottish nationality'.[26] The monument movement also inspired a considerable amount of publication on Wallace, some of it helpful and much of it dire.

Lord Rosebery, statesman, imperialist, briefly Liberal Prime Minister (1894–95) and noted patriot, had a habit of publishing his after-dinner speeches and addresses. He once perceptively referred to 'the class of minute archaeological historians who would find a savage, an almost devilish delight in winnowing the true from the false in the legends that surround Sir William Wallace, and in distinguishing all that is legendary from the few golden facts which remain'.[27] In point of fact, much nineteenth-century writing on Wallace sought to prove the authenticity of Blind Hary; furthermore, a great deal of such biographical production was produced by people who would be best described as amateur historians, who sought to recover the 'true' history of Wallace's career and who were severely critical of those writers who depended almost exclusively upon sources in Latin (as opposed to the vernacular of Hary), and who, even more deplorably, favoured evidence drawn mainly from the enemy.

John Donald Carrick was the first to produce a serious and extensive biography of Wallace. Born in Glasgow, Carrick (1787–1837) was himself a writer of broadsides who later became editor of the popular and much loved *Whistle-binkie* collections of Scottish songs and poetry.[28] This self-appointed reclaimer of the folk-history of William Wallace, thus, at one level at least, had excellent credentials for the task: 'we do not see that a great falsehood, told in the classical language of ancient Rome, should be entitled to a larger portion of public faith than a lesser one set forth in the more modern *patois* of Scotland'.[29] In post-Ossianic Scotland there was a considerable body of opinion that had little doubt that the nation's history was preserved intact by the vernacular voice. Carrick disapprovingly quotes Lord Hailes for describing Hary as 'an author whom every historian copies, yet no historian but Sir Robert Sibbald will venture to quote', a reference to Sibbald's *Relationes quaedam Arnaldi Blair, Monachi de Dunfermeleni, et Cappellani, D. Wüllelmi Wallas Militis* (Edinburgh 1705), which consists large-ly of quotations from Fordun. Although Hailes, who has some claim to be regarded as Scotland's first true medievalist, loftily dismisses Hary as 'an author who either knew not history or who meant to falsify it', he was nevertheless hugely impressed by Wallace. There is genuine pathos in his concluding statement on the Champion's career:

> Thus perished Wallace, whom Edward could never subdue. In his last moments, he asserted that independency which a whole nation had renounced. It is singular that Edward should have pardoned, favoured, and even trusted, the persons who had often made, and as often violated, their oaths of obedience; while the man who never acknowledged his sovereignty fell, the single victim of his resentment.[30]

Hailes' insistence upon sound historical method did not blind him to patri-otic heroism.

Several writers were to follow Carrick, whose book remained phenome-nally popular throughout the century, in largely rehashing Hary. One such was James Paterson who in 1858 produced *Wallace and His Times*, later issued in a third edition as *Wallace The Hero of Scotland* (1881). Although crit-ical of Carrick, Paterson shared the former's contempt for supposed schol-arly disparagement of the vulgar. Because Hary 'became the instructor of the people in all that related to their much-venerated martyr to freedom, the learned must forsooth doubt the facts so patent to the unlettered'. Paterson was completely convinced of Hary's accuracy, modestly suggest-ing that his own efforts might be regarded 'somewhat in the light of a national service', as he, 'with fearless hand', attempted to 'transfuse the poetical narrative of the Minstrel into prose'.[31]

Also in 1858, Thomas Smith Hutcheson anonymously published his *Life of Sir William Wallace or, Scotland Five Hundred Years Ago* at Glasgow, a work inspired by the National Monument movement but which opens with a eulogy of the Barnweill Monument in Craigie parish, Ayr, built in 1855. The book was intended as 'a faithful narrative, compiled from the highest authorities, and adapted for universal appreciation, being free from the many antiquarian references which encumber the greater portion of former biographies, [tending] greatly to distract the general reader's attention'. Hutcheson was convinced that if all existing accounts of the hero were destroyed it may be said 'of Wallace as of Burns that . . . a biography as complete as any extant could easily be written from the memories of his countrymen'. In his view Wallace was, quite simply and incontrovertibly, 'the most perfect model of the Patriot Hero the world has ever beheld'.[32] Hutcheson helpfully appended a *Bibliotheca Wallasiana*, which clearly demonstrates that between 1799 and 1858 the majority of Wallace items appeared as poetry, plays or fiction, suggesting perhaps that the Guardian was more of a literary than an historical phenomenon.

One other publication often overlooked or underrated was William Burns' enjoyable, monument-inspired study of the Scottish War of Independence, which discussed Bruce as well as Wallace. He was motivated by comments on either side of the debate, ranging from those who thought no monument was necessary because Wallace already had, and would always have, 'a monument in every Scottish heart, an altar at every Scottish hearth'; others regarded Wallace as 'a mythical personage, not susceptible of identification', like Arthur, Merlin or Odin, 'of whom so much old romance, and modern nonsense had been uttered, that cautious people were apt to shun his name in history'.[33] Burns was interested in how national distinctions evolved and in such questions as whether certain places were possessed of an historical atmosphere. For example, he wonders if there was some atmospheric connection in the west of Scotland between Wallace and the Covenanters. What made him hilariously apoplectic were the remarks on Scottish history by biased (and ignorant) English commentators. Almost worse were Scotland's own historians with whom he engaged in almost equal measures of polemic to those lavished on wrong-headed English writers. Burns did not pretend to original research but did achieve a reasonably even-handed treatment of material available in print, at least until his rather overblown final chapter on the effects of the wars.

It is noteworthy that there was something of a flurry of activity in the production of literary *Wallasiana* around 1810. In that year Miss Holford's *Wallace; or, the Fight of Falkirk: a Metrical Romance* went into a second edition. She may have had her English audience in mind in fixing upon one of the most dismal episodes in Wallace's career, which was neither poetic nor romantic since, from their perspective, a victory over a warrior believed to be invincible was truly a triumph. The author at least displays the virtue of realising that Falkirk was not all down to Wallace as she provides pen por-

traits of other combatants on the Scottish side where, once again, aristocratic envy, particularly on the part of the dastardly John Comyn, con-
tributes to the defeat. Wallace is introduced as being as patriotic as he is
stoic, and we know that his unique qualities will enable him to survive the
disaster at Falkirk just as they will strengthen him during the final horror at
Smithfield, conveniently foreseen courtesy of the muse:

> Oh, Wallace! Thy bold unruffled brow
> Speaks the calm of a noble mind;
> Thou hast drunk of the wave at the ebb and flow,
> Thou stand'st like an oak, while tempests blow,
> Unbent by the wavering wind!
> 'Mid the bursting flame, or the midnight flood,
> 'Mid horror's wildest scene,
> When the brooks of thy country are swollen with blood,
> Unshaken, thy soul still holds her mood,
> And thy brow is still serene!
> In the heat of destruction's fatal day
> Thy cheek it wax'd not pale,
> Though the soul of a friend still flitted away
> On every passing gale;
> Nor on their heads, how dear soe'er,
> Dropp'd from thine eye one funeral tear,
> Nor heav'd thy heart one farewell sigh,
> As the soldier met his destiny;
> Nor private joy nor grief he knows,
> Whose bosom is fill'd with his country's woes![34]

1810 was also, of course, the year in which Jane Porter's pioneering *The
Scottish Chiefs* was published, an important contribution to the developing
genre of the historical novel and four years ahead of Scott's *Waverley*. That
same year Lachlan Macquarie was settling in as Governor of New South
Wales. On a visit to Tasmania in 1811, he dubbed a 'wild romantic' spot on
the North Esk River, 'Corri-Linn Cascade, so named by me in honor of the
Patriot Chief of Scotland'.[35] It may be thought that to invoke the freedom-
loving Wallace in Van Diemen's Land, the mainly white population of
which consisted of convicts, was somewhat rash on the part of a crown ser-
vant. Corra Linn was where Wallace was hiding when he learned of the
death of his wife in Chapter 4 of *The Scottish Chiefs*. Macquarie, however,
was probably indebted to William Wordsworth rather than Jane Porter or
Henry the Minstrel, specifically by his 'Lines Composed at Cora Linn in
Sight of Wallace's Tower', inspired by his visit to the Falls of Clyde with his

sister Dorothy in 1803. Australia did not forget Wallace whose statue, endowed by Scottish miner James Russell Thomson of Airdrie who died in 1886, was erected in Ballarat Botanic Gardens. The statue, unveiled in 1889, was modelled on the physique of Donald Dinnie, 'Scotland's Greatest Athlete', from Deeside, Aberdeenshire, who happened to be resident in Melbourne at that time.[36] The inscription by Francis Lauderdale Adams:

> O Wallace, peerless lover of thy land
> We need thee still, thy moulding brain and hand.
> For us, thy poor, again proud tyrants spurn,
> The robber rich, a yet more hateful band[37]

represents grim verse that nonetheless has a particular resonance in view of the revolt at the Eureka Stockade in 1854, an iconic moment on the road to the Australian self-image of egalitarianism and an event that was ironically caused in part by the un-Wallace-like naked opportunism and greed of another Scot, David Armstrong.[38]

Wallace continued, and continues, to be much celebrated in verse. As well as Burns, Robert Southey, Robert Tannahill, John Jamieson and the indefatigable William McGonagall were moved by the muse, while modern poets still find Wallace an attractive theme. Perhaps inspired by Thomas Campbell's 'the sword that seemed fit for archangel to wield, / Was light in his terrible hand', William Freeland produced the rather questionable *The Sword of Wallace*:

> Great was the day that my maker dipped my steel in sacred fire,
> And forged me with hammer and anvil that rang like a freeman's lyre;
> When my future chief stood o'er me and saw me tempered well
> To the music of the Minstrel who gave me the battle-spell.
> Ah! then I leapt into being in my glorious master's hand,
> And he whirled me aloft and kissed me and called me his holy brand.
>
> Yea, holy I was, like Wallace, whose lofty and godlike mind
> Dreamed ever with me of Freedom and the weal of kith and kind.
> We loved each other like lovers, and living side by side,
> He fondled me like a husband, I thrilled to him like a bride;
> And often in secret he grasped me, and swore by the Holy Rood
> To strike, not for England's evil, but only for Scotland's good.[39]

Freeland was the instigator and main inspiration behind the campaign that would result in the creation of the Chair of Scottish History and Literature at the University of Glasgow.[40]

Elspeth King has made extensive studies of the entire Wallace phenomenon, turning the Smith Gallery at Stirling into a moving shrine to the hero in the process.[41] Here, she comprehensively surveys the material culture of Wallace, the majority of which she has been personally responsible for unearthing. That there was also an English cult of Wallace may surprise some, but Colin Kidd magisterially demonstrates its existence and the impact thereof upon the matter of nineteenth-century Britain. David Caldwell courageously scrutinises the Wallace Sword in search of imprinting by the hero to reach a judicious conclusion that is far from negative. Richard Finlay, the leading historian of twentieth-century Scotland, investigates the creation of a nationalist icon. Lizanne Henderson appends a select bibliography of *Wallasiana*, somewhat reduced for reasons of space. She gratefully acknowledges, as does the editor, the financial assistance of the University of Glasgow's History department in the preparation of this bibliography.

W. Barrymore's play, *Wallace* (1817), has the hero's execution take place off stage while his wife runs around screaming as she supposedly observes him being hanged, drawn and quartered. Professor Robert Buchanan, later in the century, wrote plays that were not intended to be performed. His Wallace is led off to execution while Edward I remains behind, stunned and morally defeated, while the Scottish nobles are appropriately inspired to draw freedom's sword.[42] Another play that might be cited among literally dozens on the theme is Charles Waddie's *Wallace or The Battle of Stirling Bridge*, which was written in the 1850s but which had still not found a producer by 1890. Couched in cod-Shakespearean blank verse, the play contrasts Wallace's pure unselfish struggle for freedom with the self-interest and jealous disaffection of the Scottish aristocracy, one of whom describes the patriot's campaign as a 'servile rising':

> Our glorious freedom hath endured so long, –
> From Fergus unto Alexander's death;
> That, like the channel of a mighty stream,
> The disposition of the land is fixed
> And moulded with the current of the wave.
> Nor till as many generations pass
> Of crouching slaves can nature be subdued.[43]

One of the most successful Wallace plays ever written was probably that by Sydney Goodsir Smith, first produced at the Edinburgh Festival in 1960, originating as a radio broadcast the previous year. At the stage production, in the trial scene, the exchange between Edward I and Wallace concerning the Stone of Scone brought a cheering audience to its feet. Wallace predicts that within a year a new king (meaning Bruce) will be inaugurated at Scone, to which Edward retorts that prophecy asserts that whoever sits on the stone shall rule the Scots and since it is now at Westminster that means himself. 'The Stane ye hae / Is no the richt Stane, as weill ye ken', cries Wallace; what the prediction actually states is that the Scots will rule where the stone is situated![44] Therefore, Scotland will ultimately triumph in London! The 1985 revival did not generate quite the same enthusiastic response, and the play, which contains some powerfully written passages, has certainly not been performed as often as it deserves. As one of the epigraphs to the text, Smith printed a brief quote from a leading article on the Nuremberg trials and executions that appeared in the *Manchester Guardian*, 16 October 1946, – 'Could any Englishman doubt that justice was done, if brutally, when Wallace was executed?'

When Alexander Brunton of Inverkeithing printed a sixteenth-century English version of the Wallace story in 1881, he took the opportunity to include a few appendices designed to refute some of the more idiotic allegations (as he believed) of historians. Like Carrick and Paterson, he deplored the assertion of John Mair that Latin sources were preferable to vernacular accounts; like them, he thought that Hary's version was superior to any other, challenging even the well-disposed Hutcheson for misrepresenting the poet. He refuted statements in a number of English sources on the grounds that 'it is injudicious to expect a just and fair account of any man's character from his enemies'. Brunton wrote as a sort of no-nonsense Scottish commercial man who measured, quantified and tested everything, distrustful of the academic approach of published historians and reliant upon his own common sense in the solution of historical problems. He was of a type that formed the backbone of Victorian Britain; his successors still feed the correspondence columns of *The Herald* and *Scotsman* newspapers, and historians, as well as Scotland as a whole, are the richer for their contributions, since Scottish history is much too important to be left to the historians.

Brunton's approach is best brought out in his discussion of Stirling Bridge. He attempts to calculate how many English troops could have crossed the bridge on the basis of at least one chronicler's assertion that two horsemen could ride side by side, a space that would permit three infantry to march abreast. He calculates that, marching at three miles an hour, 15,840 troops could have crossed per hour; however, since he believed the bridge to be twice as wide as reported, then he reckoned 31,680 per hour could have crossed and, potentially, even using the more conservative estimate, marching from earliest dawn until 11a.m., 102,960 could have reached the north end of the bridge!

He next tackles the matter of the flaying of Cressingham, an episode that had already caused Lord Hailes some amusement. Brunton points out that all the sources that mention the different variations of this atrocity are English and all disagree as to the articles manufactured out of the epidermis:

> One says into 'saddles', another into 'girths for horses', a third 'into a sword belt', a fourth writer says that 'they cut the skin into small fragments', while a fifth writer declares that his skin 'was converted into thongs'. If the skin was made into saddles, it could not be made into the four other articles. If it was cut into small fragments, how could it be converted into saddles and all the other things? If converted into girths for horse, all the rest cannot be true.

Furthermore, Brunton questions how many Scots would have been involved in flaying the victim since three or four persons could not work on the body at once. Why on earth would they wish to use such material when there were plenty of others, such as the hides of slaughtered horses, to hand? If they were busily pursuing the vanquished how could they stop to indulge in such a practice? How could fleeing Englishmen look behind them to see the atrocity in progress? The tanning and fitting of skin for manufacture is such a lengthy process that all Englishmen must have quit Scotland before it was completed. In short, the episode never happened.[45] Brunton has plenty more to say but, most importantly, he provides English translations of a number of documents. He represents the type of Scot who, having supported and paid for the building of the National Monument, now demanded some ownership of Wallace's history as well and who further democratised Scottish historiography in the process. In their story, the singer was almost as important as the song. Hary seemed as much one of themselves as Robert Burns, and what both poets offered was identity, recognition and pride in their own self-worth.

There is still some support for the view that Hary must preserve some genuine historical material, as indeed he probably does, but one person's wheat is another's chaff and separation is always extremely difficult where any source that was once in oral circulation is concerned. The ballads could be cited as a parallel. That said, it is surprising that hardly any ballads about the hero have survived, *Gude Wallace* being a rare example. Is it possible that Hary subverted the need for ballads by incorporating most of those that existed in his own day into his text? Many current historians (even one or two in this volume!) are reluctant to completely abandon Hary. The populist tradition survives in *Braveheart*, the movie the script of which Randall Wallace derived from Hary, via Hamilton of Gilbertfield. Hary is also the inspiration for most of the 'historical' material in James Mackay's opportunistic *William Wallace Braveheart* (1995), which unconsciously demonstrates the worthlessness of such an approach. The modern folklore spawned by the movie is adequately, if inadvertently, indicated in Lin Anderson's hope-lessly overstated essay.[46]

What is striking is that for 700 years Scots have been discussing the Wallace phenomenon and the nature of commoners and kings, of virtue and nobility, of patriotism and commitment. It is a remarkable fact that almost every single commentator from the fourteenth century to the end of the nineteenth discusses a fictional meeting between Wallace and Bruce on opposite banks of the Carron following the defeat at Falkirk. Bruce suppos-edly asks Wallace why he defied the might of Edward I while rejecting the advice of the Scottish nobility, to be told:

> When I saw my countrymen, through your inactivity, destitute of leaders, subjected by a barbarous enemy, not to slavery only, but to butchery, I pitied their situation, and undertook the cause you had deserted; and their liberty, fortune, and safety I will never forsake, till life leave me. You, to whom ignominious slavery with security is dearer than honourable liber-ty with danger, embrace the fortune you so much admire. I, in the coun-try which I have so often defended, shall live free, or freely die; nor shall my affection leave me, but with my last breath.[47]

Each time this passage, or a version thereof, was scrutinised, in genera-tion after generation, readers were privy to a confrontation between a kind of patriotic folk worth: honour and sacrifice on the one hand and, on the other, the quisling opportunism of the blood royal. Although the event was in no sense historical, it lingered in Scottish minds as one of the great lega-cies of the Wallace era, through time conveying assumptions that became virtually innate.

Yet it was probably all so different in Wallace's own time when the Scottish nobility were no doubt just as suspicious of the hero as were the English. As I have previously suggested, readers of Sallust's *Jugurthine War* might have recognised in the life and career of William Wallace certain echoes of the acts and deeds of Gaius Marius, the 'man of the people' of commoner birth, who mercilessly attacked the sloth, arrogance and love of luxury displayed by the Roman nobility. 'Indomitable on the battlefield, he was frugal in his private life, proof against the temptation of passion and riches, and covetous only of glory.' His aristocratic opponents distrusted and condemned him for his lack of pedigree and breeding, and thus he was judged by the very people who could comfortably rely on the protection of lineage, patronage and family if they made mistakes in the execution of office. Marius, however, depended on his own abilities rather than those of his ancestors, on experience rather than book-learning, convinced as he was that virtue, 'the only thing that no man can give to another or receive from another', was the only true nobility. He rose to the rank of consul before, as was inevitable, power utterly corrupted him.[48] It is quite likely that Wallace was also a victim of similar prejudices which dictated that, according to the values and assumptions of his contemporaries, there was no way that the hero could ever have truly overcome his supposed humble birth and have been allowed to succeed; that far from being a hero he was an embarrassment, possibly even one that had to be removed before Robert Bruce could make his bid for the throne. In a world that believed in the Great Chain of Being, where everything had its natural place, Wallace's actions threatened the very fabric of the cosmos. In another era he would have been accused of turning the world upside down. Too dangerous for his own time, he became the Scottish hero of all time, the humble Scot who would teach kings and nobles where their duty lay, while he himself would live free or freely die for the liberty of his nation.

2

Sir William Wallace: What We Do – and Don't – Know[1]

Fiona Watson

The William Wallace we know today is a man of steel, fashioned from a dearth of hard facts and copious quantities of Scotch mist. His reputation, outlined in detail by Blind Hary in the fifteenth century and provided with an international stamp of approval thanks to his celluloid depiction in 1995, puts him squarely in the league of super-folk heroes. But unlike those other medieval champions, Robin Hood and William Tell, Wallace was most definitely flesh and blood. And his reputation derives as much from his martyrdom – the first but not the last in these bitter Anglo-Scottish wars – as by the extraordinary things he did to incur the wrath of Edward Plantagenet.

The lack of verifiable evidence, or even relatively certain supposition, for the life and deeds of the man is both a blessing and a curse. It is a blessing for those who wish to use Wallace as an emblem for a cause since he is a sufficiently blank canvas to tolerate being commandeered even by contra-dictory ideologies, including both nationalism and unionism. Blind Hary knew exactly what he was doing when he picked the victor of the battle of Stirling Bridge as the epitome of unequivocal anti-English sentiment. Although Wallace's comparatively obscure origins, his credible claim to be a man of the people,[2] was also part of the attraction, the lack of a well-rounded life story makes it far easier to portray him in black and white.

This lack of information is obviously a curse for those interested in the frustrating business of uncovering the 'truth' about the historical William Wallace. On the one hand, there is likely to be little more hard evidence to find (although the 'rediscovery' of the Lübeck seal does remind us that small miracles are possible). On the other hand, Hary's story has muddied the waters so deeply that even unambiguous facts stand little chance if they contradict commonly held beliefs about the man. We know now that Hary got the name of his hero's father (and his brother) completely wrong – he was not Sir Malcolm Wallace, but plain Alan Wallace – yet we are still pre-pared to give the poet credence on many other points that are either un-likely or totally unsubstantiated. This may well do Sir William an injustice.

It may do our folk-history an injustice too. It is perhaps going too far to suggest that Hary completely made up large parts of his story, but it would be helpful if we could at least admit the possibility that he fictionalised some of it. What is perhaps more important, however, is the likelihood that he engaged upon a systematic reworking of the widespread oral traditions that had sprung out of the war, attributing them solely to Wallace.[3] In other words, Wallace became Everyman (and woman), a participant in any and every adventure celebrated in story and song all over the country from the half-century or so of protracted warfare between Scotland and England. His cry for freedom has now reverberated convincingly around the world, but it was echoed by thousands of other Scots men and women in his own time. Their stories, too, surely have the right, where possible, to be given proper historical scrutiny. And Sir William himself, whose formative influences and personal motivation will most likely always be hidden from us, is no less of a man, or even a hero, if we let the facts occasionally speak for themselves.

My purpose here is to examine what we currently do know, with reasonable certainty, about Sir William Wallace and to highlight the areas that remain obscure. His early life is a mystery, although, as Professor Duncan shows, we are on a rather firmer footing these days as far as his immediate family is concerned. Sir William's father's name was Alan, and he had not received the honour of knighthood, presumably because he was not sufficiently wealthy. If Alan was still alive in 1296, the evidence so far suggests he may have been a tenant in Ayrshire, an area that, according to Hary, was certainly familiar to young William.[4] We do not know, and may never know for certain, however, that this was Wallace's father. Other members of the wider Wallace family, most particularly the Wallaces of Riccarton who went on to acquire the Ayrshire estate of Craigie and the Renfrewshire estate of Elderslie, provided a network of kin and acquaintance with the very highest in the land. The Stewarts, through whose service the Wallaces came to Scotland in the twelfth century, were certainly known to maintain strong links with the higher echelons of the family whose lords they were.

This does not imply that William Wallace lived his early life in the company of great men. As a younger son of a minor member of the gentry class, he was presumably subject to the same uncertainty over his future as many others in a time of population pressure. He would have had to earn his own way in the world, traditionally either through the Church or as a professional soldier. He chose to do so as an archer, but in the forests and on the moors of southern Scotland rather than in any army. That he was proud of his occupation is graphically illustrated by the fact that he used the bow as his emblem on his seal. There is perhaps evidence that, like that other great folk hero, Robin Hood, who also frequented the depths of a labyrinthine forest, William Wallace lived on the margins of society and the law. If he is indeed the same man described as a 'thief' by an English army court in 1296 in the company of an Englishman, Matthew of York, then William was already an outlaw even before he became involved in politics.[5] We will doubtless never know for sure that this was the future Guardian. Before we get too squeamish at the thought of the great patriotic hero being indicted for common theft (*in absentia*), however, it is surely believable in the context of his later life that he did not necessarily fit into the conventional order of medieval society.

So, we do not know for sure what Wallace was doing in 1296, when war finally broke out between Scotland and England, but we do know that he soon took great offence at English impositions upon the Scots from August 1296.[6] He was not alone. After an initial shell-shocked acquiescence in new English forms of government, which included unprecedented degrees of taxation, Scotland proved contumacious. By early summer 1297 Edward's officials were finding it extremely difficult to fulfil their duties, up to and including extracting sufficient revenue to pay their own wages.

The chronicler Walter of Guisborough asserts that the Scots began their 'perfidious rebellion' some time in May 1297 and William Wallace is assumed to have been its leader. The western border county of Cumberland, however, was already on red alert against 'the coming of the Scots' in April.[7] Presumably this expected attack followed the infamous incident at Lanark, where Wallace killed the sheriff, Sir William Heselrig, romantically described by Hary as an act of revenge for the murder of Wallace's wife. He then raised the men of Clydesdale, including the renowned noble hooligan Sir William Douglas.[8]

But there is a pattern to what Wallace did in those early days that suggests a greater degree of deliberation behind his rebellious activities. Just because the people of Cumberland were expecting him does not prove that he actually went south. What he certainly did do, and this may have been soon after the attack on the sheriff of Lanark, was to head northeast, targeting the English justiciar, William of Ormesby, who was holding a court at Scone. Ormesby was forced to flee precipitously, leaving his baggage behind.

It is surely no coincidence that Wallace attacked two members of the English administration in reasonably quick succession. Heselrig and Ormesby may just have been unlucky. It is not infeasible that Wallace happened to be in the Lanark area when he decided to make an example of the local Edwardian law officer. Equally, he may have heard about Ormesby's court, which was supposedly taking homage and fealty from local people, and decided to take a step up from sheriff to justiciar. But this implies that he was already plugged into a very effective network of communication since Scone is over seventy miles away from Lanark. Intriguingly, it is worth noting that the robbery of which this William Wallace may, or may not, have been the perpetrator took place in Perth, just down the road from Scone. It is just possible, but not yet proven, that Ormesby might have been one of the justices before whom the 1296 theft case was heard. Was it revenge in both cases? We will doubtless never know but it is an intriguing coincidence none the less.

Wallace certainly seems to have ended up in Perth soon after his disruption of Ormesby's court since Guisborough notes that he was visited there by a number of messengers who arrived 'in very great haste on behalf of certain magnates of the kingdom of Scotland'.[9] Despite the chronicler's unhelpful vagueness, we can presume that these magnates were members of the Bruce 'party' rather than the Comyn 'party' who had backed King John Balliol. The Bruces and their supporters, who had acquiesced in Edward's invasion in the hope of gaining the Scottish Crown in place of Balliol, were currently at liberty, unlike the Comyns. We know that they launched an attack on English forces in late May and thus the arrival of messengers in Perth may provide evidence of collusion between their activities and Wallace. William, however, did not join their planned uprising, although Douglas now left his company to do just that.

According to Guisborough, Wallace set about killing many Englishmen north of the Forth before coming south to the safety of Selkirk Forest, besieging a number of castles on the way. There were quite a few royal castles reasonably close to Perth, including Forfar, Clunie and Kinclaven, as well as the major royal castles of the southeast, which he certainly besieged later in 1297.[10] He also inspired others to take action: Macduff of Fife was said to have joined Wallace's rebellion and may have been responsible for the recapture of Cupar Castle, which we know was in Scottish hands before the summer of 1298.[11]

But we should be wary of ascribing all castles captured at that time to Wallace, however active and effective he was in expelling English officials from their posts in certain parts of the country. Another rebellion was about to break out in southwest Scotland, under the leadership of the staunchly patriotic Bishop of Glasgow, Robert Wishart, the young Bruce, Earl of Carrick (the future king), and James the Steward. The ostensible justification for the uprising was the widespread rumour of imminent demands for military service for Edward's continental campaign and the mandatory acquisition by the Crown of wool and hides to be sold to pay for the same venture. These levies, which were causing great annoyance in England, absolutely outraged the 'middling sort' in Scotland, who were quite unused to them.

As leaders of a section of the Scottish nobility, albeit disassociated from the Scottish king, Wishart, Carrick and the Steward intended to convey their right to represent the Scottish people and their grievances. Or at least that's what they told Edward I once the rebellion had fizzled out. But they did achieve a degree of success in disrupting the English administration, including the recapture of castles in the southwest.[12] The rebellion came to an end at Irvine on 7 July 1297 after a month of negotiations. According to Guisborough, however, these Scottish nobles, who also demanded a return to the ancient laws and customs of their land, 'took so long in discussing concessions with frivolous points, so that Wallace could gather more people to him'.[13] Although it is hard to imagine Wallace taking orders from these noblemen, it discredits no one to suggest that the communication that we are fairly sure took place between them at Perth was not necessarily a one-off event. The eyes of the English administration were on the aristocrats. In the meantime, the humble Wallace could start to plan a more serious military challenge to Edward's regime from the safety of Selkirk Forest.

There must also have been communication between Wallace and another uprising taking place at the same time, this time in the north. In late May 1297, the young Andrew Murray, who had escaped from an English prison, gathered a force together at his castle of Avoch on the Black Isle. On 26 May they succeeded in capturing a contingent led by a deputy of the English constable of Urquhart Castle on Loch Ness, following which the Scots proceeded to besiege the castle. In a tacit acknowledgement of English difficulties in holding the north particularly, Edward ordered the release of a number of Scottish nobles, including the two most important members of the Comyn family. They seem to have been charged expressly with putting down any insurgency in the area, where they were major landowners. Whether or not they were sincere in their attempts to do so, Urquhart earned only a temporary release, falling to Murray and his men at some point in the summer. By the time of, or shortly after, Murray's victory with Wallace at Stirling Bridge, all the English-held castles in northern Scotland, including Urquhart, Inverness, Banff, Elgin and Aberdeen, had been recaptured.[14]

With the capitulation at Irvine in July, most of the senior members of the English administration believed that the Scots had given up their rebellious ways. The apparent exception was the Treasurer, Hugh Cressingham, who was well aware of the gathering of men in Selkirk Forest and the difficulties faced by English officials elsewhere. But the king's lieutenant in Scotland, the Earl of Surrey, was far from committed to his duty, and Cressingham was forced to wait anxiously in Berwick as events unfolded beyond his control.

At some point during the summer, Wallace and his men emerged from Selkirk Forest, and he recommenced his attacks on English-held strongholds. He supposedly besieged the royal castle of Dundee immediately before the battle of Stirling Bridge. This is perhaps corroborated by a burgess of the town, one William Doddingstone, who later sought recompense from Edward I for twelve sacks of wool stolen by Wallace 'by force of arms during the war'.[15] On hearing that Cressingham had finally managed to assemble a fresh army from England to combat the very definite continuing unrest, Wallace then allegedly left Dundee, ordering the burgesses to 'kepe that castle rycht straitly'.[16]

Wallace must certainly have moved north of the Forth, at the very least, in order to rendezvous with Murray. We have no idea where or when exactly the two armies met up, although Perth seems most likely if Murray was coming down from the Inverness area. We also have absolutely no notion how many men they each brought with them, although we can perhaps surmise that these were small but reasonably well-disciplined forces, given how effective they proved to be and not just at Stirling. It should also be noted that neither man had the authority to call out a 'Scottish' army on behalf of King John. We are on slightly surer ground with the English contingent, led by Surrey. There is no evidence that his army was much larger than the force numbering 300 horse and 10,000 men mustered by Cressingham earlier in the summer.[17] We assume that this was considerably more than the Scots had to offer.

That the two armies would meet at Stirling was only common sense, since the bridge across the Forth there was the main north-south route. Wallace and Murray led their men southwest from Perth, coming past Sheriffmuir in the Ochil Hills before descending towards the Carse of Stirling. The English were on the southern bank, their commander, Surrey, enjoying the hospitality on offer at the castle. Surrey's arrogance, hastened on by Cressingham, in letting the cavalry cross the narrow bridge to a carefully judged ambush on the far bank provided the backdrop to another victory for David over Goliath. The date was 11 September 1297. Although the English commander could have complained that the rules of war permitted the opposing army to line up for battle in safety, a moment's reflection would have suggested that there was more than one set of rules in this war.

The news of the English army's inconceivable defeat at the hands of the Scots reached London by 26 September 1297, two weeks later. Surrey was immediately ordered south to explain himself to the regency government.[18] At the same time, writs of summons were issued to a number of northern English lords and thirteen Scottish magnates, including John Comyn of Badenoch and seven earls, commanding them to ride against the rebels with as much force as they could muster.[19] The Comyns certainly did not respond; nor did James the Steward. The Earl of Carrick was not even asked to participate, indicating the extent of doubts about his loyalty. The battle of Stirling Bridge had given hope back to Scotland. Unfortunately, it also reunited England, which had been teetering on the brink of civil war in the face of Edward's continuing high-handed demands for men and supplies for his near-constant campaigning.

As the English government struggled to maintain even a tenuous grip on the northern kingdom, the leaders of the Scottish army at Stirling Bridge were equally keen to capitalise on their victory and remove any remaining Edwardian officials. Stirling Castle, hurriedly resupplied after the battle in which its constable, Sir Richard Waldegrave, and other members of the garrison were killed, fell soon afterwards. Sir William fitz Warin, the new commander, had already faced Andrew Murray as constable at Urquhart, which had presumably, therefore, fallen before the battle.[20] As 'the gateway to the north', commanding the western end of the Forth, Stirling Castle was of great strategic importance.

Scotland north of the Forth was effectively cleared of all Edward's men and remained in Scottish hands for the next five years or so. The southwest also seems to have been restored, temporarily at least, to Scottish control, judging by the lack of references to the area in English sources. But the southeast proved harder to recover in any permanent fashion. In the months following the battle, the Scottish army, presumably led by Wallace,[21] besieged the great medieval castle at Roxburgh. It did not submit, although only thanks to the arrival of an English army under the disgraced Surrey in February 1298. Wallace succeeded in gaining control of Berwick town, but not the castle, although he had to relinquish it to Surrey soon afterwards. However, the smaller castle at Jedburgh did fall for rather longer and received a Scottish garrison under the command of John Pencaitland.[22]

Wallace and his men were certainly extremely busy over the winter of 1297–98. As well as relieving Scotland of its foreign masters, Wallace was keen to take the war across the border. According to the anonymous chronicle of Bury St Edmunds, the army that invaded Northumberland in 1297 was led by 'a certain Maleis along with William Wallace'. Professor Barrow has argued convincingly that this 'Maleis' was probably none other than the Earl of Strathearn, whose family 'had considerable interests in north Northumberland'.[23] Wallace's army had presumably swelled with troops supplied by Scottish noblemen who now felt that they could come out openly again in the fight against England. Whether or not that made Wallace any more effective is a moot point.

Wallace's activities over those difficult winter months must also be seen in the context of the fact that he, and the English government in London, were expecting the arrival of an English army, summoned for a muster at Newcastle on 6 December. For a variety of reasons, however, including Surrey's usual tardiness, it did not arrive until February. Although this resulted in the saving of Berwick and Roxburgh from the Scots – an important, if unspectacular, success – the English campaign was halted once instructions from Edward himself arrived. The king was not prepared to rely on Surrey or anyone else to lose his battles for him – they were to wait until his return from the Continent when he would take charge personally. The filtering through of this news was probably what prompted Wallace to cross the border again, leading to the 'battle' at Stainmoor.[24]

As Guardian, Wallace was clearly absolutely dedicated to removing the English from Scotland and, if Falkirk had worked according to plan, keeping them removed.[25] But he certainly did not neglect the other, administrative aspects of his job. It was his instructions that brought about the election of William Lamberton, chancellor of Glasgow Cathedral, to the bishopric of St Andrews. And although we might detect the hand of Robert Wishart, Bishop of Glasgow, behind the selection of the man, it is to Wallace's credit that he could take advice when necessary.[26]

As Professor Duncan has intimated, he also did not ignore the need to maintain Scotland's links with the outside world, writing to Lübeck and Hamburg, along with Andrew Murray, even before he became Guardian. This, together with the only other extant charter of the period – the one granting the constableship of Dundee Castle to Alexander Scrymgeour, dated 29 March 1298 – indicates that Wallace had access to functioning administrative machinery, including the chancery.[27] Whatever his origins, this new, dynamic leader certainly commanded the power of government, whether or not the nobility as a whole supported him.

The muster date for the English army was set for 17 June, later postponed to 25 June, at Carlisle and later changed to Newcastle.[28] The northern counties were not asked to contribute anything, attesting to Wallace's success in causing havoc and mayhem in the area. The Scots seem to have withdrawn north of the border, presumably to start preparing for the arrival of the English king. Their leader was now their Guardian, and a knight as well. The banner of King John had flown proudly above his army, and the English, now very nervous about Scottish tactics and whether or not they would actually give battle, as a proper feudal army should, had learned that the terrible defeat they had inflicted on the Scots at Dunbar was not the end of the matter. On 19 July,[29] the sheriffs of the northern English counties were ordered to investigate 'as secretly and circumspectly as possible', whether or not the Scots were planning yet another expedition across the border. Preparations were also made in case they were sighted, including the collection of wood and turf for beacon fires. It was also anticipated that any Scotsmen living in these counties would be imprisoned, suggesting that Wallace was suspected of being able to call on the support of his fellow countrymen whilst in enemy territory.[30]

The chroniclers are all full of stories about the famine that afflicted Edward's army as it made its way along the southern bank of the Forth in the early summer of 1298. According to Guisborough, the king's supplies failed for almost a month because 'contrary winds' prevented his ships from following them up the firth.[31] This apparent reliance on provisions from the south suggests that the Guardian had opted for a scorched-earth policy, meaning that no one would benefit from the harvest in Lothian that year. If so, we have some tentative evidence for a deliberate policy of enticing the English into Scotland under difficult conditions in the hope of rendering Edward's large army much less fit to fight. At the last minute, however, supplies did arrive, Wallace's whereabouts were reported to the king by the pro-English Earls of Dunbar and Angus, and the English dashed quickly through Linlithgow towards Falkirk and the Scottish position.

Was Wallace caught on the hop? If so, then this surely implies a shocking disregard for elementary levels of reconnaissance. An English army of over 20,000 men is not easily missed, even if it is intent on marching quickly under an effective commander. It is also quite clear that the Scottish Guardian had his men arranged in an effective battle formation, poised in their schiltroms at the top of a slope, an ideal position for an infantry force intent on repelling cavalry. If Wallace had wished to avoid battle, surely he could have allowed his men to slip away at the first intimation of the English army's approach. It makes more sense to suggest that he allowed his location to become known, having some assurance in the strength of his position and the expected hunger and fatigue rife within Edward's forces. The odds were perhaps still against him, but he had done everything he could to narrow them. And he was not Bruce, whose reputation would have been damaged but certainly not destroyed if he had decided not to fight at Bannockburn. Wallace's *raison d'être* was victory in warfare, and he was perhaps under pressure from all sides – from the reluctant nobility to his own men – to inflict defeat on the Hammer of the Scots himself. But as with so many things concerning the elusive William, we will never know.

His defeat at Falkirk was not through lack of bravery on the part of the men dug into the schiltroms. The Scottish cavalry fled, the Scottish archers from Selkirk Forest, led by Sir John Stewart, cut down supposedly to a man.[32] Wallace himself left the field, although in what precise circumstances we do not know, but he must have been aware that his brief career in the centre of the political limelight was over. According to the Scottish chronicler Wyntoun, he resigned from the Guardianship, although perhaps that was merely a pre-emptive action since the Comyns were almost certainly looking for the first opportunity to reassume their pre-eminent position in Scottish politics.[33] The battle of Falkirk did as much to expose and break the uneasy relationship between the Scottish nobility and the Guardian as it did to restore English morale. Four days after the battle, Edward I arrived at Stirling Castle, which succumbed to him within a fortnight. The king seems to have been determined to wipe out as much of the preceding year's losses as he possibly could, sending cohorts of cavalry to various parts of the country, including Perth, St Andrews and Ayr.[34]

It was not that simple, however. What Wallace – and others, but especially Wallace – had done was not just win a battle and take the war to England. He had shown that it was not inevitable that Scotland should succumb to England's great military strength; that there were ways to fight a war to restore independence that, although not strictly orthodox, would at least provide the hope of victory.

Wallace was in an extremely ambivalent position in the aftermath of Falkirk, but the one thing he was highly unlikely to do was nothing. One possibility is that he continued with the strategy that he had employed over the previous winter, presumably with men more immediately loyal to him. The northern English counties certainly seem to have suffered Scottish attacks even after Falkirk, judging from the fact that the Sheriff of Cumberland failed to render his accounts in York on 30 October 1298 because:

> during the present war between the king and the Scots, who lately invaded the said parts and caused much damage and put them in much danger so that the county could not be without its sheriff . . .

He managed to come to the exchequer on 16 November 1298 but immediately 'returned to those parts to save them from damage or danger from the Scots'.[35]

Stirling was also under attack by the autumn of 1298 as the Scots sought to disrupt the castle's supply lines to English-held positions in the southeast. Indeed, the evidence for Scottish activities after Falkirk shows that there was, if anything, an increase in their use of less traditional warfare. Although Wallace was presumably not responsible for all of it, it is quite likely that he played a leading role, whether or not he was authorised to do so by the new Guardians, Robert Bruce, Earl of Carrick, and John Comyn, younger, of Badenoch, who, although representing the two most important noble factions of the time, found it extremely difficult to work together. We do not have any definite information on Sir William's activities until more than a year after Falkirk, when a spy brought news of an extraordinary incident that supposedly took place at a Scottish council meeting at Peebles on 19 August 1299. According to that account, Wallace was intending to leave the country without the permission of the Guardians. This provoked a squabble between Sir David Graham, a Comyn man, and Sir Malcolm

Wallace, William's elder brother, who, interestingly, was associated with Bruce.[36] Whatever the full ramifications of that incident, which are far from clear, we can assume that Wallace was still in the country, but not for much longer. Intriguingly, we also have an oblique reference to him from perhaps around the same time. In 1307, John Sampson, the English constable of Stirling Castle between 1298 and 1300 (when the castle fell to the Scots), claimed expenses for losses incurred during that time. This included a horse, killed 'on *a* [my own italic] St Bartholomew's day [24 August] when William Wallace came to take away our supplies'.[37] Unfortunately, this could refer to either 1298 or 1299 but, either way, it is clear evidence that Wallace had certainly not laid down the gauntlet following his defeat at Falkirk.

Despite the accusation levelled during the Peebles council meeting, Sir William must have had the permission of at least a part of the Scottish government since he could not have travelled without the requisite safe-conducts.[38] Wallace's trip to the Continent is perhaps one of the most interesting aspects of his career – it is certainly not the action of a mindless thug. Unfortunately, it is also the period about which we know the least. It is possible, but by no means certain, that he visited Norway, France and Rome during his four years away from Scotland. If he visited Norway, it is interesting to note that Haakon IV's mother, still resident in Bergen, was none other than Isobel Bruce, sister of the Earl of Carrick.[39]

We are on surer ground with the assertion that Wallace visited the court of Philip IV, thanks to the survival of a letter of 7 November 1300 from the French king to his envoys in Rome demanding that they should help Sir William with his business there.[40] We do not know for sure that he made it to the Holy See, but if he did, then he surely would have found himself wishing for the taxing certainties of the battlefield as he watched lawyers on all sides of the argument debate the case for and against Edward's acquisition of Scotland. This was the high point of Scottish diplomacy: in 1299, the Scottish ambassadors had succeeded in persuading Pope Boniface VIII to order the release of King John Balliol from the Tower of London into papal care. In 1300–01, they were able to argue successfully for what amounted, in effect, to John's liberation. This development finally persuaded Bruce, politically marginalised within Scotland by the Comyns, to return to Edward's peace. Unfortunately, we have no idea what role, if any, Wallace played in these crucial deliberations.

But Scottish success in Europe was ephemeral. Changing political circumstances among the great powers – England, France and the papacy – saw the Scots left out in the cold. By the end of 1302, there was no hope of Balliol's restoration with the help of a French army. In 1303 Edward – freed from any diplomatic restraint – launched yet another campaign across the border. But this time he intended to strike north of the Forth for the first time since 1297.[41]

By then Wallace was already back in Scotland. What is most interesting about his activities after his return before the summer of 1303 is not that he resumed the harrying of English forces but that he did so in the company of other noble commanders. What is equally interesting is the fact that most of these commanders were supporters of the (sole) Guardian, Sir John Comyn. As we have already noted, Wallace apparently left Scotland in 1299 in the face of bitter opposition from Comyn. The Wallaces were, if anything, under the protection of Bruce, whose political ambitions were virulently opposed by the Comyns, supporters of King John and their own pre-eminent position in Scottish politics. Yet Sir William seems to have returned to Scotland prepared to work directly with the Comyn-led government. It is also noticeable that the contemporary English sources, which are almost all we have to work with for this period in Wallace's career, usually manage – as they had not done before 1299 – to accord him his knightly status. It is a great pity that we do not know more about his activities on the Continent.

In mid-June 1303, at the same time as Sir Simon Fraser and Sir Edmund Comyn of Kilbride were reported to have crossed the border to wreak havoc around Carlisle, Sir John Moubray[42] and Sir William Wallace were marching through Galloway. They reputedly had 'attracted to them most of the Galwegians', a state of affairs that doubtless hugely irritated Edward I, who had spent the past five years carefully restoring his position in the southwest. On 23 June, the day on which the letter detailing Scottish activities was written, Moubray and Wallace's force was on the offensive against the English garrisons in Caerlaverock and Dumfries, reportedly 'coming to destroy Annandale and to join Sir Simon Fraser and his company'. It was greatly feared that this combined force would then threaten Carlisle yet again.[43]

Scottish tactics during the campaigning season of 1303 revolved sensibly around stretching English resources as far as possible. The main English army, it should be remembered, was in the northeast, striking deep into territory that had been effectively held throughout most of the war by the Scottish government. Although a force under Sir Aymer de Valence had been left in the south, it and the contingents defending the border were badly provisioned with men, 'because almost all the men-at-arms and footmen are with the king'. Supplies were similarly affected. If the Scots could reduce Dumfries and Caerlaverock, even temporarily, then that would go a long way to compensate for any successes that Edward might achieve in the north.

Unfortunately for them, the officials of the great English war machine managed, although perhaps only just, to maintain enough men and supplies in the right places to keep even their demanding master reasonably content. In 1303 Edward succeeded in not only striking into the Comyn heartland of the northeast but wintering in Scotland to deprive the Scots of the chance to undo his good work. Wallace, Moubray and Fraser were kept at bay by Valence, his army refreshed by men-at-arms, including Bruce, diverted from the main English army.[44] By September many of the Scottish leaders felt it was time to begin negotiations. Sir John Menteith and Sir Alexander Menzies went to Valence at Linlithgow, but they were heartened by the sight of so many starving Irish soldiers and 'broke off their business by reason of the scarcity that they saw among the said people'.[45] Their hope was short-lived, however, as Edward bedded down for the winter in Dunfermline. The Scottish government now had few places to hide and even fewer from which it could maintain its administration and vital links to the Continent. Comyn finally sued for peace on behalf of the Scottish political community at the beginning of 1304.

But not everyone agreed with surrender, although those who held out were only a tiny minority. However, they were sufficiently effective during the spring of 1304 to warrant the attentions of a force numbering several thousand men under Sir John Segrave and Sir John Botetourt. Edward also demanded that certain Scottish nobles who now held office within his administration should work hard to bring the rebels in. The Earl of March, presumably at his castle at Dunbar, was strongly reproved for having 'let the enemy go'.[46] But around 10 March the two Sir Johns finally managed to 'discomfit' Sir Simon Fraser and Sir William Wallace at Happrew near Peebles, thanks to information on their whereabouts provided by a local spy. Unfortunately for the English, neither Scottish leader was captured.[47]

With the surrender agreement under his belt, Edward now looked forward to a parliament at St Andrews where, among other things, Wallace, Fraser and the Scottish garrison of Stirling Castle were declared outlaws under Scottish law.[48] This was probably also the occasion of a grant made to the king's 'dear valet' of 'all the goods and chattels of whatever kind he may gain from Sir William Wallace, the king's enemy'.[49] The name of the beneficiary was first written as Edward Bruce,[50] but this surname was deleted and that of Keith substituted. There is perhaps nothing particularly sinister about the change of beneficiary, but the fact that the Bruces do not appear to have been rewarded with much in the way of property or offices for their early re-attachment to Edward suggests that the English king was now distancing himself from that ambitious family. But it is undoubtedly fortunate for the reputation of the great hero king, Robert I, that his younger brother did not profit at the expense of the other great hero of the period.

It is also interesting that no mention was made of any lands belonging to Wallace. The spy present at the Peebles council of 1299 stated that Sir David Graham demanded the forfeiture of Sir William's lands and property as punishment for his unauthorised trip abroad. We presume, given his position as a younger son, that Wallace did not hold land through his own family. He may, of course, have benefited personally whilst Guardian, and who could blame him – once he became a knight, he would have needed a regular income to keep him, his horse and equipment in good shape. On the other hand, the spy may have got the details of the shouting match between Graham and Sir Malcolm Wallace wrong. Once again, we just do not know.

Throughout the long process of bringing Scotland to a final peace in 1304–05, the English king was particularly careful to ensure, as far as possible, that each stage in the proceedings was accomplished with the active participation of the Scottish political community and according to Scottish laws and customs. The next major step was to bring about the surrender of Stirling Castle, which was duly achieved, under extremely unpleasant circumstances, on 24 July. Edward insisted that the besieged remain until he had fully tested his fine new weapon, Warwolf, and he considered the hanging and disembowelling of every single member of the garrison, a course of action from which he was dissuaded by his wife.[51]

Sir Simon Fraser seems to have accepted which way the wind was blowing at some point between the St Andrews parliament in March, when he was explicitly condemned as a rebel, and the reduction of Stirling Castle. On the day after the garrison's submission, Edward ordered the people of Scotland, but especially Sir John Comyn, Sir Alexander Comyn, Sir David Graham and Sir Simon Fraser:

> To make an effort between now and the twentieth day of Christmas [13 January 1305] to take Sir William Wallace and hand him over to the king so that he can see how each one bears himself whereby he can have better regard towards the one who takes him, with regard to exile or ransom or amend of trespass or anything else in which they are obliged to the king.[52]

It is hard to imagine how many of these men, but especially Fraser, must have felt about being forced to hunt down a man who had lately been their comrade-in-arms. There is a presumption, of course, that Wallace would never have submitted to Edward no matter what he was offered, which leads us to a discussion of the conditions negotiated by Sir John Comyn at the beginning of the year. In many respects, Edward tried hard to be accommodating, within the limits of his steadfast belief in the righteousness of his claim to be overlord of Scotland, and therefore his anger and frustration towards those who had opposed him since 1297 are understandable. So long as the Scots were prepared to grovel a little and acknowledge unequivocally his sovereign rights over them, the English king would not exact the full revenge to which he felt he was entitled. Almost all the notable rebels, including Comyn, were promised their lives and liberty and the enjoyment of their property. Many would, it is true, be asked to serve varying periods of time in exile or pay a fine, depending on how personally Edward felt offended by their behaviour. Sir Simon Fraser and Thomas Bois were offered the harshest conditions (which may have prompted Fraser to continue his resistance), probably because both had served in the English administration before defecting and were therefore guilty of a personal betrayal in Edward's eyes.[53] As the above extract indicates, however, even these punishments might be ameliorated if they worked hard to prove their loyalty.[54]

But there was an exception. Wallace was not mentioned by name until negotiations were well underway and the finer points were being dealt with. It was Edward who brought up the issue of the former Guardian, and his message was simple and devastating: he was 'to be received to the king's will and ordinance'. In other words, the general conditions, guaranteeing life, limb and freedom from imprisonment, were not to apply and Sir William faced the unenviable task of throwing himself on Edward's mercy, a quality that many, including the garrison at Stirling, had found in short supply. In the final document, the potential vagaries of royal clemency were given further emphasis with the injunction that Wallace was to submit 'to the will and grace of the king, *if it seems good to him* [my italics]'. It was anyone's guess as to whether Edward would find it good.[55] This uncompromising position, combined with Sir William's obvious commitment to the cause for which he had fought so fiercely, made it almost inevitable that he would do anything other than kneel abjectly before King Edward.

Time was running out. Once Fraser had submitted, it is likely that Sir William would have found it increasingly difficult to find somewhere safe to lay his head, never mind from which he might operate a resistance movement. There is no direct mention of him between the episode at Happrew in March 1304 and the following September, when Thomas Umfraville, Constable of Dundee, and other members of the garrison, gave chase to him 'beneath Yrenside [Ironside]', a hill behind Dundee.[56] Perhaps Wallace was looking for help from his old comrade-in-arms, Alexander Scrymgeour, to whom the former Guardian had granted the constableship of Dundee castle nearly seven years earlier.

Once again Wallace disappeared, this time for nearly a year until 3 August 1305 when men of the Keeper of Dumbarton, Sir John Menteith, finally captured him, supposedly at Robroyston near Glasgow. Sir John has gone down in history as the ultimate Scottish Judas, although he had certainly been a leading member of the patriotic cause until the submissions of 1304. In some ways he was unlucky that Wallace was found within his jurisdiction; it certainly seems likely that many other Scots, from the highest to the lowest, would have done the same.[57]

The charges brought against Wallace can also be read as a list of his successes as a leader of the resistance movement and then Guardian, particularly with regard to the holding of Scottish parliaments and the maintenance of the Franco-Scottish alliance.[58] A mere twenty days later, Sir William was brought to 'trial' and executed at Smithfield.[59]

If William Wallace had left us his thoughts in the face of his imminent execution, he might have done worse than pre-empt Mary, Queen of Scots with the famous words, 'In my end is my beginning'. That Wallace had an extraordinary career prior to his early death is not to be doubted – he is one of the very few real-life heroes of the pre-modern period to have come from his level of society. But those exploits were as nothing when compared with what has been claimed for him in the centuries since 1305. There is, of course, considerable overlap between the historical Wallace and the man of myth, but it is remarkable, too, how often it is necessary to distinguish between them. What I have tried to do here is to present, with a degree of brevity, what we do know about the man, ignoring much of the uncorroborated evidence of Blind Hary, and to highlight the areas where there are significant gaps. It would be wonderful to think that, in time, some of these gaps might be filled, but the trouble with Wallace is undoubtedly the infuriating lack of source material for critical moments in his life.

I have also tried to provide a degree of context for Wallace's activities. This is partly in order to help to explain what he was up to, but perhaps more particularly to try to alleviate the impression, now overwhelmingly present in our minds post-*Braveheart*, that Sir William operated more or less alone with a small band of loyal followers. As I have already argued, to fix our gaze so single-mindedly on this one man, however important he was as an inspiration in his own time and subsequently, is to diminish the contribution and achievements of countless others, both known and unknown. This is a complicated period in history – like any other – and those who lived through such a desperate war are owed our honest attempts to understand their actions, even when they do not behave as we might wish. That too is a freedom worth fighting for.

3

William, Son of Alan Wallace:
The Documents

A. A. M. Duncan

It is a moot point whether the achievement of William Wallace in his life-time is as significant as his reputation, enhanced by myth and literary romance passing as history, was to be over the succeeding seven centuries.[1] In my judgment, the reputation-myth ceased to be of contemporary signif-icance in the last decades of the nineteenth century as defence of the 1801 Union seized the centre ground in British politics. Here I turn from the fic-tion to look at Wallace in the few contemporary texts he has left to us and to set them in the context of their time. We can still learn about the real man from the exercise and may even confirm something of the legend-encrusted reputation.

Wallace is named as the author/sender of four documents the texts of which survived in various conditions to the nineteenth century and survive today. The earliest, and the only one to survive in the original, is a letter by 'Andrew Murray and William Wallace, leaders of the army of the kingdom, and the community of the kingdom' to the mayors and communes of Hamburg and Lübeck, probably one to each city, a month (11 October 1297) after the victory of Stirling Bridge. Murray had been wounded at that battle and was to die in the next few months,[2] so cannot have been – was not – the leader of any subsequent army. The kingdom's community was associated with them as sender, for leaders of the army alone would not be recognised as rulers or representatives of the kingdom; in other letters they claimed to act in the name of King John, accepted domestically as the rightful king. There must be a suspicion that omission here means that over-seas his name would arouse doubts or even derision. I shall return to this letter in greater detail shortly.

Murray and Wallace were still both nominally leaders of the army that invaded northern England when, on 7 November 1297, they issued to the canons of Hexham Priory a letter of protection under pain of life and limb, probably in return for promise of a payment – blackmail – for delivery of which they gave safe-conduct to a single canon.[3] But the sole leader of the army was Wallace, carefully retaining the fiction of Murray's participation and acting in the name of King John. In the hostile chronicle that preserves the two letters, the ruthless hand of Wallace is evident in his orders to behead the sacrilegious Scots who had seized the chalice of the priory.[4] The failure to apprehend them is usually taken as evidence of a failure of authority, and the desolation caused elsewhere by the campaign as a lack of strategic ability. Yet war was usually waged by pillage and destruction to impoverish the enemy, very rarely by pitched battle, and the reliability of the chalice story is to be judged by the conduct of the Scots in 1296, commanded by their earls, who, according to the same chronicle, 'in the morning, when they had looted [Hexham Priory] of virtually all its goods, set it on fire and burned not only the church but also the monastery with the whole township, an unheard of crime'.[5] Our judgment should surely be that Wallace's blackmail showed better judgment and more authority in 1297 than did the earls' conduct in the previous year.

The fourth document was an original charter published as an engraving by James Anderson in 1739.[6] Dated at Torphichen on 29 March 1298, William Wallace knight, Guardian of the kingdom and leader of its army *(ductor exercitus)* in the name of King John by consent of the kingdom's community, grants heritably lands near Dundee and the constabulary of the castle of Dundee, by consent of the kingdom's magnates, to Alexander called Skirmisher (Scrymgeour) 'for his faithful service and his succour given to the kingdom in carrying the royal banner in the army of Scotland at the time of making these presents' (the charter). In the Hexham letters the 'Guardian and leader' hold office 'by consent of the community', a less active role than the 'choice' *(electio)* of earlier and later guardians. The first bands of rebels in 1297 may indeed have 'chosen' their leaders;[7] but the 'community' (and the charter shows this meant, in practice, the magnates) accepted their authority on sufferance – very unwillingly according to 'Fordun'.[8]

There is no doubt that Murray, by an agile strategy, led a successful rebellion in the province from which came his name, and that farther south Wallace too showed a determination to end English occupation wherever he could attack it with advantage. Their successes in different regions contrasted markedly with the craven capitulation by Carrick and the Steward at Irvine on 7 July 1297. But in his very full account of events south of the Mounth, Guisborough tells of Bruce, the Steward, the Bishop of Glasgow, the (awful) William Douglas and William Wallace as leaders but makes not one mention of Murray;[9] in particular, messengers sent to the Scots to persuade them to surrender at Stirling met only Wallace. The *Lanercost Chronicle* has the same view of the Scottish command – it was Wallace's alone.[10] The name of Murray occurs in only one account of the battle of Stirling Bridge, when 'Fordun' comments that on Wallace's side, 'of the number of nobles only Andrew Murray, father of the noble Andrew [Guardian in the 1330s], fell wounded' – no mention of command nor of death.[11] The inquest of 1300 finding that he was slain against Edward I's peace at Stirling[12] is assumed to exaggerate the speed of his death after the battle in 1297, although it is just possible that he survived to fall at the siege of Stirling in 1299. To survive eight weeks from Stirling Bridge on 11 September until 7 November 1297, he must have had great stamina under treatment, but since he is not known to have *done* anything after that battle (unlike Wallace), the traditional view that he took a long time to die is probably correct; he was not leading armies anywhere.

This surely makes his recognition as leader in association with Wallace the more remarkable. We should see it, and the title, not as a preliminary to, but as a consequence of, the unique victory at Stirling, which made them leaders of the kingdom's army for the next campaign, taking a Scottish army to attack England. This intention may have been decided, and the title agreed, at Haddington about 11 October 1297. Attribution of leadership to Murray must have underestimated the seriousness of his wounds, but even so his unfitness suggests that Wallace was required to accept a noble associate as his senior colleague as the price for 'consent' to his authority and using the title officially, that is, especially in summoning men to the host in the name of King John.[13]

The surrender of Dundee Castle by the terrified English garrison soon after Stirling Bridge would demand a Scottish constable for the castle, but Scrymgeour's heritable grant thereof came later, after a vital duty performed in the army. In November 1297, as we have seen, Wallace ravaged northern England, but in December the English attacked Annandale, and about 25 February 1298 took and burned Annan. Wallace, it is generally said, waited in Scotland for Edward's invasion. But according to Bower, after an exchange of defiant letters with Edward I, he took an army to Stainmoor (in Cumbria). As the English under Edward I approached, the Scottish hotheads wished to ride out to win their spurs but Wallace sternly imposed discipline, and the Scots advanced in unbroken line, causing the English to flee, when once again Wallace forbade the breaking of ranks in pursuit. This 'victory' is unambiguously dated to 20 March 1298, despite which detail, because Edward I cannot have been present, modern writers have wholly discounted the episode as at best belonging to the autumn of 1297 – when he could not have been present either.[14]

Edward I is evidently an accretion to the narrative, for Bower himself comments: 'the English say that their king was not present in person, but someone else in a gleaming suit of armour'. Whoever this commander was (probably Sir Robert Clifford, who was in Carlisle), such an encounter on 20 March fits with an army's return to Scotland, the magnates holding together until 29 March at Torphichen, when Alexander Scrymgeour was rewarded by the grants made in this charter 'for his faithful service and succour given to the aforesaid kingdom'. The kingdom had been named only in the charter's address (*custos regni, communitas regni, homines regni*), for otherwise the emphasis throughout is upon the king in whose name the grant is made; Alexander's homage is to the king, as his faithful service could have been, but that was not possible with 'succour', even though it was in carrying the royal banner. So 'service and succour' were given to the 'kingdom'.

'Succour in carrying the royal banner in the army' suggests 'saving the day' not 'leading the troops to victory', a military rescue, long after Stirling Bridge but understandable after Stainmoor (20 March), at 'the time of the making' of the charter (29 March) although not on its actual date. The Bower narrative, touched already by the growth of legend about Wallace, shows that, avoiding an encounter, Wallace prevented a possible disaster by firm discipline. My own suggestion is that the Scots had been caught in a difficult situation, perhaps with an English force between them and the border (as in 1327), and that Wallace's discipline got them home under a royal banner carried in the army. Those words, *portando vexillum regium in exercitu Scocie*,[15] suggest that the succour given was that the banner was always with them.

The displayed 'royal banner' would bear the royal arms, the 'lion', which in that word was coming to symbolise the kingship of the Scots. A royal banner had been unfurled in the absence of the king by the army defeated at Dunbar in 1296 when the son of Sir William Sinclair, 'who carried the banner of the lord king of Scotland', was killed.[16] On both occasions, 1296 and 1298, the banner was surely an assertion that this army marched in the name of King John and hence was the army of the kingdom. But in 1296 he was an honoured prisoner of his magnates, in 1298 a captive of the English king, despite which, to his subjects, he was still 'the illustrious prince, the lord John, by God's grace noble king of Scotland'.[17] The banner carried by Alexander Scrymgeour was a defiant proclamation that the English king had not extinguished John's kingship. It must have seemed vital that it should not fall into English hands.

It may be too that the banner itself had a numinous significance, for it was surely that concealed by the Bishop of Glasgow in his treasury, presumably from the battle of Falkirk, until 1306, when it was taken out and sent to Scone for the inauguration of Robert I.[18] When and how it acquired its special significance we do not know, but the oriflamme of the French king may have been a role model for this Scottish banner. Kept in the treasury of Saint-Denis monastery, the oriflamme was reputed to bring victory to the king, who took it with him on campaign. Thus it went with Louis IX to Egypt, where it was pretty certainly lost to the enemy. This difficulty was met by producing a replica oriflamme to be blessed for the occasion; replicas were lost again at Crécy and Poitiers.[19] What probably made the Scottish royal banner special was ecclesiastical safekeeping and an episcopal blessing, making it a holy object, if not relic, that offered to Wallace, who cherished holy altar vessels, the hope of a victory and a responsibility to keep it from an enemy's hands. Hence its preservation in Glasgow's treasury and a concern in 1298 lest it be captured. But it is striking that Scrymgeour's service for his lands was to be as constable of a castle, with no mention of being heritable bannerman, a right and duty that came to the family from Robert I, perhaps because only a king might grant it.[20]

As the 'leader of the army', Wallace attacked the English kingdom, as in Northumbria, in November 1297 and again in Cumbria in March 1298, when he still calls himself *ductor exercitus*; this duty would not be changed by the death of Murray. But between the Hexham writs of 7 November 1297 and the charter of 29 March 1298, Wallace also became Guardian, a new responsibility, to protect and defend the Scottish kingdom. In the revised shorter version of his work Bower added a whole passage on this:

> He was appointed Guardian of the kingdom not so much by election as by divine intervention, for by a wonderful vision it was shown to various persons worthy in the faith that the most holy apostle Andrew, protector and patron of the kingdom, by hand committed a bloody sword to William Wallace, strictly commanding him to use it everywhere in defence of the kingdom by expelling the English.[21]

Wallace had expelled the English speedily in October 1297 without becoming Guardian; but defence and expulsion had first become a need again about the end of January 1298, when a large English force relieved Roxburgh Castle, so that in February the Scots descended to burn Roxburgh, Haddington 'and almost all the good towns south of Forth lest the English should find harbour in Scotland' – anticipating an incursion, and with good reason.[22] A major English invasion had indeed been intended but was postponed in February on King Edward's orders to await his return from Flanders. About late January, I suggest, Wallace had been charged with Guardianship to defend the realm. By March the threat of invasion had receded and Wallace led his attack on northern England, an invasion, so not as Guardian but in his capacity as 'leader of the army'.

Behind Bower's elevating tale, we may read the vigorous support of St Andrew for Wallace, urged by the canons of St Andrews, the English in their convent roughly expelled by Wallace, their bishop dead in French exile on 20 August 1297. The invoking of so powerful a saint may have played no small part in the elevation of Wallace – but it also suggests overcoming doubts about Wallace's appropriateness. If there was an 'election' by the community, it was probably in a small gathering, although a prominent Scottish earl did confer his knighthood.[23] As Guardian and knight, Wallace may himself have conferred knighthood upon his older brother, Malcolm, a knight by 1299, and upon Alexander Scrymgeour, a knight by 1306. Of the 'bloody sword' we shall hear again.

I return now to the Lübeck letter, the discovery of which we probably owe to Georg Friedrich Christoph, Baron Sartorius von Waltershausen, author of a history of the Hanseatic League, in three volumes published between 1802 and 1808, in which he surveyed sources, remarking that he had recently been informed of documents at Lübeck but doubted that anyone could give a satisfactory account of them.[24] Nonetheless, before his death he evidently worked, or had work done, upon them for his collection of source materials, including the letter, 'edited' (*herausgegeben*) by J. M. Lappenberg in 1830.[25] The texts seem to have been the responsibility of Sartorius and contain some misreadings, although in case of doubt an engraving of the words in the original was provided in notes. Misreadings were corrected in an appendix, probably Lappenberg's contribution, where he was working from a 'facsimile' of the letter. In 1829 Lappenberg had communicated the existence of the Murray-Wallace letter to a correspondent in England who was told, or assumed, that he had found it, according to the garbled account that appeared in print in 1830.[26] Lappenberg sent a copy of the letter, 'from the records of Lubec', which reached John D. Carrick to be included in his *Life of Sir William Wallace of Elderslie* (1830), with text and translation in Appendix H.[27] This was reprinted in Joseph Stevenson's *Documents Illustrative of Sir William Wallace* (1841), but before publication he obtained from Lübeck a 'facsimile tracing' of the letter, presumably by the engraver of the 1830 edition, and included a lithograph in this volume.[28] It may have been reproduced elsewhere in the nineteenth century but did not win a place in the *National Manuscripts of Scotland*. A more correct text was published from the original by the *Verein für Lübeckische Geschichte* in the *Urkundenbuch* of Lübeck in 1843;[29] it was republished occasionally later in the nineteenth century.

As far as I can tell, the first photograph was published when, in 1911, the archives of Lübeck sent the letter to the Scottish National Exhibition, held at Kelvingrove Park to raise funds for a chair, or chairs, of Scottish History and Literature in the University of Glasgow.[30] It was exhibited there in the Palace of History, in a vast collection of artefacts of which a catalogue was published in one volume or, for the truly dedicated, in two volumes with copious photographs, including of the front and back of the letter.[31] What the public made of the letter, or of the twenty-seven editions of Hary's *Wallace* displayed nearby, is not recorded.

In 1912 the letter was returned to Lübeck, whose archives were reportedly put in a mine for safety during the 1939–45 war and rumoured to have been taken later to Russia. At a conference in the 1960s, the archivist told me that he had heard stories of documents blowing about a Polish railway station but had been unable to find out more; that they had been destroyed turned out to be a false rumour. Eventually they were handed over to the German Democratic Republic and housed at Potsdam, to be returned to their proper home in Lübeck after the reunification of Germany. The letter was generously brought again to Scotland in 1999, for exhibition for three months in the new Museum of Scotland. The courtesy of this loan of a document that belongs, as do all letters, to the recipient was exemplary. With a few others I was permitted to examine it closely at the end of the exhibition.[32]

It is a parchment rectangle with eight lines of writing in Latin, directed to the mayors and communes of Hamburg and Lübeck, intimating that Scottish merchants have told of their favourable attitude to Scotland and its merchants, gives thanks for this and invites them to let it be known to their merchants that they can have free access, with their merchandise, to Scottish ports, because 'the kingdom, thanks be to God, is recovered by battle from the power of the English'. After 'Farewell' and the date 'Hadsington', 11 October 1297, an addition asks the German towns to promote the business of John Burnet and John Frere, 'our merchants', as they would wish the business of their merchants to be promoted. There is no evidence that these letters promoted a bustling trade between Germany and Scotland;[33] on the contrary, merchants of Lübeck loaned £400 sterling to the English government, for which they were repaid on 20 August 1300.[34]

But this is an original letter, challenging the historian to learn from all aspects of it, not just its text but the layout, handwriting, method of sealing, seal(s) and folding for dispatch. He might even find the stains of a sea voyage – although not in this case. The handwriting of this letter is in neat straight lines but is very small – a marked contrast to the Scrymgeour charter – and suggests to me the work of a ledger clerk. Moreover, the addition was not written as a postscript on this letter, for the ink and writing show no change; this letter, including the addition, was copied from a previous version, which, it is reasonable to suppose, was the letter to Hamburg. The copying may have taken place after some interval of time, for the place date, Hadsingtona, shows an error that could scarcely have taken place at Haddington.[35]

At the bottom of the letter two tongues were cut, one about one centimetre broad to carry sealing, the other below it, narrower, to act as a tie around the folded parchment. The folding is clear: the top three lines were turned down, the right-hand end folded over, then again and again, until the document was reduced to a sixth of its original size; the narrow tongue was taken around the document and knotted with itself. Either before or after folding, beeswax was placed around the tongue and impressed with a seal of about four centimetres diameter on the obverse and a smaller seal on the reverse. The claim in 1843 that there had been two seals must have been a guess from the two senders, for there was absolutely no trace of another seal when I examined the original – particularly on this point.[36] The sealed and folded document could be carried in a purse.

We might expect the seals to be those of Murray and Wallace, but the evidence is more complex than that. The obverse represents a cheaply or hurriedly made matrix by a craftsman of no great skill, for although the charge is a shield of the royal arms, lion rampant with double tressure flory counter-flory, a wyvern at the top and on each side of the shield, the lion is manifestly off-centre. The legend has been punched on the matrix with curves and straight lines, not individual letters, and its reading is uncertain. The standard reference work offers SI[O]I . . . SCOTT[ ]VM . . . EG;[37] I first read S'OI . . . SCOTIIORVM . . . [R]EG, with the tail of an R before EG. The apostrophe could be a damaged I, giving SIGI[LLVM]; a following word – REGNI or COMMVNITATIS is called for – is wholly lost. While possible, an expanded reading as SIGILLVM COMMVNITATIS SCOTTORVM REGNI seems to me to clash with showing the lion, the king's arms. The oddity of SCOTI-IORVM suggests that the original intention was SCOCIE (as on the 1286 seal), changed for reasons now undiscoverable but which cramped what followed. This is now a short gap, for about five letters before [R]EG, so not room for the DEPVTATVM REGIMINI suggested by the 1286 seal, unless abbreviated to DEPVT REG. That is my best conjecture. In putting forward an expanded reading of SIGILL*VM* REGNI SCOTTORVM DEPVT*ATVM* REG*IMINI*,[38] I confess to being influenced by the 1286 seal, with its shield of the royal arms, but I think it likely that the men of 1297 would also have been so influenced.[39]

My reading of this seal was made from a cast identified by Ashby McGowan of Glasgow, a learned student of the history of William Wallace, in the Mitchell Library, Glasgow in 1998.[40] Gilt copper casts of the two sides of the seal attached to the Lübeck letter are sunk in a wooden block, and a label on the back states 'Made by P. Sinclair Rae. Glasgow. 1912', at that time a dental technician in Maryhill, Glasgow.[41] Mr McGowan sought to interest in his discovery those who should be concerned; he wrote to myself and failed to receive a reply, for which I tender my apology. He has since published his views on the seal and Wallace.[42] With the impending arrival of the original in Edinburgh in 1999, a sympathetic journalist at *The Herald*, Lesley Duncan, took note of his information, inspected the casts and, via Ted Cowan, called on myself for help.

Our attention was concentrated upon the seal on the reverse, no better in workmanship than the obverse. Here, the smaller seal, about twenty-three millimetres in diameter, is struck off-centre on the wax. The charge is a bow and string, before the bow is stretched, with a broad arrow protruding to the edge of the legend with the fletching between bow and string. Two fingers of a hand grasp the string and the arrow behind the fletching,[43] but not the bow. About a fourth of the legend is lost after the + at the top, but the bottom sector reads clearly as FILIVS, requiring a name in the nominative, without *Sigillvm*; that name ended in VS. There are no spaces between words but the following ALANI, with reversed N, is certain. It was only when I made out W as the next letter that Mrs Duncan suggested 'Wallace' to me, and I was able to decipher that name with ligatured WAL, the W sharing the stroke (/) with the A, and the L formed by extending the bar of the A. The following A is large, so that after letter I there was no space for the final S; it was crammed within the charge, touching the bow. The whole (with hyphen inserted by me to show the change of register) reads . . . VSFILIVSALANIWALAI-S.[44]

It was not unknown for men to use the seal of a relative or lord if perhaps they had none, but this document calls for the seal of Murray or Wallace. The name *Willelmvs* fits the space for the lost first name and *Andreas* will not do. I complete the legend as [WILLELM]VS FILIVS ALANI WALAIS, 'William son of Alan Wallace', and claim it as the only known impression of his seal, unrecognised since the document was first printed by Sartorius in 1830. Its modest size surely places the creation of the matrix before Wallace became leader of the kingdom's army. And it demolishes the names given by literary sources for William's father; he was, we can be sure, Alan Wallace.

Another version, to be sent to Hamburg, may have borne the seals of the community and the wounded Andrew Murray,[45] or that of Wallace; the destruction of the Hamburg archives in the eighteenth century means that we cannot be sure. It does seem probable to me, however, that the decision to add the postscript on the Hamburg letter, and to write to Lübeck, a Baltic port less accessible than Hamburg, came after the letter to Hamburg had been written and would be prompted by the identification of two merchants going to the two ports, perhaps one to each. The writing and misspelling suggest that one of the merchants may have written the Lübeck letter.

To return to seals. In 1296, after the fall of King John, Edward I, having collected on his travels in Scotland fealties from about 126 individuals and some burgh communities recorded in forty-five documents sealed by those submitting,[46] ordered the further collection of a wide range of submissions with sworn fealties recorded and sealed. The fealties were recorded in groups of between one and 100 (rarely more) persons on one parchment, usually from more than one sheriffdom but grouped according to sheriff-dom.[47] Seals from these persons were appended, four or five on one string, the strings attached to the documents. The result was fifty-eight (possibly more) documents of submission and fealty with multiple seals.[48]

How was this done? We do not know. The basis seems to be the sheriff-dom,[49] but names from a sheriffdom will appear in groups, each group associated with another or others from other sheriffdoms, these making up one of the fifty-eight documents. All these are dated at Berwick, 28 August 1296, but the number of names is so great that the fealties seem to have been sworn locally at different times. Yet on 25–28 August, in response to royal writs, groups of between twelve and fourteen men from each of six sheriffdoms compeared at Berwick to make a retour on the possessions of the late wealthy widow Elena la Zouche.[50] Many of the men named swore fealty according to the submission documents – of the Ayrshire thirteen, ten did so. They may have brought to Berwick lists of those who had sworn fealty in the sheriff court, with their seals, to be written up into formal documents at Berwick.

The documents subsequently decayed badly or completely, often leaving only a trayful of seals for each one. Fortunately, between 1300 and 1306 three comprehensive enrolled copies of the 103 (45+58 in the two preceding paragraphs) ragman texts had been made, each called (apparently only since *c.* 1700) a Ragman Roll (here the RR).[51] If the RR copies are reasonably faithful, then these documents were drawn up by English administrators. Further work on the original fragments might throw more light on how the documents were created.

The RR is the record of submission by some 1,500 men and a few women and should (but does not always) correspond to the names on the surviving seals.[52] Some 870 seals were catalogued by Bain, about 160 (18 per cent) showing arms; more recently, Dr B. A. McAndrew has published a more careful catalogue of 912 seals,[53] and suggests about 20 per cent (180) showing arms. Of the 912, 64 are ecclesiastical, 7 of towns, 17 of women (88 in all),[54] and on about 35 the charge (but not necessarily the legend) is damaged or obliterated. Of the remaining *c.* 650 (912–(180+88)), many lack or have fragmentary legends and cannot be associated firmly with a name in the RR but nonetheless show the devices of laymen who were sigilliferous but not armigerous.[55]

These were the men significant enough to have seals, free, propertied, who might serve on the assize in the sheriff court,[56] who could execute a land sale or purchase, and who were in the region where Edward's armies and garrisons dominated the native inhabitants – the overwhelming preponderance of names from south of the Forth is unmistakable. They were probably drawn from suitors of the sheriff court in each sheriffdom, the middling folk who in 1297 feared that Edward I would tax them and send them on military service to France.[57] Some were fairly humble in status.[58] The devices on their seals were varied and of unknown appositeness. Many employ the fleur-de-lys, some the hunting horn, but a surprising number use the lion rampant (common also in England). Otherwise, birds and the bestiary comprise most of the repertoire: hedgehog, squirrel, rabbit, hound, stag, boar, lamb, even a rhino (McAndrew No. 3486).

Among the names occurring in one ragman text copied to the RR is that of Alan Wallace, a strong claimant to be father of William. This original ragman text, now gall-stained into illegibility[59] (which I call Text 13, the first figures in McAndrew's list of its seals)[60] in the RR version lists 91 names in groups from eight sheriffdoms south of the Forth, plus Perth.[61] Some of these names are found elsewhere in the RR and must have sealed more than one document.[62] Seven names, including Alan Wallace, come from Ayrshire, two of them, but not Alan, found elsewhere in the RR.[63] The corresponding seal found with others from Text 13 shows a curlew, with S ALANI WALAYS (No. 1332).

Would it were that simple! For there is another seal, a fleur-de-lys with the legend S'ALANI WALIS, used twice (Nos. 3465, 3574), one unidentifiable with any part of the RR, the second (No. 3574) with other seals from a document copied in the RR with 75 names, from the sheriffdoms of Ayr (56), Lanark (7) and Dumfries (12). This includes two Wallaces in Ayrshire: Adam (not Alan) and Nicholas.[64] The former name could be a RR miscopying of 'Alan', or Adam could have borrowed Alan's seal; in either case, the evidence is that either Alan had two seals or else there were two men called Alan Wallace in the county. There are other examples of this 'same name, two seals' conundrum, for which there can be no certain resolution with the present state of our knowledge.[65]

But what can be said is that Text 13 was one of two unique in form, for in the RR it describes all those named as 'tenants of the king', as another document describes the men named as 'tenants of the bishop of St Andrews'.[66] These were men who could lose their lands by forfeiture to the English king because their lords, King John and Bishop William Fraser (an author of the Franco-Scottish treaty and still in Paris, where he died in 1297), had engaged in plotting with King Edward's enemy, the king of France. These documents name persons selected for a particular reason – liability to forfeiture. Since they pretty certainly did not lose their lands, we may conjecture that after they were assured of this they swore fealty, some for a second time – and this may explain a multiplicity of sealings by Alan Wallace.

The RR does not name the holding(s) of Alan (or anyone else), and we must be content with knowing his name and his sheriffdom, ignoring Blind

Hary's *Wallace* of the 1470s, which names William's father as 'Sir Malcolm' and his tenancy as 'Elrislie'. The fourteenth-century chronicle, printed as 'Fordun', is more persuasive – that although he was thought ignoble by the magnates, Wallace's forebears were of knightly status. His elder brother was knighted and had a sufficient patrimony that passed to his descendants,[67] for William did indeed have a brother, Malcolm, a knight in 1299, and it is likely that they were descended from the Wallaces of Riccarton, a knightly family. What became of Malcolm is unknown, but another brother, John, was executed by the English in 1307.

William has a rightful place in what we make of the history of Scotland. From May 1297 for some fifteen months his career is reasonably documented. But before 1297 it can only be remarked that he did not seal any known ragman fealty, perhaps because he abstained or refused, or because he was not a suitor of the sheriff court. According to 'Fordun', he 'rose from his hiding places' in 1297, while English sources for the most part denigrate him as 'a common thief, . . . often outlawed', 'a bloody man, formerly a leader of thieves', and even 'deserter of piety, plunderer, sacrilegious one, arsonist, and murderer, cruel as Herod, debauched as Nero'.[68] But there is one English source, the chronicle ascribed to William Rishanger, monk of St Albans, that is specific:

> When Edward returned to the south of his kingdom . . . all the Scots by common assent chose and made their leader and recruiter a certain man called William le Waleis, of ignoble family, so that they could renew the war against the king of England – in vain.
> *How the Scots chose William le Waleis to be their leader and recruiter.*
> At the same time there was in Scotland a certain young man called William le Waleis,[69] an archer, who sought his sustenance by bow and quiver. Born and brought up of a lowly and poor family, since he had tried out his audacity in many places, as is the way of strong men, he sought leave from the Scots that he might meet the English and halt their army by his bow, and, so that they would help him, and he would protect their army. He promised them by a sworn oath, that if leave to meet with them was given him, he would take all England and lead them to London, and so deliver up the whole kingdom of England by force. . . . On the spot all the Scots chose the said William le Waleis, of ignoble family, and appointed him leader and recruiter over their army.

This chronicle breaks off about 1300, and the above section, although the *frustra*, 'in vain', shows that it was written after the battle of Falkirk in July 1298, shows no awareness of the capture and death of Wallace in 1305, over which English writers were wont to gloat. The repetition in it is striking, and the content of the second paragraph, with its absurd boasts, speaks not only of its English origin but also suggests a popular poem of the kind preserved in the chronicles of Pierre Langtoft and perhaps written soon after Falkirk. The comment on Wallace's ignoble birth in 'Fordun' is here reiterated; what is new is his strength and his occupation as an archer. His archery skill had been gained not in war but in the pursuit of game for the pot, and if he was criminalised before 1297 (and this depends on a mention of him or a namesake as 'thief' in 1296),[70] this could have arisen from poaching. But the occupation is surely confirmed beyond a peradventure by the device on his seal of a bow and string, with arrow.

Among the ragmen seals, Patrick Archer, another royal tenant in Ayrshire, shows a stringed hunting horn above a bow and arrow,[71] while William de Kinmonth and Duncan Baird (Nos. 3383, 3503) show an archer or bow and arrow shooting at a stag. The bow alone, however, occurs nowhere else among the 600 non-armigerous seals; and the absence from Wallace's seal of emblems of the chase – the stag, the hunting horn – suggests that his pursuit was, or should have been, small game. The broadhead arrow depicted on the seal was the weapon not of war but of the hunt; the device on his seal was chosen with care as relevant to Wallace's status and profession as an archer.

For long the history of archery[72] accepted a development from the 'short bow', known before the late thirteenth century, to the longbow developed then, which gave the English a superiority over lesser races on the battlefield – as over the Scots at Falkirk in 1298. But the few references to short bows are to those intended for women or children; the short bow, supposedly in general use before the late thirteenth century, was a category invented by Sir Charles Oman in the nineteenth century. Archaeology has provided ample evidence for the existence of bows longer than 168 centimetres (5 feet 6 inches) and as long as 192 centimetres (6 feet 3 inches) in the tenth and eleventh centuries.[73] The artist of the Bayeux tapestry, following the stylised iconography of an earlier age, depicted bows much smaller than the archers, but in the lower margin of the battle scenes gave the Norman archers unstylised bows of their own height. From the twelfth century there is less archaeological evidence until the dozens of bows and arrows recovered from the *Mary Rose*, sunk in 1545, but there is enough to show that the bow of adult height was the usual equipment in both chase and battle, from at least Viking times until the sixteenth century. Such a bow would be the equipment of William Wallace.

The *Mary Rose* examples have permitted the construction of replica bows that differ in many respects from modern archery examples, where a modern longbow will store about 50–70 pounds in energy. For this:

an archer uses well-controlled muscle power, the greater part of the work being done by the arm and shoulder muscles ... The pull on the fingers of the drawing hand corresponds to the weight of the bow, the left hand holding the bow, and the left arm, being fully extended but not locked. The effect of the natural elasticity of the bow is to swing the bow-arm across the chest so, to counteract this, the shoulder muscles have to develop a pull of about 300 lb (136 kg) force ... The resulting force across each shoulder joint ... is greater than three hundredweight (152.4 kg).[74]

The physical development of a professional archer, practising daily, as he/she must, with such a bow, would be remarkable.

The weight (that is, stored energy) of the longbows of the *Mary Rose*, and of earlier fragments showing that the type had long been known, is 110–170 pounds, at least double the weight of the modern longbow; the enormous energy stored in the drawn bow would allow a range of 300 metres, while the feathering of the arrow would cause it to rotate, so, holding a straight course, to achieve a remarkable accuracy of aim. The energy to achieve this was stored by human effort. Repeated drawing and firing (and shooting ten arrows per minute was not at all unusual) would lead to striking muscular development of the shoulders and arms. The skeletons from the *Mary Rose* that can be associated with archery tackle are described as 'huge . . . not *necessarily* tall, but massively boned' with changes to the shoulder blades that *could* be the result of working with heavy bows.[75]

Now, it can be argued that the ignoble of thirteenth-century Scotland would be more familiar with plough and harrow than longbow and arrow, and that their bows, if any, would be less well made, less powerful and less demanding than the yew bows bought for Henry VIII of England. But imported yew bows of quality were indeed possessed by the ignoble in England *c.* 1300, and there is no reason to think that they did not also reach the Scots in the thirteenth century. Our sources do not permit us to test whether the peasantry were skilled archers or not, but scepticism on this surely cannot apply to William Wallace who 'sought his sustenance by bow and quiver', and who would need the most effective implement of his day in both range and power for his hunt, with a lifetime of using it from an early age to perfect his expertise. A broad, powerful man.

That is how he appears in later narratives. In Wyntoun he is 'of stature . . . strang and stout', and later 'manlyk, stout and lyberalle',[76] descriptions that were perhaps only conventional, although it is notable that 'lang', tall, is not among them. Bower in the 1440s remedied this, sketching a man 'tall, with the body of a giant . . . broad shouldered and big-boned', but these words were borrowed from a much earlier description of Charlemagne, already used by him.[77] This was also the source of the vivid description of a seven-foot-tall Wallace, with 'great limbs' and 'hard muscles' in the full-blown romance-life by Blind Hary,[78] a man who fought with the sword. Just once he gives us Wallace the archer, in the context of a fictitious encounter with the English near Cargill (Perthshire):

A bow he bair wes byg and well beseyn	*well looked after*
And arrows als bath lang and sharpe withal	
No man was thar that Wallace bow mycht drall	*draw*
Rycht stark was he . . .[79]	

He shot down fifteen of the enemy before running out of arrows, but his men were not good archers, preferring to fight in close encounter with sword and spear.

Other atrocities were alleged by English sources: that the Scots bound and threw old men, clerics and women into rivers, and Wallace himself was about to preside at such an occasion when the clerics were saved by the intervention of some magnates. One source tells us that after the battle of Stirling Bridge his men showed a lively hatred when they flayed the skin of Cressingham, the English Treasurer, killed in the battle, and divided it into small parts; but another source that Wallace himself 'caused a broad strip [of the skin] to be taken from head to heel to make therewith a baldrick for his sword' – a savage gesture of triumph.[80] How much truth there was in these stories we cannot know.

But there was ample justification for portraying Wallace as a man of the sword in the leadership he gave from 1297, described in the account of his career in the last document to be considered: the record of his offences and sentence on 23 August 1305 preserved by a contemporary London annalist. I give references to the paragraphs of the translation provided here. He first tells us something of Wallace's entry to London and then his being conveyed to Westminster Hall where he was crowned with laurels in derision because he had once claimed that he should wear a crown there (§1). The annal also claims that when the offence of treason was read out, 'he answered that he had never been a traitor to the king of England but granted the other crimes charged against him'. The justification for this, that Wallace had never sworn fealty to Edward, is entirely modern.

The official record does make it plain that the king, by his *ordinacio* enjoined on the justices,[81] had informed the specially appointed justices of Wallace's offences (§2) and that they then pronounced the penalties incurred by the offender. The king's authority – his record — sufficed to make guilt absolute, and the final clause of the offences (before sentence) denying the opportunity of defence or response (§7) makes it clear that no evidence was led and that Wallace was intended to be silent throughout. His rejection of treason, which is the annalist's name for the sedition and felony of the charges,[82] is not in the official record. But in 1322 the trial of Thomas, Earl of Lancaster, began with the judge saying, perhaps in English: 'Thomas, at the first our lord the king and this court excludes you of [from] all manner [of] answer. Thomas . . . you have ridden with banner displayed . . . as a traitor', to which Lancaster did riposte that he had never been a traitor – and was ignored.[83] This may represent either the procedure of 1305 or an unsuccessful attempt to bar repetition of Wallace's riposte. In any case, there can be little doubt that he did speak out, perhaps on the first charge, perhaps towards the end when, as an outlaw, he was said to have no right to speak. If, as is likely, the whole proceedings were conducted in insular French,[84] the accused might pick out the recurring *sedition* and *felonie* and make his protest; the details of the rest would be incomprehensible to him unless he had acquired that language, which is doubtful.

So there would be only charges and sentence. Of the twenty or more opponents of Edward I who were executed for treason, only two suffered the penalty, inescapable later, of being drawn to execution, hanged, disembowelled and quartered. Some elements were imposed in different cases: for example, the 296 persons drawn and hanged in 1279 for clipping the coinage, or Llewellyn ap Gruffydd, leading the Welsh against Edward I, killed in a skirmish with an English platoon, whose head was cut off to be displayed on the Tower of London. But in 1283, David ap Gruffydd (brother of Llewellyn), who had enjoyed Edward's favour and rebelled against him, was sentenced to be drawn to execution because he had betrayed the king, hanged alive for killing English noblemen, taken down, disembowelled and his entrails burned because he had done this at Easter, and his body quartered, the pieces despatched to be displayed as a warning to others – probably in Welsh towns. Only beheading is not mentioned, but as his head was displayed at the Tower, that too was inflicted upon him, although we do not know at what point.[85]

The record of the judgment on Wallace, well summarised and discussed in recent scholarship,[86] relates each element in his punishment to asserted crimes (§8). For acting as though king in Scotland, and for his other felonies against the king, seeking his death (§3–4), he was drawn to the place of execution; for his robberies, homicides and felonies (§4–5), he was hanged and disembowelled;[87] as an outlaw (§7), he was beheaded; for his injuries to the church (§8) caused by blasphemous thoughts arising from his bowels, his entrails were burned; and finally, his head was to be displayed in London, and his body quartered and a part displayed on the gibbet at Newcastle, Berwick, Stirling and Edinburgh (§9). The correspondence with David ap Gruffydd is not exact, and in the circumstances consistency was not up for debate, but the two punishments were clearly meant to be identical; it is likely that the Westminster chronicle is correct when it places the burning of entrails before the beheading, as evidently happened with David ap Gruffydd (§10).

Yet the contrast with, for example, the other Edwardian *cause célèbre*, that of Thomas Turberville in 1295, is striking. He told Edward's secrets to the French king (when the two kings were at war), urged the possibility of the Welsh and Scots rising together, and left a trail of treasonable correspondence, yet was merely – forgive the word – hanged for it and left on the gibbet until his body disintegrated.[88] The sentence on Wallace makes it quite clear why he, and presumably David ap Gruffydd, were treated with such ferocity: his corpse was quartered because he had committed felonies not only against King Edward but also against the people of England and Scotland, and the quarters were therefore displayed before them. The logic of this statement is that the people would rejoice in justice manifestly done, but the act, limited to these two men, had nothing to do with logic; it was to 'put fear into and to warn' the rebellious of the awful fate that awaited them if they followed another such leader. The chunks of flesh were intended to cow the subject peoples, the Welsh and the Scots.

But one detail in the charges against Wallace, relating to the death of the sheriff of Lanark at the beginning of Wallace's public career, seems to have escaped comment (§4). The Latin claims that Wallace 'attacked, wounded and killed William de Heselrig, sheriff of Lanark, who [held *or* was holding][89] the pleas of the king in open county court', and *postea, in contemptum ipsius regis, ipsum vicecomitem sic interfectum frustatim dimicavit. Dimicare* here carries the unusual meaning 'cut up',[90] as required by the rare *frustatim*, 'in pieces'.[91] Hence, 'afterwards in contempt of the king he cut up the sheriff, slain thus in pieces'.

The gesture is unknown to writers of the time or later. 'Fordun' knew little or nothing of the early Wallace, save that he killed the unnamed sheriff of Lanark in that town.[92] Only with Wyntoun, writing soon after 1400, is there acknowledgment that: 'Of his good deeds and his manhood / Great tales and songs are made', and that all his deeds would fill a 'great book'.[93] Wyntoun shows no knowledge of Wallace the archer; rather, he was a swordsman, brawling with the English in Lanark because they taunted him for the 'sword both sharp and long' with which 'it was his use then for to gang', to which Wallace's bawdy ripostes, 'sa said the prest that served thy wif' and 'thi dame[94] was swyvit [sexually compromised] or [before] thou was borne', led to the predictable riot, exchanging 'dint for dint', from which Wallace escaped with his mistress's help.[95] Then the unnamed sheriff, the king of England's 'lufftennande',[96] came to Lanark, had her arrested and executed, to Wallace's anguish. He gathered thirty men, entered the town by night, burst into the sheriff's lodging, seized him by the throat in his bed, crying 'the woman's death of yesterday I shall quit thee now', and, dragging him downstairs, killed him (from what follows) with his sword.[97]

This source agrees with 'Fordun' in killing only one man, so we can reject the version of a battle against an English company given in *The Wallace*[98] and accept that the assault could well have taken place at night, as Wyntoun describes. 'Holding the king's pleas' in the charges describes the reason for Heselrig's presence at Lanark and makes the offence an attack upon the king, for the sheriffs and others appointed by Edward are described as 'holding his place', *locum suum tenentes*, making the same point and leading to the charge that Wallace in sedition to the king acted feloniously 'in perpetrating his death'. It is striking that this point had somehow reached Wyntoun when he described the sheriff as the king's 'lufftenand'.

But neither Wyntoun nor any other source knows the savagery of those two Latin words *frustatim dimicavit*, 'he hacked the slain sheriff in pieces', which so justify the belief recounted by Bower that St Andrew gave Wallace a bloody sword. They show us that in 1297 he was already a man of the sword, secondly, a seeker after vengeance fuelled by hatred, and therefore, thirdly, a man moved by a terrible personal outrage. If I am right in seeing him moved by a personal affront in taking vengeance on Heselrig, then we must surely give some credence to the essential of Wyntoun's story: that Heselrig had killed a woman dear to William Wallace.

Thus what he did to Heselrig's body in 1297 was done to his own in 1305. The precedent of David ap Gruffydd's execution shows that the quartering was not an innovation, not introduced as repayment for the violation of Heselrig's corpse, which was regarded as 'contempt of the king'. Yet although the sentence on Wallace makes no connection between the two violations, it seems possible, even likely, that there was one, after the dismemberment of Heselrig was cited to justify that of Wallace. Three weeks after the latter's execution, Edward began discussions within parliament with some English prelates and magnates and a delegation of ten leading Scots, on the 'form of peace' that would settle the government of Scotland and which resulted in the *Ordonnance* of early October 1305. To these Scots, among them the betrayer of Wallace, Sir John Menteith, whom Edward appointed to a vacant place on the delegation, the execution would be very immediate – his head looked down upon them at the Tower – and some may even have been in London when it took place;[99] to recall his atrocity might remind them of his lowly origins and justify the quartering of his body.

It is a possibility, but no more, that it was feared that the Scots might protest on religious grounds. In 1299 Boniface VIII, in the bull *Detestande feritatis*, denounced with characteristically immoderate language the practice of treating the bodies of nobles and persons of rank who died distant from their desired place of burial to a process whereby they 'were cruelly disembowelled and frightfully severed into pieces'.[100] These were boiled, the flesh separated from the bones and the latter sent to be buried.[101] The pope's denunciation was aimed at noble ranks[102] and not at those who might suffer quartering at Smithfield. It was also ineffective – we need only recall that the corpse of Douglas, killed in Spain in 1331, was dismembered and boiled, his flesh buried there, his bones brought home to Douglas kirk.[103]

But in 1305 Edward I was mending fences with the papacy and its compliant new occupant, Clement V (elected 5 June 1305), sending a well-prepared embassy to Clement, partly to secure release from promises given domestically in 1297–1301, and the revocation of the bull *Clericis laicos*, and partly to have Robert Winchelsey removed from the archbishopric of Canterbury. So hopeful was Edward of a new relationship that in the month of Wallace's execution he told the Bishop of Hereford that he intended to petition the pope for the canonisation of Thomas Cantilupe, bishop from 1275 to1282, and did so early in November 1305.[104] He may have judged that it would be well to give the Scots no case (based upon the condemnation in *Detestande feritatis*) with which to stir up Clement against him, as they had stirred up his predecessor, 'that Roman priest', Boniface VIII; hence, perhaps, the implication that by his act Wallace earned the same treatment.

If the later picture of Wallace's physique doubtfully represents a tradition passed down in tales and songs,[105] I offer the much firmer judgment that – by tradition or by chance – it is close to the truth about the man revealed by his seal. William Wallace the archer must have been strong of arm and broad of shoulder well beyond the average of his time, and skilled of eye and hand. When this man of lowly birth came to lead a people in arms and to defend their kingdom, bow and arrow would give place to the sword with which he is endowed in literature and shown in sculpture. But Wallace in temperament was a man of his time and of his non-chivalric origins, a man of vengeance who killed the sheriff of Lanark and hacked to pieces his corpse, a deed returned in full measure by his judges.

Appendix. William Wallace: The Judgment of 23 August 1305

Modern accounts of the trial of Wallace, particularly those by Professors Bellamy and Barrow and Mr Andrew Fisher,[106] have set the event in a convincing context. Here, from the London annalist, who included the record of proceedings, is a translation of the key contemporary account of what happened seven hundred years ago, followed by a brief excerpt from a chronicle kept at Westminster Abbey, giving details of Wallace's execution. I have broken the texts into paragraphs and added numbering thereof.

1. From *Chronicles of Edward I and Edward II*, ed. W. Stubbs, I, 139–42:
[*Annals of London:*] In the same year on 22 August, Sir William Wallace, knight, born of Scottish birth, came to London; a multitude of men and women met him and he was put up in the houses of William de Leyre, citizen of London, in the parish of All Saints *ad Fenum*.[107] The next day, Monday, the eve of St Bartholomew, he was led on horseback to Westminster; with John de Segrave and Geoffrey de Segrave, knights, the mayor, sheriffs and aldermen of London leading and following him, with many others on foot and horseback. In the Great Hall of Westminster he was placed on the south bench, crowned with laurel leaves inasmuch as it was commonly said that in past times he had claimed that he should wear a crown in that same hall. Forthwith he was called to judgment and charged by Sir Peter Malory, justice of the lord king of England, as a traitor to the said king; he answered that he had never been a traitor to the king of England, but granted the other crimes charged against him. At length the said Peter with other justices pronounced the judgment in the order which follows.

2. [*Summary of letters patent:*] Edward I to John de Segrave, Peter Malory, Ralph de Sandwich, John de Bakewell and John le Blound mayor of London, appoints them justices at the prison of London to deliver William Wallace 'according to the ordinance on the matter enjoined by us upon you'. All or four or three of them are to deliver him 'in the aforesaid way'. John de Segrave, who has custody of William, is to cause William and his *attachiamentum*[108] to come to the appointed place at the appointed time. At Raurethe [Rawreth, Essex], 18 August, regnal year 33 [1305].

3. [*The proceedings:*] Trial at Westminster before John de Segrave, P. Malory, R. de Sandwich, John de Balewell and J. le Blound mayor of the king's city of London, on Monday, the eve of St Bartholomew, in the 33rd year of the reign of King Edward son of Henry.

William Wallace, a Scot and coming from Scotland, taken for sedition, homicides, depredations, arsons, and other divers felonies, came, and after the justices recited how, after the aforesaid lord king had taken the land of Scotland by arms against John Balliol, the prelates, earls, barons and others of that land, his enemies, by forfeiture of the same John and by his conquest he had reduced and subjugated all Scots to his lordship and royal power as their king, had received the homages and fealties of prelates, earls, barons and many others and had caused his peace to be proclaimed through all the land of Scotland and had ordained and appointed keepers of that land in his place, sheriffs, provosts, baillies, and others his agents, to maintain his peace and do justice to all according to the laws and customs of that land.

4. the aforesaid William Wallace, forgetting his fealty and allegiance, pondering every possible felony and sedition against the said lord king, and having joined and allied to himself an immense number of felons, arose and feloniously attacked and assaulted the keepers and agents of the said king, and feloniously and against the peace of the said lord king attacked, wounded and killed William de Heselrigg, sheriff of Lanark, who [was holding][109] the pleas of the said king in open county court, and thereafter, in contempt of the same king, he cut up piecemeal the said sheriff [who had been] killed thus.

5. Thereafter with the largest possible throng of armed men gathered to him and his felony, he attacked the cities and castles of that land, and caused to be sent out his writs through all Scotland, as though [they were] the writs of the superior of that land, and he ordered his parliaments and musters,[110] all the keepers and agents of the lord king having been thrown out of the land of Scotland by the same William. Not wishing to be curbed by such wickedness and sedition, he advised all the prelates, earls and barons of his land belonging to his party that they should submit to the fealty and lordship of the lord king of France and give him help to the destruction of the kingdom of England.

6. Also taking with him some of his fellows he entered the kingdom of England, namely the counties of Northumberland, Cumberland and Westmorland, and all whom he found there in the king of England's fealty he feloniously killed by various kinds of death; he feloniously and seditiously assaulted, burned and devastated religious men and nuns dedicated to God, churches built to the honour of God and his saints and with them the bodies of saints and other relics honourably collected in them; he spared none who used the English language but inflicted [upon] all, old and young, wives and widows, children and babes the worst death which he could devise.

7. Thus he persevered every day and hour seditiously and feloniously to encompass the death of the said lord king and the manifest weakening and destruction of his crown and royal majesty. And although after such immense and horrible deeds, the lord king with his great army had invaded the land of Scotland and had defeated the said William, who bore a banner against him in mortal battle, and his other enemies, and had granted his firm peace to all of that land, and had mercifully caused the said William Wallace to be recalled to his peace, the same William persevered seditiously and feloniously, harmoniously and eagerly,[111] in his afore-noted wickedness, refused to submit himself to the lord king's peace and to come

to it, and so was publicly outlawed in the court of the said lord king as a deceiver, robber and felon according to the laws of England and Scotland; and it is, and is believed, unjust and in disagreement with English laws for anyone outlawed thus and placed beyond the laws and not afterwards restored to his peace to be admitted to defend his position or to answer.

8. It is decided that the said William, for the manifest sedition which he feloniously contrived to bring about his [the king's] death and to weaken and destroy his crown and his royal dignity, bearing a banner in mortal battle against his liege lord, shall be drawn from the palace of Westminster to the Tower of London and from the Tower to Aldgate and from there through the middle of the city to Elms[112] and for the robberies, homicides and felonies which he carried out in the kingdom of England and land of Scotland, shall be hanged there and afterwards taken down. And because he was outlawed and not afterwards restored to the lord king's peace, he shall be beheaded and decapitated. And afterwards for the dreadful wickedness which he did to the church, in burning churches, vessels and feretories [shrines] in which the body of Christ and the bodies of saints and their relics were collected, the heart, liver and lung and all the bowels of the said William, from which such perverse thoughts proceeded, shall be put in the fire and burned.

9. And also because he had done the aforesaid sedition, depredations, arsons, homicides and felonies not only to the said lord king but also to the whole people of England and Scotland, the body of the same William shall be cut and divided into four quarters, and the head thus severed shall be put on London Bridge in the view of those passing both by land and water, and one quarter shall be hung on the gibbet at Newcastle upon Tyne, a second quarter at Berwick, a third quarter at Stirling and the fourth quarter at St John's Town[113] to put dread in and to warn all by-passers and observers.

10. From *Flores Historiarum*, ed. H. R. Luard, iii, 124
[A Westminster Abbey chronicle:] On the eve of St Bartholomew's day he was condemned to a very cruel but well-deserved death. First [he was] dragged through the streets of London at horse's tails to the very high gibbet made for him, on which [he was] hanged by a noose and afterwards let down half alive; next his genitals [were] cut off and his intestines eviscerated and burned in a fire; finally when his head [had been] cut off and his body cut in four parts, the head was affixed on a stake on London Bridge; the quartered limbs were sent to parts of Scotland.

4

The Battle of Stirling Bridge:
An English Perspective

Michael Prestwich

At Stirling Bridge on 11 September 1297 the Scots under the inspirational leadership of William Wallace won a quite extraordinary victory. The Edwardian war machine, which had achieved the conquest of Wales and had routed the Scottish host at Dunbar in 1296, was revealed as vulnerable. The English warhorses proved to have hooves of clay. My purpose is firstly to set the battle of Stirling Bridge in its military context: how surprising was it that an ill-equipped army of Scottish foot soldiers should have been able to defeat an English host? Secondly, I will examine the political significance of the battle from the English point of view. It was fought at a time of major political crisis in England and had a considerable bearing on the outcome of the disputes between Edward I and his opponents.

At the time of Stirling Bridge, the English under Edward I were highly experienced in war. The various campaigns in which Edward's armies had been involved had provided the king and his officials with immense experience in organising campaigns. They knew how to recruit men and how to organise the logistics of a campaign. It was no easy task to collect the vast supplies of victuals needed and to organise their transport. The financial mechanisms for funding war were tried and tested. The English were, however, relatively inexperienced in battle. It was more than thirty years since the two great civil-war battles of Lewes and Evesham. The Welsh wars had seen the English triumph in two battles, Irfon Bridge in 1282, and Maes Moydog in 1295, but neither was a full-scale engagement. In each case, English cavalry backed up by infantry had been successful against relatively ill-equipped Welsh forces, which lacked above all heavy cavalry. Nor had it all gone the English way, for the Welsh themselves had won one engagement, in 1282, near the Menai Strait. War against the French began in 1294, but neither side relished the prospect of battle, and there was no full-scale set-piece engagement. In Scotland, when war began in 1296, the English first engaged in a ferocious sack of Berwick, demonstrating a wholly unexpected and unacceptable degree of savagery. The subsequent campaign witnessed one field encounter, at Dunbar, when Earl Warenne's forces defeated the Scottish army, routing a cavalry charge and destroying with it the main aristocratic military strength of Scotland. Edinburgh Castle resisted briefly, and there followed a military promenade around Scotland. This must have persuaded the English that the Scots were unlike the Welsh and would not offer serious resistance.

Following this triumph, the English did not expect war in Scotland in 1297, but their high-handed policies soon provoked rebellion. The main rising began in May, when William Wallace killed William Hesilrig, sheriff of Lanark, who, according to the official record, was presiding over the court in which the king's pleas were being heard.[1] This was followed by a rapid raid on Scone, to attack William Ormsby, the English justiciar of Scotland. There was widespread support, both aristocratic and popular, for the rising. By 10 July Hugh Cressingham was informing the king that none of the English officials in Scotland could raise any money because of extensive hostility. Later in the month Edward was told that only Berwickshire and Roxburghshire were under proper control.[2] Yet at the first sign of English military reaction, when Henry Percy and Robert Clifford marched north from the western border to Ayr, the Scots began to negotiate terms. At Irvine, in July, James Stewart and William Douglas offered surrender. Wallace, however, was not to be dealt with so easily. In addition, there was a widespread popular rising in the north, headed by Andrew Murray.[3]

The English did not respond effectively to the continued resistance until late August, when an English army under Earl Warenne, assisted by Hugh Cressingham, marched north from Berwick to Stirling, presumably intending to move on farther northwards. Warenne was a man of considerable military experience. He had fought in the Welsh war of 1282–83 and was there again dealing with the rebellion of 1287. He commanded a substantial retinue in the final Welsh war, that of 1294–95.[4] His main military achievement had come more recently still, for it was he who had commanded the English troops who achieved the striking victory over the Scots at Dunbar in 1296. Warenne had no enthusiasm for Scotland. He declared that the climate was bad for his health and that he could not possibly remain in the country, preferring to stay in the north of England.[5] Early in August 1297 an attempt was made to replace him; this may have been because he was proving inadequate and incompetent in Scotland, but it is more likely that the king wanted him to take part in the forthcoming campaign in Flanders. Brian FitzAlan of Bedale was approached but protested that he was too poor for such a task: 'In my poverty, I could not keep the land in peace to your profit and honour, when such a lord as the earl cannot hold it in peace with what he receives from you.'[6] It must have been with a heavy heart that Warenne marched towards Stirling.

Stirling was the lowest point at which the River Forth could be crossed, and with its castle it was a key point in English strategy. If the northern rising was to be dealt with, the army must pass the stronghold. When Warenne advanced towards Stirling, Wallace was engaged in besieging the castle at Dundee; he and Murray must have decided that Stirling was the best point at which to intercept Warenne's force. From the Scots point of view, not only was it the obvious place to prevent an English advance farther north, but there were also many tactical advantages in challenging the English there. The narrow bridge limited English mobility; in addition, the meadows and fields on the north bank were unsuitable for the use of heavy cavalry.[7] The Scots could observe the English manoeuvres and control the position from high ground to the north.

The problem presented to historians by most medieval battles is that of reconciling divergent versions. In contrast, Stirling Bridge was fully recorded by only one chronicler, the English Walter of Guisborough, and the problem is to decide how much credence to give to his account.[8] According to him, Warenne advanced to the town of Stirling, where he was met by James Stewart, the Earl of Lennox and other Scottish magnates. They asked for some assistance, so that they might somehow be able to subdue their fellow Scots. After a few days they returned to Stirling and promised to come back the following day with forty men-at-arms. As they rode off, they encountered an English foraging party; Lennox attacked them, striking one foot soldier in the neck with his sword. The English troops were understandably agitated, accusing the Scottish magnates of treachery and breach of faith. Warenne promised action and issued orders that the army was to move out on the next day, 11 September, to cross the Forth. Duly, first thing in the morning, many of the infantry marched over the bridge. They were soon ordered back because Warenne himself had overslept. When he finally arose, he knighted some of his men, a traditional move on the eve of battle. Meanwhile the infantry advanced again across the bridge, only to return once more because James Stewart and the Earl of Lennox had arrived without the promised cavalry forces. Two Dominican friars were sent to negotiate with the Scots; Guisborough reports Wallace as declaring that he and his men had not come to make peace but to fight to vindicate themselves and to free their kingdom. 'Let those who wish climb up here, and they will find us ready to trim their beards.' There was much discussion in the English ranks as to what to do; some hotheads were in favour of an immediate attack on the Scottish position, which was on high ground. Sir Richard Lundy, who had surrendered to the English earlier in the year at Irvine, gave sensible advice. The bridge was too dangerous to cross, since the men could go only two abreast; the Scots would then attack from the flank when they reached the bank. Instead, Lundy offered to take a force across a nearby ford, where sixty could cross in a line, enabling him to attack the Scots from the rear, while Warenne and the remaining force crossed the bridge. It is easy, with hindsight, to condemn the English commanders for their response; it was, thought Warenne and Cressingham, far too risky to split the English forces in this way. There was much debate as to what to do, but Cressingham persuaded Warenne to proceed over the bridge. The English probably expected the Scots to face them formally in battle; a surprise attack was clearly not anticipated.

Given how narrow the bridge was, the troops must have taken a long time to move across it. Among the first to advance was the standard bearer of the king (it is not clear why this man was not in Flanders with Edward I), together with those of Earl Warenne and the notable Yorkshire knight Marmaduke Thweng. Once a number of English had made their way over the bridge, the Scots attacked, rushing down from the heights, and their pikemen seized the end of the bridge so that no one could cross in either direction. Thweng and his men charged into the Scottish ranks, with some success, but the numbers opposing them were too great, and none of the other English cavalry followed their example. After a struggle, Thweng was able to force his way back over the bridge, but a large number were slain by the Scots. A few Welshmen swam to safety, and one knight was able to force his horse into the water and across the river. Hugh Cressingham was killed. Warenne himself had not crossed the bridge, and once Thweng returned over it, he ordered it to be broken and burned. Thweng was put in charge of Stirling Castle. Promising faithfully to return with reinforcements in ten weeks, Warenne, no doubt thoroughly dispirited, made his way to Berwick as fast as he could. Many of the English were not so lucky. The retreating baggage train was caught by Stewart and Lennox, who naturally had turned to the patriotic cause once they saw how successful Wallace and his men had been. Many of the fleeing common soldiers were caught and killed by the pursuing Scots.

Walter of Guisborough's account of the battle is exceptionally detailed. He added colour to it by providing vivid dialogue that can hardly be relied upon as a verbatim account of what was said. No direct indication of his sources is given, but the important role accorded to Marmaduke Thweng is very striking. The chronicler gives a detailed and dramatic account of how Marmaduke's nephew, unhorsed and wounded in the battle, asked for help. Marmaduke told him to climb up behind him, but he lacked the strength. Another member of the Thweng retinue then dismounted and helped the unfortunate man to mount, so that they could all ride safely to the bridge. This suggests that Marmaduke, or one of his followers, could have provided much of the information; this is made more likely by the fact that the Thweng family had close connections with the priory at Guisborough where Walter wrote.[9] Other chronicles do not provide sufficient independent evidence with which to test Walter's account. A briefer but essentially similar version was provided, for example, by a St Albans chronicler.[10] The main hint of an alternative account is provided by Thomas Grey in his *Scalacronica*, relying on what he had been told by his father. He has it that it was the Scots who broke the bridge rather than this being done on English orders.[11] The Scottish tradition is startlingly uninformative, recording little more than the bare fact of victory.[12]

There has been little questioning of Walter's narrative of Stirling Bridge, but significant doubts have been raised over his account of the battle at Irfon Bridge in Wales in 1282. J. Beverley Smith noted that this has 'a disturbing similarity' to Stirling Bridge. In both cases there was a bridge, a nearby ford and an attack from the flank or rear. As with the account of Stirling Bridge, that of Irfon Bridge is enhanced by vivid dialogue. Smith does not directly question the accuracy of Walter of Guisborough's version of events in Scotland but argues that his version of the Welsh battle has to be treated very cautiously.[13] It may be that Walter's account of Stirling Bridge is more credible than that of the Welsh battle, for it was written nearer the time, but if he was capable of being inventive in one case, he may also have taken liberties in the other. Such elements as Warenne's creation of new knights, and his sending friars to negotiate with the Scots, are features that might be expected in any battle account and could well have been added for effect.

One obvious reservation about Walter's account concerns the numbers involved. He puts the size of the English force at about 1,000 cavalry and 50,000 infantry. Reinforcements under Percy totalling 300 horse and 80,000 foot soldiers were, according to the chronicler, dismissed by Cressingham on the grounds that he had sufficient troops and did not want to spend unnecessarily. The Scots force was put at 180 horse and 40,000 foot.[14] These numbers are not credible. There are, unfortunately, no surviving payrolls for the English army; they may have been lost with Cressingham in the battle. There are no indications that there was substantial recruitment for the army in Scotland, and Guisborough's figures are no more than the wild imaginings of a typically innumerate chronicler. It would be dangerous to hazard a guess as to the size of Warenne's force, but it is worth noting that the king at this time had with him in Flanders a total of almost 900 cavalry and some 8,000 infantry.[15] Warenne must have had a much smaller force than this at Stirling. Indeed, the chronicler Bartholomew Cotton stated with considerable plausibility that the English army was too small, since many had decided to abandon the expedition when they were convinced by the promises of the Scots that they were about to make peace.[16]

Walter of Guisborough is surprisingly vague about the casualties at

Stirling. The total number he puts at about a hundred cavalry and 5,000 infantry. Hugh Cressingham is the one and only victim of the Scots he names; fat, proud and arrogant, he died what the chronicler clearly considers a deserved death. Cressingham was an unpopular official who had been Queen Eleanor's steward – for all her reputation, she had been a harsh landlord. He was the man who would have been regarded as responsible above all for the harsh financial aspects of English rule in Scotland. In a touch of horror, Wallace's men flayed his corpse, and distributed pieces of his skin as mementoes.[17] Peter Langtoft in his chronicle adds the deaths of Robert de Somerville and his eldest son, but although he states that many noble men were also killed, he provides no more names.[18] Others who died in the battle included Robert Delaval and Richard Waldegrave, constable of Stirling Castle.[19] There can be little doubt that a considerable number of foot soldiers lost their lives, but it seems possible that knightly casualties were indeed at a low level. The normal reason for this was that knights were worth more alive than dead, given the value of their ransoms. In this case, however, there is no evidence of ransoms paid by the English, and the answer may be either that few English knights in fact crossed the bridge or that their armour and equipment protected them.

The battle of Stirling Bridge witnessed the rout of a conventional English force, with its heavy cavalry, by a force of foot soldiers. Many successes for infantry over cavalry would follow in the fourteenth century. In Scotland there was Bruce's first real triumph against the English, at Loudon Hill in 1307, and, of course, Bannockburn in 1314. Other successes for infantry forces included those in Flanders, with Courtrai in 1302 and Arques in the following year. In England there was Boroughbridge in 1322. Once the English had grasped the point that a line of dismounted men-at-arms assisted by archers was virtually unbeatable, there came a whole succession of celebrated triumphs, from Dupplin Moor and Halidon Hill in 1332 and 1333 respectively through to Crécy and Neville's Cross in 1346 and Poitiers a decade later.[20] It is important to stress, however, that Stirling Bridge stands out from these infantry victories as untypical; its tactics did not provide a precedent for these later battles. In the great majority of cases, an army reliant on its foot soldiers established a strong defensive position, using ditches or pits to provide a defence against cavalry attacks. It was at Falkirk in 1298, not Stirling Bridge in 1297, that Wallace's tactics presaged the infantry successes of the future. There, he made a major innovation by using the formation of the schiltrom. This was a dense circle of pikemen that formed an almost impenetrable obstacle to the English cavalry. On that occasion the tactic was, of course, unsuccessful, but at Bannockburn in 1314 the story would be a very different one. The English developed different infantry formations from those used by the Scots, notably the wedge of archers and the line of dismounted men-at-arms. The archers, placed on the flanks, were important in hindering and breaking up any attack before it reached the defensive line of dismounted knights and men-at-arms with its full impetus.

The rush down the slopes towards the bridge at Stirling therefore does not fit the later pattern of infantry successes. The English defeat in 1297 was not a classic set-piece battle; Warenne and his men, although aware of the Scots presence, did not expect to be attacked as they crossed the bridge. If Guisborough reported Wallace's words to the friars correctly, the expectation was that the English would have to advance somehow up to the Scottish position to engage them. As it was, there was no time to draw up lines of battle. This was more ambush than open battle. Indeed, for Walter of Guisborough, it was not a battle but a *confusio*.[21] Stirling Bridge was not the only ambush that the English suffered in 1297; earlier in the year at Bellegarde in Gascony the English army under the Earl of Lincoln was caught by surprise as it made its way out of a wood in the evening. The unprepared English forces were routed by a French army under Robert of Artois; many infantry were killed and a significant number of knights captured.[22]

The English defeat at the hands of the Scots at Stirling Bridge undoubtedly came as a shock to contemporaries, but it should not be regarded as particularly surprising. It was not the first time that English troops had suffered at the hands of less well-equipped opponents close to a bridge. The battle had a distinct resemblance to the English defeat at the Menai Strait in 1282. Then, English troops under Luke de Tany, many of them mounted knights, were advancing towards a pontoon bridge that Edward's engineers had constructed over the strait. They were in a spirit of high confidence at the end of a raid into Snowdonia, but their enemies were waiting, unseen by them. Choosing their moment brilliantly, the Welsh came down on the English from their position high on the hills. They were on foot, and, lacking the sophisticated equipment of the English, most of them were probably armed with spears. The English force was caught as part of it was crossing the bridge. One knight forced his horse to swim for safety, but at least sixteen others were killed, as were many men-at-arms. This was a major disaster: the news reverberated throughout England. Accounts of the engagement differ in detail. It may be, as Walter of Guisborough has it, that the Welsh, aided by a high tide, prevented the English from reaching the bridge and drove them into the sea.[23] Alternatively, the English knights, driven back by the Welsh, did succeed in reaching the bridge but, in their haste to cross, overloaded it. In this version, the barges supporting the roadway began to sink, and it was only a very few who managed to swim to safety. The loss of so many knights in a single engagement was a great shock to the

English; the way in which the chroniclers recorded the casualties shows that this was not regarded as an accident of war but as an unprecedented catastrophe.[24]

The parallels between the fight at the Menai Strait and the battle of Stirling Bridge are not, of course, exact. There is a striking contrast between the many casualties listed on the occasion of the Welsh battle and the few recorded for Stirling Bridge. Like the Scots in 1297, however, the Welsh had shown that English cavalry forces were vulnerable to an unexpected infantry attack. They demonstrated, as Wallace would do, the helplessness of a force as it moved across a bridge. The defeat in Wales was perhaps the first real manifestation of the effectiveness of infantry against heavily armed cavalry, but the lesson that the Welsh taught Luke de Tany and his men in 1282 was not to be learned for fifty years. It would need a whole succession of infantry triumphs before the message sank in.

The disaster at the Menai Bridge, together with that at Bellegarde in Gascony, shows that the English by 1297 did not have the kind of record of invincibility that they would achieve later, in the Hundred Years War. Even so, the defeat at Stirling Bridge was startling. The obvious explanation is that there was a fatal failure of command. Earl Warenne appears to have displayed a monumental degree of stupidity, which puts him alongside the Earl of Cardigan in the roll call of disastrous English commanders. Hugh Cressingham demonstrated the obvious fact that accountants do not make generals. Peter Langtoft places the blame squarely on him for attempting to cross the bridge with too small a force.[25] The English did try to find excuses for the defeat: spin doctors are not a purely modern phenomenon. According to a poem on the Scottish wars, Warenne was the first across the bridge, boldly and heroically driving into the Scottish formations, but he was driven back by treachery, not by force of arms. Lennox and Richard Lundy were named as the traitors.[26] Although the form of their treachery is not described, the accusation was presumably that they changed sides once the engagement began, although it could relate to the negotiations and discussions that took place before the battle.

One view, expressed by a medieval commentator, of the effects of Stirling Bridge was that it saved the kingdom of France from potential disaster, in that it led Edward I to abandon his campaign against the French in the Low Countries.[27] It is, however, most unlikely that Edward would have achieved much success against Philip IV of France. His army was too small and his allies unreliable. In practice, the consequences of the battle for the English were very different. It was fought at a time of acute political uncertainty and difficulty in England, and ironically did much to help resolve the crisis that Edward I faced.

There were several strands to the opposition that confronted Edward in

71

1297, but a common factor was resentment at the heavy burdens imposed on the country as a result of war, burdens that were made more acute by the fact that this was a period of bad harvests and high prices. War with France had begun in 1294; in that year there was a Welsh revolt, while 1296 had seen the campaign against John Balliol in Scotland. There were separate issues relating to the taxation of laity and clergy. Novel demands for military service in 1297 aroused much hostility, and very few troops were recruited. Prises, compulsory seizures of foodstuffs and of wool, were much disliked.[28] Edward was determined, come what may, to lead an expedition to Flanders, and was prepared to ignore both constitutional niceties and the pleas of impoverishment that came from his subjects.

Scotland provided Edward I's opponents, notably the Earls of Norfolk and Hereford, Roger Bigod and Humphrey de Bohun, with an excellent argument in their case against the king. In the summer of 1297 the English reaction to events in Scotland was very limited. Late in June 1297 the English government sent £2,000 north to Hugh Cressingham, but this was no more than a loan, to be repaid out of Scottish revenues by 1 August. Such a requirement shows that there was no awareness of the scale of the problem. Cressingham protested on 10 July that the situation was impossible; English officials in Scotland were not in any position to collect funds, given the multitude of continuous and daily troubles that they faced.[29] In the so-called 'Remonstrances', drawn up by the opposition at the end of July, it was pointed out among other things that the Scots had already begun to rise in rebellion and that if Edward were to go abroad, the rising would intensify.[30] The argument was a good one, but the king was not to be diverted. Rather than make concessions to his opponents, he instituted a new tax of an eighth, with assessors and collectors appointed on 30 July. A wool seizure was also ordered. On 20 August the exchequer was told to proceed with a new tax on the clergy. Two days later Edward embarked at Winchelsea and sailed for Flanders the next day. His was a most remarkable display of obstinacy: he was determined to carry out his plans come what may.

Edward left a country seething with indignation. The government was under the nominal leadership of the young Prince Edward, but in practice Reginald de Grey led the council. The two earls, Bigod and Bohun, appeared with an armed force at the exchequer on 22 August and prevented the collection of the tax of an eighth.[31] There was an atmosphere of imminent civil war. The events and debates that took place in September are not well recorded, but there was evidently much alarm. A number of meetings were held in an attempt to settle the political disputes. Knights were asked to attend a meeting at Rochester on 8 September with the king's son. In writs dated 9 and 15 September respectively, the prelates and magnates were summoned to attend parliament in London on 30 September and knights of the shire on 6 October.[32] At the same time, military preparations began. Sheriffs were asked to retain men in royal service and to muster at London.[33] Royal castles were put in a state of defence. At Tickhill in Yorkshire, for example, iron bars were fitted to prevent access to the drawbridge, for which new ropes were bought. A new lock was fitted to the gate. The walls were repaired, the ditches recut, and thirteen crossbowmen and twenty archers hired.[34] The situation in England was critical.

The king made no move to resolve matters. The grievances that had led to the crisis were not tackled. Edward's attention was fixed on his war against the French; perhaps he hoped that if he achieved some signal success, the means he had adopted to finance his campaign would be seen as justified and his opponents confounded. Yet the situation in the Low Countries was not encouraging for the king. His own army was small. A letter of 18 September shows that he expected the man regarded as the chief English ally, the German ruler Adolf of Nassau, to join him shortly, but in the event Adolf neither met Edward nor sent troops.[35] Many of Edward's other allies had been defeated on the eve of the English king's landing. The townspeople of Bruges and Ghent were less than eager to support Edward. He left Bruges because of rumours that the citizens were about to rise in support of the French, and at Ghent he faced repeated troubles with the local inhabitants.[36] Not only, therefore, was the political situation in England very serious, but also the military position in the Low Countries was critical.

The triumph of the Scots under Wallace at Stirling Bridge, fought on 11 September, was the catalyst that transformed the situation. It is not clear how quickly the news travelled, but it must have been known within a very few days. The first indication that the government was aware of what had happened, however, is an instruction, issued on 21 September, to take Hereford Castle into the king's hands, as the previous keeper was Hugh Cressingham.[37] On 24 September the council in England wrote to Roger Clifford, instructing him to give all his assistance to Warenne. This letter refers to bad news about the condition of Scotland, which strongly suggests that news of the defeat was known.[38] A letter in Edward's name, written at Ghent on 5 October, suggests that the king may still have been unaware of the defeat at that date. It notes that Earl Warenne and Hugh Cressingham had testified in their letters that John de Vaus had done well in royal service in Scotland and had promised to go to Flanders to serve the king there. The government at home was asked to restore Vaus' lands to him.[39] The terms of the letter would surely have been different if Cressingham's death had been known. Edward's reaction to the news from Scotland is not recorded, but it is easy to guess at the initial fury of this irascible man. The French alliance with the Scots had yielded effective results, while his own allies had not achieved any worthwhile success against the French. The odds on a successful outcome to the war were becoming longer. There must have been wise heads suggesting that what was urgently needed was for the king to cut his losses and agree to a truce with the French, so that he could return home to deal with the problems created by Wallace's success. At the same time, Edward was still optimistically expecting help from his German allies. Even as late as mid-October, after the truce had been agreed, there were still hopes that Adolf of Nassau, king of the Romans, would join Edward with his troops.[40]

The council in England was surely determined to try to settle the political disputes so that full attention could be paid to Scotland. Edward's opponents in England must have felt the same way. The news of the defeat proved the point that they had made in the Remonstrances; they had been absolutely right. The situation in Scotland had indeed deteriorated badly once the king had left the country for Flanders. They must have considered that they were under a strong obligation to redirect whatever forces they had gathered against the possibility of civil war to the defence of the north and revenge against the Scots.

The defeat at Stirling Bridge therefore paved the way for the king in Flanders to agree to the truce of Vyve-St-Bavon on 9 October and for the government in England to agree on 10 October to the issue of the *Confirmatio Cartarum*, which conceded in very general terms much of what the opposition had demanded. The change of mood in England was very striking. It was possible to obtain a grant of a new tax of a ninth, equivalent to the loathed eighth, with no apparent difficulty, on 14 October.[41] Arguments with the clergy ceased. Attention turned to the problems in the north. On 18 October new appointments were made to command in Cumberland, Westmorland and Northumberland. On 23 October levies of almost 30,000 infantry were ordered; the troops were to muster at Newcastle on 6 December. In the same month contracts for three months' service were agreed with the two opposition leaders, the Earls of Hereford and Norfolk, and with Warenne, Warwick, Gloucester and Henry Percy. A prise, or seizure, of victuals was authorised in November.[42] Such prises had been a major issue for the king's opponents, but there was no hostility to the measure now that it was so obviously necessary. Various military operations took place, of which the most important was the relief early in the new year of Roxburgh and Berwick, but a winter campaign was difficult, and further activity was halted, for a request came from Edward, who was still in the Low Countries, asking the earls to delay until he could lead the expedition in person.[43]

One consequence of their success at Stirling Bridge was that the Scots began to raid England, establishing a base at Rothbury from which to operate. The Scottish operations began in the second half of October, but it seems likely that Wallace himself was not involved until the following month. On 7 November he was at Hexham and then moved his forces west, burning and plundering. Later in the month he returned to Northumberland and soon went back to Scotland.[44] Although damage was extensive, the Scots could not take any castles apart from the minor one at Mitford. As Walter of Guisborough would have us believe, St Cuthbert successfully defended Durham by organising severe weather conditions. Reports of this raid did much to turn Wallace into a figure of hate for the English. There were various stories of what happened on the raid into England. It was alleged that English priests, their hands tied behind their backs, were forced to jump into a river to drown. Boys were burned alive in schools and churches. Choirs of naked English men and women were made to sing for Wallace's amusement.

News of the Scottish ravages in the north of England must have re-emphasised the message that the defeat at Stirling Bridge had given to Edward I. The situation in Scotland must have been a factor in persuading him to agree formally to the settlement of the crisis in England by means of the issue of the Confirmation of the Charters. It was abundantly clear that the urgent problem was that presented by the Scots and that the political problems in England had to be resolved. The changed mood in England was displayed very clearly in the new year, once Edward had returned. The king was able to organise a new campaign against the Scots on a massive scale. The defeat at Stirling Bridge was avenged within less than a year, for in July 1298 Wallace and his followers were overwhelmed at Falkirk. The schiltroms were broken, and the bubble of Wallace's astonishing reputation was pricked. Once defeated, he could not continue to play the leading role in resistance to Edward I.

It is no longer fashionable to regard battles as decisive. The effects of the Scottish victory at Stirling Bridge were, however, both striking and unexpected. Without Wallace's victory at Stirling, Edward I's position would have been very different. He would have been under far less pressure to come to terms with his political opponents in England. Success in Flanders against the French was most unlikely, and the political crisis of 1297 might well have developed into civil war by the autumn of that year. As it was, Stirling Bridge was a signal triumph for the Scots, but it was a deceptive one. The victory must have given Wallace a false sense of what he could achieve. Defeating Warenne's unprepared forces was quite a different matter from facing a full-scale English army under Edward I at Falkirk in 1298, but the Scots clearly believed that they could repeat the trick of the previous year and that their schiltroms could rout Edward's formidable forces.

Stirling Bridge was without doubt a remarkable success, but the consequences of the battle were not what the Scots would have wished. It led to a reinforcement of Edward I's position in England and prepared the way for the English triumph in battle at Falkirk.

5

John Duns Scotus and the Idea of Independence

Alexander Broadie

The Franciscan priest John Duns Scotus was born in the Scottish border village of Duns in about 1266. He must have excelled in his studies, because when he was, at most, in his early teens he was taken to the Franciscan centre in Oxford to continue his education.[1] He remained there as a teacher of philosophy and theology for most, if not all, of the following two decades or so, and then in 1302 moved to the University of Paris, where he continued to teach and write. It seems to have been at this point that he developed his political theory. That theory, composed during the last years of William Wallace, provides what may be a clue to Scotus's attitude to the dispute between Scotland and England over the right to rule Scotland.

Elsewhere I have suggested that it was a coincidence that Scotus was exploring the power of the human will and the concept of freedom while a war of independence was being waged in Scotland.[2] I no longer think it a coincidence. The dispute between Scots and English must have informed in a particularly vivid way Scotus's youthful experiences in the Borders, given the military and political turmoil that then marked the Scottish borderlands, and it may also have informed his experiences during his years in Oxford, a centre of legal and theological excellence to which King Edward I turned for guidance in the preparation of his case for his right to rule Scotland. It would not be surprising if these experiences impacted on his philosophy.

However, I do not wish to discuss here the question of what motivated Scotus's interest in political theory and in particular the question of the origin of political dominion, although it should be said that Allan B. Wolter, OFM, the leading Scotist scholar of the past half-century, has suggested that Scotus's interest arose from his active involvement in the dispute between Pope Boniface VIII and Philip the Fair concerning the origin of the French king's ownership both of his political authority and of his feudal possessions.[3]

Whether or not this explanation of Scotus's interest in the question is to be preferred to the explanation (not considered by Wolter) that Scotus developed his political doctrine with an eye on the political relations between Scotland and England, the fact remains that whatever the reason for his interest, his ideas might still have been taken up by Scots who were actively engaged in the political process that in due course led both to Scottish independence and to the document that most famously defined that independence, the Arbroath Declaration. For Scotus was much the most outstanding Scottish philosopher and theologian of his day, and it would be natural for the Scottish leaders to turn to him, or at least his writings, to see what help he might provide in the articulation of the arguments they sought to construct in justification of their acts. Here I shall be comparing Scotus's ideas with the ideas of those at the forefront of the movement for Scottish independence and shall not seek to resolve any of the related problems concerning historical causation.

To put flesh on these considerations, I wish now to take the first steps towards arguing that Scotus's political doctrine impacted on the content of at least two major Scottish documents, the Declaration of the Clergy (1310) and the Declaration of Arbroath (1320),[4] which were penned during the twelve years that followed his death in 1308.

SCOTUS'S CONCEPT OF FREE WILL

Scotus was the great philosopher of freedom in the Middle Ages. This description of him is particularly merited in view of what he has to say of freedom at the level of the individual, but there is a formidable unity in his thinking as a whole, and it is therefore not surprising that in his political theory the emphasis is on a concept that we would now identify as that of national independence, a kind of freedom that bears a strong formal resemblance to the individual sort. I shall therefore first expound his concept of individual freedom before expounding his concept of the kind of freedom that characterises a community.[5]

Scotus identifies two sorts of act of will, one of which he describes as natural and the other as free. To deal first with natural will: biological creatures such as us desire certain things by our very nature. Above all we desire to stay alive. When we are threatened with death it is almost as if the organism then takes over and does whatever it can or must in order to maintain itself in existence. If we are choking, we fight for breath; if a lethal blow is aimed at us, we try to ward it off; if we are starving, we reach out for food. That is how we are by nature. The desire to stay alive takes charge and impels us to act. Beyond this most basic desire there are other desires: for warmth, for sleep, for company, and so on. We are dealing here with biological imperatives that we have to obey if we are to function well as the biological creatures we are. Scotus speaks of the 'will' in this context, for by our nature we will to obey these imperatives. And for obvious reasons he calls this 'natural will'.

But the will to obey a biological imperative can be thwarted. We can say 'no' to it, for we are not merely passive beings, so constructed that we must sit back and let nature take its course. For there is another principle in us, one that Scotus terms 'free will'. That we can reject a biological imperative is demonstrated by the fact that we can say 'no' even to the imperative that we stay alive. For people can overcome their natural fear of death and instead voluntarily become martyrs in a religious cause, voluntarily fight for their country or voluntarily commit suicide. In such cases the will is active but it is plainly a different principle of action from the principle of natural will. Although hungry, I do not necessarily eat food that is to hand, for I may know that the food belongs to someone else and that taking it without permission is therefore theft. In such an act of forbearance I display my freedom.

There are two aspects to our freedom, one negative and the other positive. The negative aspect is our independence from nature; that is, we are not determined to act by any act of nature. In particular, we can always do as morality demands even if the moral demand conflicts with a demand of nature. And where we do act as nature demands, but do so only in light of the judgment that the act is morally permissible, then we have acted not because nature has demanded the act but because our conscience has sanctioned it. Hence, even to act according to nature is to act freely so long as we act in light of our moral judgment and not simply because of a natural urge.

The positive aspect of our freedom concerns what Scotus terms our 'openness to opposites', the fact that whatever we actually do in a given concrete historical situation, we could in that same situation have done something else instead. Possibilities open to us are real live possibilities. Our future is not predetermined. What in fact transpires does so because we have realised one of the several genuine possibilities. We are independent, therefore, in the double sense that we are both free *from* nature and free *to* realise one of the several mutually opposed possibilities that are always open to us. Of course, there is a sense in which dead matter can produce opposite effects. For example, the sun can bleach some things and blacken others; it can melt some things and harden others; but the point is that what it bleaches it cannot, in those same circumstances, blacken; what it melts it cannot, in those same circumstances, harden. In that sense, far from having power the sun is powerless, for it cannot do other than precisely what it does do. We human beings are quite otherwise. We can do otherwise than we do, and this is because we are, in the way just described, independent of nature. Our principle of change lies within us, with our own judgments and choices. The principle is not imposed from outside.

SCOTUS'S CONCEPT OF INDEPENDENCE

It is upon this concept of individual independence that Scotus proceeds to construct a concept of independence in the political sense. His political theory occurs in the context of the theological question whether a thief can be truly penitent if he has not made restitution.[6] This might seem an odd context but it is not really so, for restitution of property to its rightful owner naturally raises a question about the origin of property rights, and that question is a central one in political theory. As Scotus puts the question: 'What is the source of distinct ownership such that this may be called "mine" and that "yours"? For this is the basis of all injustice through misappropriation of another's property and consequently of all justice in restoring it.'[7] It is natural to think that Scotus had in mind such things as an ordinary thief might steal, but I wish to hold in the background the thought that Scotus might also have had in mind a non-ordinary thief, such as a king who had stolen another country and who also (as with the ordinary thief) cannot be a true penitent unless he restored to its rightful owners the property he had stolen.

The source of property rights, argues Scotus, cannot lie in the 'state of innocence', the state of nature prior to the Fall, for there was then no mine or thine; instead, everything was held in common. Scotus invokes in support of this claim a proposition in the *Decretals* of Gratian: 'By the law of nature all things are common to all.'[8] They are common to all because, as Scotus puts the point, such an arrangement will contribute to a peaceful and decent life and will provide needed sustenance.[9] In the state of innocence a person would not seek by violence to take from another what another needed for life or comfort. It is therefore only after the Fall that property rights come into existence.

According to Catholic theology, the loss of innocence involved a radical change in human psychology in the direction of covetousness and a willingness to use violence against one's neighbour. In the state of innocence there are no oppressors. After the Fall oppressors are part of the human scene and their presence has to be dealt with. A covetous and violent person would not only take more than he needs of the things that have been held in common, he would also be willing to use violence to withhold them from another who has a genuine need of what the covetous person has needlessly appropriated. In the face of this new psychological reality, it becomes necessary to divide up what has previously been held in common. The division could not be by natural law, since that law, as already stated, sanctioned the common ownership of things, and hence positive law was required for the task. A legislator is therefore required, and Scotus argues that the legislator must possess two qualities, prudence and authority.[10] Prudence is needed for the obvious reason that the legislator's job is to form a correct judgment as to the principles of division that would result in a decent and peaceful life for the citizens, and such judgment involves the exercise of practical right reason, that is, prudence. Furthermore, authority is required because prudence by itself is not enough. The mere fact that the legislator is prudent does not imply that others will attend to him. The word of a legislative authority must be sufficient to bind others also, and for that he must be recognised as having just command over others.

But from where is this just command to come? It is in his answer to this question that Scotus moves into territory that is also occupied by the Declaration of the Clergy and the Declaration of Arbroath. According to Scotus, authority takes two forms. The first, parental, is entirely according to nature, not according to any human convention or voluntary arrangement. Hence, even in the state of innocence the parent has a right to command and the child has a duty to obey; and after the Fall it remains a part of the natural order. It is simply a natural feature of parenthood. This is to be contrasted with the other kind of authority, the political. There are several differences. First, political authority is not exercised solely over members of the authority's own family, and indeed it is possible that no member of the authority's family is subject to his political command. Secondly, parental authority over a child does not cease if the child moves to a distant place, but political authority is held over people who live together in a *civitas*, a city or state, and if someone ceases to be an inhabitant of the state, the political authority that the ruler has over him thereby ceases. Thirdly, political authority can reside with either a single person or with what Scotus terms a community (*communitas*), a group to which he assigns no upper size. Fourthly, in contrast to parental authority, the justice of which is a natural endowment, political authority, as Scotus states the matter, 'can be just by common consent and election on the part of the community'.[11] While it is not by 'common consent and election' that parents justly command their children, by contrast the just rulership of a political authority derives from the choice of those who will be ruled. Scotus continues:

> Thus, if some outsiders [*extranei*: that is, people who are not all in the one family] banded together to build a city or to live in one, seeing that they could not be well governed without some form of authority, they could have amicably agreed to commit their community to one person or to a group [*communitas*], and if to one person, then either to him alone – and to a successor who would be chosen as he was – or to him and his posterity. And both of these forms of political authority are just, because one person can justly submit himself to another or to a community in those things which are not against the law of God and as regards which he can

81

be guided better by the person or persons to whom he has submitted or subjected himself than he could by himself.[12]

There are several elements in this doctrine that we have to take with us into the question concerning the major political scheme in the minds of Scottish political leaders in the two decades after Scotus devised and taught his doctrine. The first element is that of a social contract. The people are to choose their ruler by agreeing among themselves as to who the ruler should be. Secondly, and consequently, the people also choose the principle of transference of authority. This is crucial. It is not that the people choose the first ruler, and that thereafter the question of who is to rule is out of their hands; on Scotus's scheme, it is never out of their hands. It could be agreed by the people that the transference of authority could be by birth, say, the principle of primogeniture, or at the end of one ruler's rulership the people could agree among themselves as to who should be the next ruler. Thirdly, the ruler is put in place because there is a job to be done, one that requires exercise of practical right reason, that is, prudence. As Scotus says, the ruler must be able to guide the people better than the people individually can guide themselves. Fourthly, the people can choose as a ruler either a single person or a 'community'.[13] This should be mentioned if we are looking to support the claim that there is a close relation between Scotus's political theory and the politics of Scotland. For in the decades from 1286, the phrase 'community of the realm', referring to the political elite in Scotland, had become a term in rather frequent use in Scottish documents,[14] and the phrase perhaps gives particular significance to Scotus's use of the term 'community' in his description of one kind of just rulership. But whether the political authority be a single person or a 'community', the outcome is that a nation governed in the way described by Scotus is independent in the sense that, as with individual independence, the principle of change lies within and is not external. The people come together and decide among themselves and for themselves who is to govern them and what the principle of change of ruler should be.

Before moving on to the question of the relation between Scotus's political theory and Scottish politics, I should add that Scotus, in political theory as in so much else, was his own man. None of his contemporaries and predecessors produced a theory quite like his. Some did describe a form of social contract theory, although in that feudalistic age very few endorsed one, but nevertheless Scotus's form of the theory was unique, unlike that of any of his contemporaries and predecessors.

SCOTUS AND TWO SCOTTISH POLITICAL DECLARATIONS

I turn finally, and briefly, to the question of how Scotus's doctrine stands in relation to the politics of Scotland in the first two decades of the fourteenth century and in particular to the Declaration of the Clergy and the Declaration of Arbroath. First, the Declaration of the Clergy in which the clergy of Scotland declared themselves in favour of King Robert: the date of the declaration is disputed although the document itself bears the date 24 February 1310.[15] The declaration begins by affirming that John Balliol was made king of Scotland by the king of England. This is the nub of the clergy's criticism of Balliol's status, for they argue that the English king does not have the authority to determine who will be king of Scotland. Only the Scots themselves have that authority:

> The people and commons of the aforesaid kingdom of Scotland . . . agreed on the said Lord Robert, the king who now is, in whom the rights of his father and grandfather to the aforesaid kingdom, in the judgment of the people, still reside and flourish incorrupt; and with their concurrence and consent he was raised to be king, to reform the deformities of the kingdom, correct what required correction, direct what needed direction; and by their authority having been advanced in the kingdom, he was solemnly made king of Scots . . .

The declaration then refers to the cardinal virtues by which Robert Bruce is fitted to rule and be worthy of the name of king, a point to be borne in mind in view of Scotus's emphasis on the ruler's possession of the cardinal virtue of prudence. And it continues: 'and if any one in opposition claims right to the foresaid kingdom by letters sealed in the past and containing the consent of the people and the commons, know that all this took place by force and violence which could not then be resisted . . .'[16]

It is clear that the political doctrine in this document is Scotus's so far as it focuses repeatedly on the doctrine that legitimate rulership depends on the consent of the people; the '*people agreed*' upon Lord Robert; it was '*with the concurrence and consent of the said people*' that Robert was King; it was '*by their authority*' that he was set over the people. If anyone has documents to the contrary, including documents containing '*the consent of the people*', then the people were not then, that is, at the time of giving their consent, acting freely or voluntarily; their consent was extracted by force and was therefore not real consent. In light of the fact that the political theory underlying the declaration is thoroughly Scotistic, it is of particular interest that the document was presented in the General Council of Scotland celebrated in the Church of the Friars Minor, the Franciscan Church, in Dundee. In short, Scotus's own order provided the venue for the occasion.

The Declaration of Arbroath, ten years later, repeats the message that a king does not rule except by the consent of those who are ruled, for it states

83

that Robert was made prince and king 'by the due consent and assent of us all'. And it then adds a new element to the Scotistic story that we have extracted from the Declaration of the Clergy. I quote in full:

> We are bound to him [King Robert] for the maintaining of our freedom both by his right and merits, as to him by whom salvation has been wrought unto our people, and by him, come what may, we mean to stand. Yet if he should give up what he has begun, seeking to make us or our kingdom subject to the king of England or to the English, we would strive at once to drive him out as a subverter of his own right and ours, and we would make some other man who was able to defend us our king.[17]

Nothing could more clearly encapsulate Scotus's doctrine that the ruler justly rules his people solely by their choice and consent. From this doctrine it follows immediately that the ruler's authority can be transferred solely by an act of the people and not at all by an act of the ruler. Of course, the people unwilling to lose their political power, which is, above all, the power to decide who will rule, are bound to replace the errant ruler by one who will work for and not against them.

The independence of the people resides, more than in anything else, in their freedom to determine who will rule; and having determined this, the people's will is not followed by a period of passivity – their will is not switched off. They remain watchful, judging the quality of the job done by the person they have elected and ready to withdraw their consent to his rule if he fails them. In this collective act of self-determination lies their independence. It is formally the same as with the individual person, whose actions are determined from within and whose act of will is not followed by passivity – the will is not switched off. The person remains watchful, judging whether the line of action decided upon remains appropriate in all its aspects or whether it requires modification or abandonment in light of developments.[18]

I have argued that Scotus's theory of freedom is articulated in the two great declarations that were issued within a few years of his death. There remains the question of historical causation, which I am not competent to answer, of whether this identity of doctrine in the theological work of Scotus and in the declarations was a coincidence or not. But I do note that Scotus was much the most prominent Scottish philosopher/theologian of his time and that his doctrine was therefore one that the senior Scottish clergy were likely to know.

My conclusion is that while Wallace was fighting for Scottish independence, Scotus was developing precisely the intellectual framework that the

Scots within a few years would deploy in the chief documents that defined that independence. I also believe it possible that the documents in question were compiled with Scotus in mind. There remains an intriguing thought, which I have not pursued, that Scotus was actively engaged in the development of Scottish thinking on the matter of Scottish independence through discussions that he might have had with Scots whom he met at the great centres where he worked. If such discussions did indeed take place, then my suggestion, made some years ago,[19] that the relation of Scotus to the Wars of Independence was one of theory to practice, is false. Scotus may, after all, have been on the side of practice as well as theory by working to the same end as the Scottish military leaders even although by utterly different means.[20]

6

Bravehearts and Coronets: Images of William Wallace and the Scottish Nobility[1]

Alexander Grant

As Mel Gibson's *Braveheart* shows so vividly, the modern perception of William Wallace is not just as the great Scottish leader; it is also as an ordinary 'commoner' heroically maintaining his country's cause in the face of selfish feuding, craven submission and treacherous collaboration by despicable Scottish nobles, who are as much the enemies of a free Scotland as the English. Like the English, indeed, the Scottish nobility constitutes an 'other' against which the modern image of Wallace's career has been constructed. But what images lie behind this dichotomy? That is the subject of the present chapter.

I

The first issue to explore is Wallace's own status. His *Braveheart* portrayal encapsulates a twentieth-century trend in which Wallace, 'the man of the people', becomes 'a proletarian hero who – according to the modern reworking of the myth – was a victim of the class conflict'; it is, indeed, even possible to contemplate considering him as 'Scotland's first working-class hero'.[2] On the other hand, virtually every serious modern account of Wallace's career states that he came from Elderslie in Renfrewshire (or occasionally Ellerslie in Ayrshire) and that his father was the local landowner[3] – which would give him a far higher status.

At first sight, though, that would not affect the fundamental commoner–noble contrast, since in Britain lairds and gentry usually count as commoners and only titled peers (dukes, earls, and so on) are nobles. It is wrong to apply that in a medieval Scottish context, however. Restricting nobility to members of the titled peerage is a uniquely English concept (derived from the fourteenth-century division of parliament into separate 'Lords' and 'Commons', with gentry belonging to the latter).[4] This was not the case elsewhere in Western Europe. There, instead, ideas of status followed the traditional theory of the 'three estates', made up of clergy, nobility and ordinary people, all defined by function, which for the nobility was protecting the others through military expertise; hence, from the twelfth century the noble estate consisted of knights. But it also became established that normally only sons of knights could be knights. This produced the concept of inheriting knightly, or 'noble', blood, which meant that the descendants of knights, even if not knighted themselves, came to be considered noble. Since knights were invariably landowners, the eventual result was that throughout most of late-medieval Western Europe all members of landowning families with knightly ancestry were regarded as having noble status, belonging to what is often termed 'the noblesse'.[5]

In this respect, Scotland conformed as usual to the west-European norm.[6] Indeed, even nowadays those who are not peers but possess coats of arms belong, technically, to 'the noblesse of Scotland'.[7] As for the Middle Ages, despite the emergence of a Scottish parliamentary peerage in the mid-fifteenth century, lairds who attended parliaments thereafter still belonged to the second, noble, estate, along with the peers.[8] Moreover, there are countless examples of late-medieval lairds being explicitly called 'noble' – including, in 1410, John Wallace of Elderslie.[9] Thus in later medieval Scotland the family of Wallace of Elderslie was certainly regarded as noble; so, ironically, the modern Scottish image of William Wallace as a commoner despite being a son of the laird of Elderslie follows the English concept of nobility and rejects the Scottish one.[10]

Wallace's problematic status is not, however, purely a modern issue; it is also evident in medieval sources. The first known account of his origins – from the contemporary *Annales Angliae et Scotiae* associated with William of Rishanger – called him a man 'of ignoble family', and 'born and brought up from a most lowly and poor family'; when he was knighted, 'it was like making a raven into a swan'.[11] The *Lanercost Chronicle* similarly disparages Wallace's knighthood: 'When William the Welshman was made noble, the Scottish nobility became utterly degenerate.'[12] Of course, since these chronicles are English and vehemently hostile to Wallace, their remarks could simply be typical smears. Yet the earliest Scottish chronicle comment on Wallace's status, the later fourteenth-century *Gesta Annalia* II (formerly attributed to Fordun), also uses 'ignoble': that, it records, is how Scottish magnates regarded Wallace.[13] The English statements may therefore not be smears after all. Or, less extremely, the Scottish magnate perception may have stemmed from resentful jealousy coupled with the snobbish assumption that Wallace, like all non-magnates of whatever status, belonged among the led not the leaders. But whatever the case, the *Gesta*'s author strongly disagrees. The whole passage reads:

> Though among the earls and great men of the kingdom he was considered ignoble, yet his kindred shone with knightly honour. His older broth-

er was also a belted knight who held a patrimony in lands in keeping with his status, which he bequeathed to be held by his descendants.[14]

This obviously counters the idea of the ignoble Wallace by stressing his knightly lineage and especially his brother's status as a hereditary landowner.

That image was developed by Wyntoun in the 1410s and Bower in the 1440s. According to Wyntoun, Wallace:

> In sempill stait thocht he wes then,
> Yit wes he cummyn of gentill men;
> His fader wes a manly knycht,
> And his moder a lady brycht,
> And he gottin in mariage.
> His eldare brother the heretage
> Had, and ioisit in his dais.[15]

This echoes *Gesta Annalia* II, but omits what the magnates thought about Wallace, emphasises that his father was a knight (which the *Gesta* does not state explicitly), and adds the lines about his mother, possibly to counter any suggestion of bastardy. Subsequently, Bower's rewriting of *Gesta Annalia* went further.[16] He changed its introductory sentence about Wallace – 'In the same year, William Wallace raised his head as if from his hiding-places, and killed the English sheriff of Lanark'[17] – to read: 'In the same year, the famous William Wallace, the hammer of the English, the son of the noble knight [space left for the name] raised his head.' Then he inserted a long passage about Wallace's appearance and character that is not in the *Gesta* at all. Next, on the Lanark episode, he added that Wallace was 'a young knight' when the sheriff was killed. And finally, when Bower came to the *Gesta* statements about Wallace's social status, like Wyntoun he deleted the magnate perception of Wallace, replaced it with the statement that Wallace 'came from a distinguished family', and provided the name 'Andrew' for Wallace's brother.

Thus Wyntoun and Bower significantly embellished *Gesta Annalia* II's already positive image of Wallace. The *Gesta*–Bower contrast is particularly illuminating: Bower removed two potentially derogatory passages and (presumably reacting against 'ignoble' in the *Gesta* text) laboured Wallace's knightliness and called his father a noble knight. Moreover, Bower subsequently twice applied 'noble' to Wallace himself; while the final story of a hermit's vision of souls en route from Purgatory to Heaven waiting while Wallace's (by implication saintly) soul flew straight into Paradise is the ultimate in image-building.[18] With that, Bower was in fantasy land – but is his general image of Wallace any more valid? Wallace is known to have been knighted some time after Stirling Bridge;[19] so when Bower called Wallace a 'young knight' at the time of the attack on Lanark, he was either inventing or following an inaccurate (perhaps ballad) tradition. Also, he was wrong to call Wallace's brother Andrew – and indeed deleted the name from the abbreviated *Scotichronicon*, possibly because the source was unsatisfactory.[20] And the blank left for Wallace's father's name is most illuminating. As Donald Watt remarked, Bower had apparently been collecting Wallace material for some time,[21] so his failure to name the father indicates that reliable details about Wallace's parentage were not available in the mid-fifteenth century. Bower's embellishment of the *Gesta*'s image, therefore, cannot be regarded as deriving from sound information.

In the 1470s, however, abundant information about Wallace's family was at last presented, in Blind Hary's *Wallace*. According to Hary, his father was 'Malcolm Wallas . . . That Elrisle than had in heretage, / Auchinbothe and othir syndry place'; his elder brother was 'Schir Malcom Wallas, a full gentill knycht'; and he had two uncles, Sir Richard Wallace of Riccarton and Sir Reginald Crawford, sheriff of Ayr.[22] This is the first time that Wallace is associated with Elderslie, and Hary also links him with two baronial families: in the late thirteenth century, Sir Richard Wallace[23] and Sir Reginald Crawford had a similar status to lords such as Sir William Douglas. Hary, therefore, completes the process of situating Wallace within a clearly noble kin.

Unfortunately – as is commonly pointed out but insufficiently appreciated – none of Hary's information can be believed without independent corroboration. His technique was to pack his story with authentic-seeming episodes and names that mostly turn out to be anachronistic plagiarisms from Barbour's, Wyntoun's and Bower's narratives of post-Wallace Anglo-Scottish warfare; the purpose was to give the strongest impression of verisimilitude and reliability[24] – but only in the way that including real events and people in modern thrillers does. Hary's account of Wallace's kin cannot, therefore, be accepted uncritically, as has happened so often, especially regarding Elderslie; yet nor can it be automatically dismissed. Consider, for instance, Sir Reginald Crawford. He is not mentioned by *Gesta Annalia* II, Wyntoun or Bower, but occurs in Barbour's *Bruce* as being hanged in a barn at Ayr – which gave Hary a famous but fictitious story.[25] Barbour, however, did not call Crawford sheriff of Ayr, so Hary obtained that, correct, detail elsewhere[26] – probably from Crawford's heirs, the Campbells of Loudon. But does that mean Hary was correct about Crawford's relationship with Wallace? Perhaps – but equally possibly he invented the relationship to flatter the Campbells.

The same applies to Wallace's other 'uncle'. The Wallaces of Riccarton survived throughout the fifteenth century, although they were then usually 'of Craigie' – and Hary definitely knew Sir William Wallace of Craigie.[27] Although Riccarton is not recorded in Wallace possession until the 1370s,[28] it was almost certainly one of their early estates, and the Sir Richard Wallace found (without territorial designation) in the later thirteenth century is probably Hary's character.[29] Hary gave him three sons, Adam, Richard and Simon. Although there are no independent references to Richard and Simon, Adam was doubtless modelled on the Adam Wallace who fought in the fourteenth-century wars and was executed in 1337 by Sir Thomas Rokeby; significantly, Hary fictitiously included 'ald Rukbe' among Wallace's victims.[30] It therefore appears that Hary had some good family information about the Riccarton Wallaces. In addition, he mentioned another branch, the Wallaces of Auchincruive, who are first recorded in the twelfth century but died out in the late fourteenth.[31] Hary's accurate reference to them shows he had quite wide information about the kindred – and Sir William of Craigie is surely the most likely source.

But what of Wallace's immediate family, which Hary said possessed 'Elrisle' and 'Auchinbothe'? In the late fourteenth century, the Renfrewshire estates of Elderslie and Auchenbothie both belonged to John Wallace of Elderslie; these must be what Hary meant.[32] Auchenbothie subsequently went to a cadet line, but Elderslie, on the death of a later laird in 1444, escheated to the superior, namely Sir John Wallace of Craigie, father of Hary's contact Sir William – and during Hary's lifetime, Elderslie was held of the lord of Craigie/Riccarton by George Wallace, Sir William's younger brother.[33] Unfortunately, that does not mean we should believe Hary and associate his hero with Elderslie. Instead, the reverse is more likely, because, when Hary was writing, the laird of Elderslie had the same relationship to the lord of Riccarton as in Hary's poem. That coincidence looks too good to be true, especially since linking the hero with the Craigie/Riccarton family would have enhanced Sir William of Craigie's own image. Moreover, if Wallace's immediate family details were well known in the Craigie/Riccarton family, why was Bower ignorant of them? Bower's contemporary as lord of Craigie/Riccarton, Sir John Wallace, was probably prominent enough to marry a daughter of the seventh earl of Douglas,[34] and it is surely inconceivable that Bower did not consult him about Wallace's family. The likelihood is, therefore, that Hary's description of Wallace as son of the laird of Elderslie and nephew of the lord of Riccarton was an invention, designed to promote the hero's namesake, Sir William of Craigie. That may have been especially relevant in the 1470s, since by then the main Douglas line could no longer present itself as the chief upholder of Scottish independence;[35] did Sir William of Craigie (with a likely Douglas mother or stepmother) hope to step into their shoes?

A further problem about Hary's account of Wallace's family is A. A. M. Duncan's demonstration that his father was called Alan, not Malcolm as Hary states. However, Hary *was* correct to name Wallace's brother as Malcolm.[36] It is difficult to see this as a lucky guess, so presumably Hary had found accurate material somewhere. But since Bower did not know the brother's name, it probably did not derive from straightforward family information. Instead, Hary was probably using a different kind of source (possibly a ballad) that Bower either did not have or discounted; but if so, it was hardly very sound, given that Hary was wrong about the name of Wallace's father and about the brother's death in battle before Wallace's revolt began (also, he did not mention Wallace's other real-life brother, Sir John, whom the English executed in 1307).[37] Despite the accuracy over the elder brother's name, therefore, it is surely unwise to give credence to Hary's most significant statements, namely that Wallace came from Elderslie and was a cadet of the Riccarton family. And if these can be discounted, so too can Hary's specific location of Wallace within a baronial family. Like Bower, Wyntoun and the author of *Gesta Annalia* II, he must be regarded as engaging in deliberate – but unreliable – image-building.

It does not follow, however, that we must simply accept the English chroniclers' depictions of an ignoble plebeian Wallace; after all, they too had images to construct and axes to grind. Instead, more neutral contemporary images of Wallace need some thought. For a start, there is his seal.[38] Because this describes him as 'son of Alan Wallace' and does not depict a coat of arms, it might be thought to denote a much lower status than that given by the Scottish chronicles. Personal medieval seals, however, have laconic legends and usually omit descriptions such as 'knight'; the bald 'Alan Wallace' tells nothing either way about Wallace's status. Nor does the seal's non-heraldic device, for until the fourteenth century only knights had heraldic arms on their seals; esquires (even with knightly blood) employed non-heraldic images.[39] But if, as Duncan argues, Wallace's father is the 'Alan Wallace' recorded in the Ragman Rolls, then although he was not a knight, he would have counted as a landowner; the Ragman lists go some way down the social scale but do not include plebeian peasants.

More generally, consider the actual names. In Scotland the surname Wallace belonged to a landowning family normally believed to have arrived in the twelfth century; since thirteenth-century peasants did not adopt landowning surnames, it can be assumed that during the period all Wallaces belonged to the same extended kin group. The first names Alan, Malcolm and William are perhaps illuminating too. The father's is associated with the Stewarts, while the sons' (taken together) are reminiscent of the royal family. The combination of Malcolm and William for brothers seems unusual in thirteenth-century Scotland, but can be found with the sons of

Farquhar, Earl of Ross. Earl Farquhar presumably had Kings Malcolm IV and William I in mind when he named his sons;[40] did Alan Wallace too? That this question can be posed suggests Alan's status – or self-image – was at least above the plebeian.

Be that as it may, the evidence for Malcolm's name comes from a neutral contemporary source, the English spy's report about a Scottish council at Peebles on 19 August 1299. This records that 'Sir David Graham demanded the lands and goods of Sir William Wallace because he was leaving the kingdom without the leave or approval of the Guardians'; that 'Sir Malcolm, Sir William's brother, answered that neither his lands nor his goods should be given away'; that 'the two knights gave the lie to each other and drew their daggers'; and that 'Sir Malcolm Wallace [was] of the earl of Carrick's following'.[41] This is the only reference to Wallace having lands. Had he held them as a peasant, Graham should have complained to the immediate landlord; thus in August 1299 Wallace was a landowner. He might have received land to reward his achievement as Guardian, but if so, from whom? (Such a grant should have been made by the crown.) Conversely, it is not impossible that he already possessed land before 1297 – in which case, the bow and arrow on his seal might indicate that archer service or a token arrow was owed for it.[42] Moreover, was Malcolm knighted alongside his brother in 1297–98 or subsequently – or was he already a knight? There is no sense in the spy's report that Malcolm was an upstart; he stands up to, and is bracketed with, one of Scotland's leading barons. Thus it is likely that Malcolm's knighthood was well established.

But Malcolm followed Robert Bruce, Earl of Carrick, not the Steward. Since men tended to belong to their feudal superiors' retinues, Malcolm may not have held his land from the Steward. In that case the identification of Alan Wallace, Malcolm's father, as a crown tenant in Ayrshire might be especially significant.[43] Late thirteenth-century Ayrshire consisted mostly of great lordships, and the crown tenants must have been concentrated in 'King's Kyle', the hinterland of Ayr itself.[44] Since Bruce was active there during 1298,[45] it is perfectly possible that Alan Wallace's son was in his retinue. And there is a later Carrick–Wallace link: Countess Eleanor, widow of Alexander Bruce, Earl of Carrick (died 1332), married Sir Duncan Wallace, who possessed Auchincruive in Ayrshire, the earliest known Wallace property in Scotland.[46] This apparent Carrick connection makes it tempting to bracket Sir Malcolm and Sir Duncan together as belonging to the Auchincruive family – and while that must be resisted for lack of evidence, it is worth noting that although Auchincruive lay in the Stewart lordship of Kyle, it was on the edge of it and very close to Ayr. Thus it is not difficult to envisage a cadet of that family acquiring land close by, but within King's Kyle south of the River Ayr.[47] Alternatively, part of the Auchincruive estate may have been south of the river, as with 'Auchincruive Holdings' on the modern map. It may be significant that, according to Hary's story, after his father's death Wallace hid in Laigland Wood beside Auchincruive Holdings, in King's Kyle, and his nurse was from Newton of Ayr, only a few miles away.[48]

Considering neutral contemporary images, therefore, suggests the conclusion that Wallace and his brother William were more probably connected with the Auchincruive Wallaces than with the Riccarton ones. That completely contradicts what Blind Hary has led almost every student of Wallace to believe; but Hary knew the lord of Craigie/Riccarton, whereas the main line of Auchincruive Wallaces had died out a century earlier. However, the neutral images do not undermine every Scottish account. If Wallace's father Alan was not a knight (although from a knightly family) but his brother Malcolm was, that is close to *Gesta Annalia* II's statements that 'his kindred shone with knightly honour' (which avoids calling his father a knight) and that 'his elder brother was also a belted knight'. Thus, while the embellishments by Wyntoun, Bower and especially Hary should be rejected, the *Gesta* image does need to be taken seriously – and it would situate Wallace marginally within the fringe of the nobility, according to the later medieval Scottish concept.

Taking *Gesta Annalia* II seriously, however, returns us to the perceptions of Wallace as 'ignoble' among the Scottish magnates and the English chroniclers. As mentioned already, these can be ascribed to Scottish magnate jealousy and general English hostility. Conversely, it should be pointed out that the broad concept of nobility was only evolving during the thirteenth century. In that period, knighthood was the essential test of nobility, and the idea of including 'potential knights' – men of knightly blood – had not gained the general acceptance that it had in subsequent centuries.[49] Thus, whereas for the fourteenth-century author of *Gesta Annalia* II (and his successors) Wallace's knightly lineage would have made him noble, in the late thirteenth century that would not necessarily have been so. 'Ignoble' may not, therefore, have been merely a smear; it might also reflect a thirteenth-century concept of nobility that focused sharply on actual knighthood – as indicated by the way the English writers regarded Wallace as (wrongly) ennobled when he was knighted.

Thus even in his own lifetime Wallace's social status was probably unclear – which makes certainty about it impossible nowadays. Consequently, it is hardly surprising that in this respect his image has been constructed in so many different ways. But for my own part, I would argue that Wallace cannot be seen as plebeian or proletarian; he should be regarded as belonging, if only just, to Scotland's landowning, knightly, and hence noble, class(es).

II

In *Braveheart*, Scotland's cause is constantly undermined by its nobility – Wallace's Scottish 'other' – including Robert Bruce, whose treachery at Falkirk is especially dramatic. This powerfully reflects modern anti-aristocratic prejudices: present-day Scotland's landowning classes appear, to those who dislike them, to be firm Unionists with English public-school accents, so it is easy to portray them as enemies of the people in both class and nationalist terms, and to tar their medieval predecessors with the same brush.[50] Furthermore, since the nineteenth century Wallace's depiction as a commoner betrayed by the nobility has, in Richard Finlay's words, made him 'a convenient icon for radical liberals to use against the landowning classes who owed their position to birthright rather than meritocracy'.[51] That was expressed in unionist as well as nationalist terms[52] – and (as Colin Kidd shows in this volume) Wallace was even presented as upholding pop-ular 'Saxon' liberties against feudal 'Norman' oppression, making him an English as well as a Scottish hero! Thus, in the past two centuries, the dichotomy between Wallace and the Scottish nobility has had an excep-tionally wide appeal – expressed at times in highly emotive language, as in Thomas Carlyle's much quoted words:

> It is noteworthy that the nobles of the country have maintained a quite despicable behaviour since the days of Wallace downwards – a selfish, ferocious, famishing, unprincipled set of hyenas, from whom at no time, and in no way, has the country derived any benefit.[53]

Academic histories also contributed to the nobility's image. In the first research-based history of Scotland, dating from 1828, Patrick Fraser Tytler stated that 'the patriotic principle . . . entirely deserted the highest ranks of the Scottish nobles, whose selfish dissensions had brought ruin and bondage upon their country'; and that 'when an honest love of liberty, and a simul-taneous spirit of resistance, could alone have saved Scotland, its nobility deserted their country, and refused to act with the only man whose success and military talents were equal to the emergency' – namely Wallace.[54] Similarly, in 1841 Joseph Stevenson called the Scottish nobles 'a body of men, disunited among themselves, traitors to their country, and induced, by the private jealousies and prejudices of their leaders, to thwart [Wallace's] exertion, and prevent his further interference'.[55] Subsequent historians are more restrained, but their narratives nevertheless highlight noble infighting and submissions.[56] Indeed, not until Geoffrey Barrow's *Robert Bruce* – which calls Tytler's comments 'one of the hardest-dying half-truths of Scottish history'[57] – were the Scottish nobility's activities during the Wars of Independence presented more positively. And this still seems a minority attitude. Thus, although Andrew Fisher's *William Wallace* is carefully judicious, the Scottish nobility is again contrasted unfavourably with its hero. Moreover, the most recent account highlights political dissension and feuding as much as nineteenth-century writers did, and hence in effect maintains the Scottish nobility's traditionally negative portrayal.[58]

But there is no smoke without fire: the basic narrative does seem to support that image. The Balliol–Bruce succession dispute caused serious trouble in 1286 and 1290, meant that the Bruces refused to fight for the Balliol kingship and were pro-England for much of 1296 to 1306, and after 1306 caused a full-scale civil war in which the Balliol/Comyn faction joined the English against the Bruce usurper. Also, mass submissions did occur in 1296 and 1304, while in 1305 it was a Scottish noble working for Edward I who captured Wallace. Nevertheless, it is wrong to regard the Scottish magnates as different from the rest of the Scottish people. As the Ragman Rolls illustrate, lesser landowners, ecclesiastics and townsmen were just as ready to submit during crises,[59] while countless Scots of all sorts collaborated in various ways after 1296. So if Wallace stands out, it is from the Scots en masse, not just from the magnates. Focusing predominantly on the Bruce–Balliol/Comyn feud significantly obscures the overall picture.

Interestingly, in this respect Blind Hary's *Wallace* is more balanced. Admittedly, it describes several 'bad', pro-English nobles (especially 'Amar Wallange', concocted out of the *English* magnate Aymer de Valence, Earl of Pembroke, Edward I's cousin!),[60] and it narrates the story of Robert Bruce at Falkirk at considerable length.[61] Yet several Scottish nobles, such as Malcolm, Earl of Lennox, fight consistently for Scotland; and although the Comyns are extremely jealous, others, like Stewart of Bute, reject them and back Wallace – whose followers include many with late-medieval magnate surnames.[62] In general, Hary did not condemn the Scottish nobles as a whole: in his poem, they are not Wallace's collective 'other'.

Hary, however, is in a minority; the other late-medieval Scottish writers express generally anti-magnate sentiments. In its reflections on Falkirk, *Gesta Annalia* II presents the classic statement: 'we rarely if ever read that Scots were overcome by the English except as a result of jealousy among their leaders or by guile and deceit on the part of natives going over to the other side'.[63] Wyntoun says something similar, blaming the disaster on 'falset and invy'.[64] Bower repeats the *Gesta* passage verbatim and precedes it with a whole chapter of his own about the magnates' 'plot', which describes them as 'intoxicated by a stream of envy . . . saying to one another, "We do not want this man to reign over us."'[65] In the following century, Mair developed the theme: Wallace had 'the universal acclamation of the common people', but 'the Scottish nobles pursued him with a deadly hatred, inasmuch as his conspicuous valour threw their own deeds into the shade'.[66] Boece wrote much the same: in the words of John Bellenden's 1531 translation, the nobles had 'gret invy' for Wallace, 'throw quhilk raise grete sedicioun', for they conspired with Edward I and at the time of Falkirk were 'boundin to his opinioun'.[67] Mair's and Boece's histories were printed long before the *Gesta Annalia* II and *Scotichronicon* accounts,[68] and they – especially Boece's *Scotorum Historia* (1527) in Bellenden's Scots version – were what really established the negative image of the Scottish nobility so firmly in Scotland's historical consciousness.

In all these accounts of Falkirk, the Comyns are serious transgressors. *Gesta Annalia* II explicitly blames the Scottish cavalry's flight on 'the stream of jealousy which the Comyns directed towards the said William [Wallace]',[69] and this was copied and extensively developed by Wyntoun, Bower, Mair, Boece and Bellenden.[70] In the Scottish narratives, therefore, the Comyns appear to undermine the Scottish cause. That is consistent with their demonisation, which has been such a prominent feature of Scottish historiography and which, according to recent studies, was caused by a strong pro-Bruce bias in the chronicles.[71] Given that these were written under the Bruce/Stewart regime of the fourteenth and fifteenth centuries, this makes good sense.

But there is a problem: *Gesta Annalia* II and its successors actually condemn the Bruces as much, if not more, for the Scottish defeats. Consider, first, the *Gesta*'s remarks about Dunbar, in 1296:

> For all the Comyns with all their supporters stood by Balliol; but the earls of Mar and Atholl with all the force at their command adhered . . . to the party of Robert de Bruce . . . It was for this reason . . . that, according to the common view, the aforesaid earls with their armies fled unharmed from the field on the day the . . . battle was fought, and thus a great disaster befell the opposing party, and the enemy of both of them gained such a welcome and pleasing victory. And, just as afterwards when King Robert Bruce was making war, all the supporters of Balliol were suspected of treason in his war, so also in this Balliol's war, the aforesaid . . . earls with all the supporters of Bruce's party were generally considered traitors to the king and kingdom.[72]

The *Gesta*'s explanation of Falkirk is even more remarkable.[73] Initially, the Comyns' malicious jealousy, which caused their flight, is highlighted. Yet a few sentences later it states:

> Moreover, it is commonly said that Robert de Bruce, who was later king of Scotland but at that time supported the king of England, by his industry provided the opportunity for this victory. For when the Scots stood fast

in their ranks and could not be broken by force or craft, this same Robert de Bruce, making a long detour round a mountain with a force commanded by Anthony de Bek, took the Scots in the rear from the opposite side; and thus the Scots, who at the earlier stage stood unbroken and unconquered, in the later stage were cleverly overcome.

Thus Bruce is also responsible for the crushing defeat. And, in addition, the *Gesta* comments, 'alas! as a result of the arrogance and blazing jealousy of both, the noble community of Scotland lay miserably prostrate'. Since this follows a statement that both the Comyns and Wallace fled, it has been assumed that they are the targets here.[74] However, Wallace is never arrogant or jealous elsewhere in the *Gesta*; and in discussing Dunbar, the *Gesta* employs the same term for 'both' (*utriusque*) to refer to the Balliol/Comyn and Bruce factions. When the author uses *utriusque* with respect to Falkirk, therefore, he was probably blaming both factions again and was thinking ahead to Robert Bruce's treachery.[75]

Furthermore, in the *Gesta* account Wallace flees immediately after the Comyns, so the latter could not have run away early in the battle. Instead, initially the Scots 'stood fast' until the attack in the rear led by Bruce caused defeat and flight. Hence, in *Gesta Annalia* II most of the blame for the disaster falls squarely on medieval Scotland's other great hero. Admittedly, the story about Bruce begins 'it is commonly said'; nevertheless the author clearly believed it, because he continues immediately with the passage about the Scots losing only through magnate envy or natives joining the other side. Since envy is consistently attributed to the Comyns, the treacherous natives must be the Bruces. There is no Bruce propaganda here.[76]

The story about Bruce is one of the most devastating episodes in Scottish historical writing. And it is not confined to *Gesta Annalia* II; all other writers recount and elaborate on it.[77] The most famous elaboration is Bower's: that Bruce encountered the fleeing Wallace, who reproached him so bitterly that Bruce repented and eventually joined the Scots[78] – a road-to-Damascus conversion that has been repeated in every account down to *Braveheart*. But this is not in the *Gesta*, and must represent Bower's attempt to soften the main story's effect by having Wallace show Bruce the light and so, implicitly, sanction his subsequent kingship. Here is another example of Bower's image-building, this time on Bruce's behalf. It was only partly successful, however: later writers narrate the episode in ways that give Bruce much less credit.[79] And whatever the version, it is always preceded by Bruce causing Wallace's defeat. Thus in all the late-medieval Scottish accounts the Bruces oppose Wallace's leadership just as significantly as the Comyns do. Now, since Scotland's political elite can then be seen (albeit exaggeratedly) as split between the Comyn and Bruce factions, it has been easy to conclude that almost the entire elite deserted Wallace. That is the fundamental basis for the modern image of the medieval Scottish nobles.

But is the basic story true? Recent Scottish historians mostly ignore or reject it, but do not confront it head-on[80] – leaving the popular image of the treacherous Bruce virtually unchallenged. The problem is that *Gesta Annalia* II's explicit statement is not contradicted by other direct evidence. Abundant circumstantial evidence, however, proves the story to be false. First, contemporary English accounts of Falkirk do not mention Bruce;[81] had he fought for Edward I, surely they would say so, especially since he is later portrayed as England's greatest enemy. Secondly, they record instead that when Edward marched south, he found Ayr Castle burned on the orders of the fleeing Bruce: strange behaviour if Bruce had been on Edward's side (the texts might even imply that Bruce fled from Falkirk).[82] Thirdly, in 1299 Malcolm Wallace was in Bruce's retinue; would he have followed the man who brought about his brother's defeat? Fourthly and most significantly, after Falkirk Wallace was replaced by joint guardians, including John Comyn and Robert Bruce; had Bruce fought for the English, it is inconceivable that the Comyns would have accepted him as guardian.[83] It follows that the story about Bruce at Falkirk should be rejected absolutely.

So what was the author of *Gesta Annalia* II doing? Historians of the Wars of Independence take the *Gesta* at face value, but since its version of mid-fourteenth-century Scottish politics is skewed in favour of David II and against Robert the Steward,[84] its account of 1286–1306 needs to be examined in that light. When that is done, it turns out to have one overriding theme: the importance of strong kingship and the miseries caused by magnate feuding whenever that was missing. Thus, Alexander III – whose second marriage and subsequent death in 1285–86 are *Gesta Annalia* II's starting point[85] – was an ideal king, 'because he ruled himself and his people rightly', and dealt with rebels 'with such harsh discipline that with a rope round their necks and ready to be hanged . . . they were subjected to his authority'.[86] But after his sole heir, the Maid of Norway, also died, the Balliol–Bruce feud over the succession broke out and could not be settled because the nobles 'had no superior who by the strength of his power could demand the execution of their decision or compel the parties to observe it' – one reason for bringing in Edward I.[87] Subsequently, John Balliol's kingship proved unsuccessful, so 'twelve peers or guardians were appointed for the protection and defence of the liberty of the realm and the community of the same' – but the *Gesta* dates this to 1296, *after* Dunbar and John's abdication, whereas the correct date is 1295.[88] The misdating is generally treated as a slip,[89] but it was surely deliberate: the *Gesta*'s author could not countenance a magnate-dominated council removing power from a king and therefore changed the sequence of events.

Next, there is the *Gesta*'s account of Dunbar (quoted above). The defeat is blamed on desertions by two pro-Bruce earls, Mar and Atholl, motivated by the Balliol–Bruce feud.[90] In fact, in 1296 – when the Bruces were on Edward I's side – both Atholl and Mar invaded northern England under Comyn leadership.[91] Subsequently, Atholl missed the battle because he was garrisoning Dunbar Castle; he was captured there and imprisoned in England.[92] Mar probably did flee the field, but so did the Comyns and the rest of the nobility; the Scottish cavalry was apparently chased for more than twenty miles.[93] Later in 1296, Edward I took Mar to England, along with the Comyns and other magnates; there is no indication that he was treated differently.[94] So whatever Mar did at Dunbar, anti-Balliol disaffection is unlikely to be the explanation. The *Gesta*'s statement about Atholl's and Mar's behaviour at Dunbar is another fabrication.[95]

After that comes the *Gesta*'s treatment of William Wallace. As James Fraser argues, it significantly overplays his role as sole leader of the Scottish cause in 1297, especially in omitting Andrew Murray almost entirely[96] – but this fits its theme, because Wallace is portrayed as at last providing the strong leadership that the author admired:

> he in a short time subjected all the magnates of Scotland willy nilly to his authority, whether by force or the strength of his prowess. And if any of the magnates did not gladly obey his orders, Wallace got hold of him, put pressure on him, and held him in custody until he submitted entirely to his wishes.[97]

No doubt that is overstated. But, for the *Gesta*'s author, it was exactly what Scotland needed and was how the ideal ruler should behave; there are significant parallels with his account of Alexander III. Wallace, however, was not a king, and the magnates would not accept his rule: hence their envy, and, at Falkirk, his desertion by the Comyns and betrayal by Bruce.

Then, after Falkirk, *Gesta Annalia* II's political tone alters. For 1299–1305 it focuses on John Comyn of Badenoch in a highly complimentary way.[98] Bruce is not mentioned, and the Scottish war effort goes well under Comyn; he defeats the English at Roslin in 1303. The *Gesta* states that, since the outbreak of Anglo-Scottish warfare, 'there is no report of so fierce a fight in which the bravery of the Scots so shone out in warlike power'.[99] Remarkably, it devotes more space to this relatively minor battle than to Bannockburn.[100] Given what the *Gesta* previously says about the Comyns, this change of tack seems strange, but it does maintain the general theme. From 1299 to 1305 John Comyn is portrayed (erroneously) as the sole Scottish leader, and there is no Bruce complication:[101] the Scots are united once more, so the war goes well. But, finally, feuding emerges again in

1305–6, this time between Comyn and Bruce – which sets the scene for Bruce's coup d'état and Scotland's eventual unification under his rule.[102]

Throughout its account of 1286–1305, therefore, *Gesta Annalia* II shapes and distorts its narrative in order to expound its overriding theme. But the author was not writing in a vacuum: for example, a lost pro-Comyn chronicle almost certainly lies behind his account of the period after Falkirk – probably the verse chronicle from which Bower preserved four extracts, all with a Comyn slant, including these lines on Roslin:

> in the field of Roslin grace shone anew from on high,
> and so, under John Comyn, leader of the Scots
> it confounded the English and gave victory to the Scots.[103]

The story of Bruce's treachery at Falkirk might also belong to a pro-Comyn chronicle.[104] The *Gesta*, however, is pro-Comyn only after 1298; its account of Falkirk condemns them and by implication does so for Wallace's whole career. The author's main source for 1297–98, however, was presumably different – probably the (lost) ballads about the hero to which Wyntoun famously refers.[105] The story about Bruce at Falkirk could have originated as easily in a Wallace ballad and perhaps derives from an actual event, such as Wallace's 'discomfiture' near Peebles in March 1304 by an English force that included Bruce.[106] Also, ballads about Wallace may have included stories about his harsh treatment of Scottish nobles who opposed him – which would have fitted the *Gesta*'s theme.

Yet, since *Gesta Annalia* II was written under David II, why does it relate anti-Bruce, pro-Comyn material? The answer partly lies in the absence of a specific Bruce history covering 1292–1305. Robert I ignored Balliol's reign and presented himself as Alexander III's immediate heir;[107] accordingly, the 'official' Bruce view of recent history (as expressed in the Declaration of Arbroath and Barbour's *Bruce*) leaps straight from Edward I's choice of Balliol to Robert's coup d'état, omitting the intervening years and not mentioning Wallace at all. That is hardly surprising, for although Bruce did not support Edward I at Falkirk, he was on the English side in 1296 and after *c*.1302; thus, the less said about 1292 to 1305, the better for Robert I. And because the Bruce history glosses over those years, the *Gesta*'s author would have to have used non-Bruce sources for them.

But, also, as long as the Bruce right to the throne was maintained (as *Gesta Annalia* II does, albeit ambivalently),[108] David II would probably not have objected to a portrayal of Robert I as less than perfect. David had been defeated and captured by the English in 1346, and thereafter had compromising dealings with Edward III; so his Scottish opponents no doubt contrasted him unfavourably with his father. Thus, the *Gesta*'s story about Bruce fighting for Edward I at Falkirk might not have been unwelcome.[109] Moreover, David's affinity had links to the Balliol/Comyn faction, especially in connection with his queen, Margaret Logie.[110] Most strikingly, in the 1364 debate over whether John of Gaunt (Edward III's son) should succeed if David died childless, one argument was that Gaunt's wife had Scottish blood – being descended from the Comyn earls of Buchan![111] Clearly, the Comyns were not demonised at David II's court.

That said, *Gesta Annalia* II is not consistently critical of Robert Bruce: its treatment of the period after 1305, for which pro-Bruce sources were available, is much more favourable, and John Comyn's killing is blamed on Comyn's wickedness.[112] Perhaps, therefore, the author simply parroted whatever sources were available. Yet what made Comyn wicked in 1306 was breaking his oath to join Bruce in fighting for Scottish freedom. This, once more, fits the *Gesta*'s basic theme, the troubles caused by uncontrolled magnate quarrels and feuding – certainly a message that David II and his circle would have welcomed wholeheartedly. Perhaps, indeed, the whole of *Gesta Annalia* II was designed to support David II's anti-magnate policy of the later 1350s and 1360s,[113] which was at its peak at the time of the 1363 rebellion, just when the chronicle was being written. Be that as it may, the main point here is that the exposition of the *Gesta*'s overriding theme for the years 1285 to 1305 involves significant historical distortions – which include misleadingly negative portrayals of the Scottish nobility – and that this was followed and developed by all subsequent writers from the fifteenth until the twentieth centuries.

So, to conclude this section: although the modern popular image of the Scottish nobility's unpatriotic behaviour during the Wars of Independence has a medieval basis, that itself should be regarded as an artificial construct, invented initially by the author of *Gesta Annalia* II, one aspect of whose theme was the creation of an image of William Wallace in which he alone acted like a proper ruler. The modern construct of a dichotomy between Wallace and the Scottish nobility already existed as early as the fourteenth century – but the images behind it were then just as artificial as they are today.

III

Finally, let us return to William Wallace himself and to a very different aspect of his image – as illustrated initially by the story in Wyntoun's *Orygynale Chronykil* about his first main exploit at Lanark, which clearly comes from a ballad. In this story Wallace is depicted as wearing green, hiding in the woods, leading a small band of followers, and finally killing a sheriff.[114] That makes him just like Robin Hood, or indeed 'the Scottish Robin Hood', as an English commentator explicitly describes him *c*.1500.[115]

Now, according to Bower, Robin Hood stories were popular among 'the foolish common folk' of Scotland.[116] Wyntoun knew about them, too; he refers to Little John and Robin Hood under the year 1283–84.[117] But Bower redates Robin to 1265–66 (the Simon de Montfort era), when 'that most famous armed robber Robert Hood . . . raised his head' from among those disinherited and outlawed by Prince Edward (subsequently Edward I). Bower's story, not found elsewhere,[118] of Robin finishing hearing mass before dealing with a sheriff has a triple relevance: that Bower knew ballads that have been lost; that Robin defeats one of Edward's sheriffs; and that Robin's raising his head after defeat by Edward Plantagenet parallels the *Gesta*'s first words about Wallace.[119] Hence, when Wyntoun and Bower (and possibly the author of *Gesta Annalia* II) develop their images of Wallace, they surely had Robin Hood in mind – or conversely, as Stephen Knight suggests, 'Wyntoun and perhaps Bower too had Wallace in the forests as an image in which to shape Robin Hood'.[120]

Subsequently, the images develop in opposite directions. Robin was originally a yeoman, but by the seventeenth century he had risen, becoming a wronged magnate,[121] whereas Wallace originally belonged to a minor noble family and went downwards, becoming (in general belief) a commoner and peasant: that reflects interesting contrasts between English and Scottish popular culture. But there is, of course, a much greater difference: Robin is fictional, Wallace existed in real life. The fictional outlaw is benign except to enemies; a real-life outlaw threatens and frightens almost everybody.[122] So, therefore, the question must now be asked: is that what Wallace was actually like?

English chroniclers had no doubt: virtually every one portrays Wallace as a robber or brigand. Guisborough states that 'there was a certain public robber (*latro publicus*) named William Wallace', and thereafter consistently applies *latro* to him. Lanercost and Langtoft both say he was originally 'the chief of robbers' (*princeps latronum*; *mestre de larouns*). As for Rishanger's chronicle, it describes him first as 'hitherto a public robber', and then, hyperbolically, as 'a shunned, deceitful criminal, a hater of piety, a sacrilegious plunderer, an arsonist, and a murderer crueller than Herod and madder than Nero' – words with which *Flores Historiarum* largely agrees.[123] This is what Fraser aptly calls the 'chief of brigands' image,[124] and it obviously reflects intense English hostility.

Unsurprisingly, that English image is usually rejected in Scotland, but one piece of evidence suggests that it might be valid. In August 1296, Matthew of York was indicted by Christina of Perth for stealing ale worth three shillings from her house in Perth on 14 June, in the gang of a certain thief, William le Waleys.[125] Scottish historians tend to ignore this episode[126] – yet how many William Wallaces led bands of men in late 1290s Scotland? Moreover, outlaw activity can easily merge with freedom fighting, as happened in English-held Normandy in 1419–49.[127] Was that what the Perth robbery was about? When it occurred, Edward I was in Stirling, thirty miles away; he reached Perth a week later.[128] Wallace might, therefore, have been requisitioning provisions for guerrilla activity. But the alternative is at least equally likely: that Christina's indictment should be believed and that the robbery should be attributed to a gang led by the subsequent hero.[129] In that case, since outlaws commonly poached deer, might it be that the bow and arrow on Wallace's seal denote his own real-life image before he became Scotland's hero – that of an outlaw? Furthermore, one task of sheriffs was to catch outlaws; is that actually why Wallace killed the sheriff of Lanark?

Moreover, the image of Wallace as outlaw would certainly not be out of place in the Britain of his era. What has been called 'fur-collar crime' was rife in early fourteenth-century England;[130] there were countless criminal gangs whose leaders were 'for the most part . . . drawn from the gentry, the knights and esquires, the very members of society on whom paradoxically the task of preserving law and order increasingly devolved'.[131] The classic instances are two early fourteenth-century outlaw bands headed by younger sons (like Wallace) of gentry families, the Folvilles from Leicestershire and the Coterels from Derbyshire;[132] and numerous other examples could be cited.

There is no reason to believe that Scottish landowners were any better.[133] *Gesta Annalia* II's account of Scotland after Alexander III begins with the earl of Fife's murder by minor nobles[134] – illustrating not only the problems caused by the absence of royal power but also by elite criminality. And consider the Douglases. At Edward I's request, the Guardians arrested Sir William Douglas in 1289–90 for abducting an English widow, with 'a multitude of armed men'; and King John punished him in 1292 for illegally imprisoning three of his own men in Douglas Castle (one was beheaded and one died), and for imprisoning the justiciar's baillies when they levied damages on behalf of his own mother.[135] His son James – Robert I's close companion – was equally violent.[136] A generation later, William Douglas of Lothian is even more significant. Like Wallace, he rose from virtual insignificance to become a major Scottish leader during the long fightback after Halidon Hill in 1333. He did so by recruiting a band of armed men to wage guerrilla warfare from lairs in Selkirk Forest and the Pentlands; and although he fought the English, he also kidnapped and starved to death one of his Scottish rivals.[137] Wallace did not do that, but he is surely a basically similar character. In that case, *Gesta Annalia* II's statement that he 'raised his head as if from his hiding-places'[138] is highly relevant. Why did Wallace need hiding-places before his revolt began, unless he already was an outlaw? The *Gesta* implicitly supports the English chroniclers.

Furthermore, whether or not Wallace was an outlaw, he was certainly extremely tough and at times seems callous. At Falkirk, it was essential to stop the foot soldiers fleeing from cavalry attack, as normally happened in the thirteenth century.[139] Wallace apparently found a remarkable solution. According to reliable English accounts, he arranged his spearmen into large circular schiltroms and in front of these had a fence made from stakes driven into the ground and tied together with ropes. Since the schiltroms were circular, the roped stakes presumably went all the way round – which meant that the Scottish foot soldiers could not run away because they were literally fenced in.[140] Unlike the Scottish horse they fought valiantly, repelling several English cavalry attacks; but then, being immobile, they were slaughtered by the enemy's archers and slingers. The result was horrific – but Wallace's brutal strength of mind must be recognised. The flaying of Cressingham's body at Stirling Bridge might also illustrate his mindset.[141]

As mentioned already, *Gesta Annalia* II applauds that strength of mind, stressing Wallace's harshness towards recalcitrant magnates. No doubt it exaggerates, but corroboration can be found in what happened in July 1297 after the capitulation at Irvine by the bishop of Glasgow, the Steward and the young Robert Bruce, who had planned to join Wallace in rebellion:[142] Wallace attacked the bishop's palace and carried off his furnishings, arms, horses and 'sons'.[143] Barrow has remarked that 'the emotion behind this act speaks of close relations between the two men';[144] perhaps, but it also demonstrates Wallace's fury against those who let him down and a strong propensity for taking the law into his own hands – like any outlaw. Then there is the case of Michael Meigle, accused in 1305 of supporting Wallace. A jury of twenty-five Scottish landowners, mostly from Tayside, testified that (in Joseph Bain's summary):

> he had been lately taken prisoner forcibly against his will by William le Waleys; that he escaped once from William for 2 leagues, but was followed and brought back by some armed accomplices of William, who was firmly resolved to kill him for his flight; that he escaped another time from said William for 3 leagues or more and was again brought back a prisoner by force with the greatest violence and hardly avoided death at William's hands, had not some accomplices of William entreated for him; whereon he was told if he tried to get away he should lose his life. Thus it appears he remained with William through fear of death and not of his own will.[145]

The jury's statement is clearly consistent with the *Gesta*'s account of how Wallace treated Scots who defied him.

Yet in these episodes Wallace's actions are not the kind that win friends and influence people, and suggest poor man-management skills. Furthermore, they contradict medieval theories of 'noble' behaviour.[146] The concepts of 'noble' and 'ignoble' are discussed above with respect to birth and status, but behaviour is probably more important. If, as *Gesta Annalia* II states, Scottish magnates considered Wallace ignoble, that might have been not because of his birth but because of how he treated them – especially if he was the outlawed leader of a band of robbers. Certainly, if he did behave in the way the *Gesta* describes and the instances in the previous paragraph illustrate, then, despite his knightly family, they would not have regarded him as a brother noble.[147]

This must be borne in mind when we consider his tragic end. In 1304 the Scots submitted, just as in 1296. However, whereas after the 1296 submissions Wallace headed a widespread revolt, in 1304–5 he was hunted by English forces and led a band not an army.[148] Eventually, Sir John Menteith captured him. Menteith has suffered lasting infamy, but he should be seen as an administrator who recognised whoever exercised effective authority;[149] he worked for Edward I after 1304, but King Robert soon employed him, and he was a prominent signatory of the Declaration of Arbroath.[150] Thus, in his own lifetime Menteith was not condemned in Scotland. The point is that by 1304–5 Wallace's day was past. Although leading a popular revolt is admirable and indeed magnificent, if it is eventually defeated, what then? After eight years of fighting, the Scots had clearly had enough – so in 1304 hardly any of them would support Wallace against England's might. It was time to admit defeat, recognise what had happened and bring peace.

That, expressed baldly, is an argument for defeatism, which is hardly praiseworthy. Normally what is praised is the image of indomitable fighters maintaining their conflict against all odds. In Wallace's case we know, with hindsight, that Scotland did maintain its independence; therefore we can applaud his 'No Surrender' attitude. Yet surely we would generally condemn such an attitude in our contemporary world – as, for instance, most people condemn the 'Real IRA'. Moreover, if Wallace is viewed dispassionately, he could be compared with extremists in the 1990s Balkans and even with 'insurgents' (brigands or freedom fighters?) in post-2003 Iraq. Thus, on reflection, Wallace's ultra-patriotic image may not be so wonderful. His real image is much darker – and was surely rejected by the Scots in 1304–5: 'blessed are the peacemakers'. Indeed, although after his execution parts of his dismembered body were displayed in Scotland, no relics from it are known to have been preserved and no shrines were erected in his memory.[151] For all his subsequent fame, there was no contemporary cult of William Wallace.

Yet the Scottish submission of 1304–5 was not final, and England's power was, eventually, resisted successfully. Therefore – a last, counter-factual, thought – had Wallace not been captured, had he survived well beyond 1305, what would have become of him? Since he supported John Balliol's kingship so staunchly in the 1290s, he might have rejected the usurping Robert Bruce.[152] But I would argue the opposite. If Wallace really was the great patriotic hero, then – as freedom fighter rather than outlaw – his first commitment was to Scottish independence. Moreover, in 1299 his brother Malcolm followed Bruce; and, even more significantly, another brother, John, was executed in 1307, so must have been fighting for Robert I. There is no reason, therefore, to suppose that William, if still alive, would not have joined Bruce in 1306. If so, and if he had lived to witness Robert's eventual triumph, then surely he would have contributed significantly to it. In that case he, like all Robert I's close supporters, would have been handsomely rewarded. Since Wallace came from southwest Scotland, he would presumably have been given lands there – probably including some that actually went to the man whose image is virtually that of a Wallace-substitute, Sir James Douglas. But the Douglases became late-medieval Scotland's greatest magnate family. So, if Wallace had survived, he would doubtless have finished up alongside, or above, the Good Sir James in the uppermost rank of the Scottish nobility.

That is a final irony about William Wallace. His enduring modern image, which contrasts so strikingly with that of the Scottish nobility, not only rests upon the mass of artificial constructs explored in this chapter but, also, would not exist at all had he not been rejected by the Scots in 1304 and sent to that tragic death in London in August 1305. In *Braveheart*, Mel Gibson – echoing Blind Hary, who was echoing Walter Bower – depicts Wallace's death as martyrdom. Although it is difficult to accept the explicit religious imagery of those final scenes, it must remain the case that Wallace's execution was absolutely vital in ensuring that his – artificial – image endures for ever.

7

Unmapping the Territory:
Blind Hary's *Wallace*

Felicity Riddy

My subject is a poem written in the late fifteenth century by a poet known only as Hary, or sometimes Blind Hary. Hary's *Acts and Deidis of Sir William Wallace* was the most widely read of all Scottish poems for a period of some four hundred years after its composition. It was this poem that fixed the figure of William Wallace in the popular imagination and gave definitive shape to the legend. Moreover, it taught the people of Scotland a way of conceptualising the nation that includes a virulent anti-Englishness but, as I shall argue, is at the same time more than this.

Hary's *Wallace* was part of that great flowering of Scottish literature at the very end of the Middle Ages. Robert Henryson, author of the *Fables* and *The Testament of Cresseid*, was probably Hary's contemporary, while William Dunbar, poet at the court of James IV, was perhaps a generation younger but certainly knew of him. *The Wallace* was composed in the reign of James III: the sole surviving manuscript, now in the National Library of Scotland, was copied in 1488 and the poem itself must have been written a decade or so earlier, probably in the late 1470s.[1] We do not know anything about its author, Hary, or even whether this was his first name or his surname. Dunbar calls him 'Blind Hary' in his 'Lament for the Makaris', and in the early sixteenth century the historian John Mair says that 'Henry, a man blind from his birth, compiled in my infancy a whole book on the history of William Wallace, and wrote in Scottish verse, in which he was skilled . . . This man obtained an honourable living by reciting histories in the presence of the nobles.'[2] In the early 1490s there are records of a Blind Hary receiving royal gifts, and it seems certain that this is Mair's man. But it is hard to see how the author of the *Wallace* could have been blind since birth, because in compiling his poem he had clearly read a number of written sources, including Chaucer, and he alludes several times to a Latin book from which he says he is working. Of course, late-medieval reading habits were different from ours: reading aloud was still a common practice and the memory was cultivated in ways that we have now largely forgotten. We know little about how people coped with blindness in the Middle Ages.

Nevertheless, there seems to be a consensus that Hary's blindness probably came upon him some time after the composition of the *Wallace* or at least after the preparation for it.

Hary also acquired a somewhat romantic reputation as a minstrel, like the blind crowder that Sidney speaks of in the *Apology for Poetry*, although he was in fact, like the other makars of the late fifteenth and early sixteenth centuries, a bookish writer, as I have already indicated. He is not, I think, a very good poet. He writes in five-stress couplets and, indeed, is one of the earliest Scottish writers to do so. Until the latter part of the fifteenth century the staple form in Scots narrative verse had been the brisker four-stress couplet, which is the form that John Barbour had used for his long poem about the Bruce a hundred years earlier. The five-stress couplet was introduced into English in the fourteenth century by Chaucer, who used it in *The Canterbury Tales*. In the hands of a poet with a poor ear it has a deadly expansiveness: it is ample and can be wordy, and Hary's poem is ample too. There are nearly 12,000 lines of it in twelve books, starting with Wallace's birth and ending with the martyrdom in London. Although there is a certain banal, even McGonagallish quality to the writing, nevertheless the poem as a whole is driven by an extraordinarily virulent, energetic and clearly engaging nationalism (to judge by its later history) that sustains a morality of vengeance and justified murder: 'Southeron to sla he thinkis it na syne' (III.270).

In writing the *Bruce* in the 1370s, Barbour had drawn on the memories of men who had lived through the Wars of Independence or whose fathers had. Hary was writing around a hundred and eighty years after the events he describes, in the latter part of the reign of James III, and the poem seems to have been provoked by contemporary events, particularly James III's policy of peace with England during the years around 1474–78. This included various forms of rapprochement, including betrothing the future James IV to an English princess, and there was dissension within Scotland about this policy.[3]

The poem gives a voice to the dispossessed, or rather to fantasies of dispossession. *The Wallace* conveys extraordinarily well a sense of what it is like to live in occupied territory, with talentless bullies strutting about helping themselves to whatever takes their fancy, lording it contemptuously over the natives and committing acts of random atrocity. It is very good, too, at showing how in a world that is not ruled by law, anything goes, on either side. Wallace's violence is directed primarily against Englishmen or untrue Scots, and he ostentatiously spares women, children and priests. The world of the poem is one in which young men are humiliated by the temperance and restraint of their elders whose decent aim is to try to make some kind of show of normal living. When English followers of 'Earl Persie', as he is called, brazenly help themselves to a baggage horse belonging to Wallace's uncle, Sir Ranald Crawford, sheriff of Ayr, Sir Ranald receives the news philosophically:

> That is bot litill der. [harm]
> We may get hors and othir gud in playne,
> And men be lost we get them nevir agayne.' [If] (IV. 60–2)

This kind of middle-aged counsel is lost on Wallace. He accuses his uncle of cowardice, renounces his allegiance to him and pursues the thieves. He catches up with them to the east of Cathcart, kills three of them while his companions kill the other two, loots the baggage train and makes for hiding among 'trew Scottis'. Thus is the pattern established: Wallace is driven first to quick retaliation for insult or violence and then to outlawry. Wallace knows that love and marriage are not for him, or not for long: he has chosen a different course. At first he says he will not marry at all, but against his better judgment does marry the nameless daughter of Hugh Braidfoot, and they have a daughter. His wife is killed, though, by the English in retaliation for helping him escape; and his mother has long since had to flee from her home in the southwest to Dunfermline Abbey, disguised as a pilgrim, where she dies. When he learns of his wife's death, Wallace vows that ten thousand Englishmen will die for her sake, and by the end of the poem he must have achieved that aim, although the reader loses count of the dead. The Englishmen's violation of Wallace's wife is a version of their violation of Scotland. Scotland, we come to see, is his mother, wife and daughter: there is a strange episode in the second book when he is rescued by his old nurse after being slung for dead into a cesspit, and her daughter suckles him. He was not committed thereafter exclusively to a life on the run – for a period he was Governor of Scotland – but nevertheless was committed to the company of other driven and single-minded men. There was the triumph of generalship at Stirling Bridge, but after the defeat at Falkirk – which Hary turns into a victory – Wallace fought the English in France before returning to Scotland and the inevitable betrayal and martyrdom.

I say inevitable because the pattern of the betrayal and death of the hero whom Wallace's life exemplifies is offered by those other mythic lives that were so widely known in the Middle Ages: Alexander and Arthur. Perhaps it is because the contours of this myth can be seen so readily in what is known of Wallace's real-life history that he has assumed the role he has. In or about the 1460s, Hary's Scots contemporary, Sir Gilbert Haye, wrote a long *Life of Alexander the Conquerour*, also in five-stress couplets, which tells the story of Alexander's mighty conquests and his in-the-end empty dominion – empty because it all ends with his early death by poison.[4] The medieval

Alexander legend is characteristically moralised, though, and is used to provide a lesson in vainglory. The story of Arthur, however, was, like that of Wallace, used for more complex moral purposes, including the exploration of issues relating to English nationalism. By the fifteenth century, Arthur was in some sense to English history what Wallace and Bruce were to Scots. Arthur comes to the throne at sixteen and thereafter conquers the rest of Britain (including Scotland) and much of Europe, and is marching triumphantly to take Rome itself when word comes of treachery at home, forcing his return to England and the final battle that brings about his death. Arthur's story can be read as a narrative of ambition, a myth of English imperialism. Another contemporary of Hary's, the Englishman Sir Thomas Malory, uses this myth in his *Le Morte Darthur*, written around 1470, just before the *Wallace*. In *Le Morte Darthur*, Arthur's reign does not come to an end through a failure of ambition abroad but because of betrayal at home. Malory may have had England's failure to maintain its hold on France in mind when he wrote of the collapse of Arthur's *imperium*.[5] What happened in France in the first half of the fifteenth century may also be relevant to Hary's *Wallace*.

I have already said that the poem is very good at conveying a sense of what it was like to live in enemy-occupied territory. This is in some ways surprising, since when Hary was writing no one in Scotland can have remembered such a time. The territory that did experience English colonisation in the fifteenth century was, of course, Normandy, from the 1420s until the English withdrawal in 1450. A Norman chronicler, Thomas Basin, writing in the 1470s (the same decade, that is, in which Hary composed *The Wallace*), describes the kind of guerrilla warfare that is one of Hary's main subjects. It is provoked by the presence in Normandy of oppressive English garrisons, and Basin views the response of some of his fellow countrymen with contempt:

> There was also a great number of desperate and lost men who, whether through cowardice, hatred of the English, or a desire to seize the goods of others, or whether, knowing they had committed crimes, wished to escape the snare of the law, quit their fields and houses, did not live in the towns or castles of the French and did not fight in their ranks, but, like wild beasts and wolves, lived in the deepest and most inaccessible forests. . . . They especially attacked the lives of the English, massacring them when the opportunity presented itself, without any pity.[6]

Thomas Basin was a former bishop of Lisieux, writing in exile, who had collaborated, as many Normans of his class did, during the English occupation: there are plenty of figures like him in the pages of *The Wallace*, including Robert the Bruce himself, who attempt to distance themselves from the freedom fighters. I do not suggest that Hary knew Basin's chronicle, which is not the only one to record the activities of the Brigands, as they were called, but he may have heard or read stories of what Normandy had been like under English rule and this helped him to imagine an occupied Scotland. Other Norman chronicles record their hatred of Henry V for his brutality and ruthlessness in terms very similar to those used of Edward I in Scotland.

It is of course important to see Hary's *Wallace* in its immediate context as a fifteenth-century poem, and that is how I have been discussing it so far. It is also important, however, to look at the ways in which it is not a fifteenth-century poem, since it was read for hundreds of years after its composition. It had an extraordinarily long and successful run. It went quickly into print: there are fragments of an otherwise lost edition by the first Edinburgh printers, Chepman and Myller, dated around 1508–9. It was reprinted in 1570 by Lekprevik, and then twice by Henry Charteris in the late sixteenth and early seventeenth centuries, and then by Andro Hart and others throughout the seventeenth century. There were numerous eighteenth-century editions, including one by the Jacobite printer Robert Freebairn, around 1730, and a modernised one by William Hamilton of Gilbertfield, first published in 1722 and several times reprinted in the eighteenth century. This was the edition read by both Burns and Wordsworth. The printing history suggests that the poem really took off after the union of the crowns, when its bitter resentment at the loss of Scottish autonomy acquired a new contemporary resonance. It taught its readers, in a period of the anglicisation of Scottish culture, how to feel Scottish.

In 1820 the lexicographer John Jamieson re-edited it from the manuscript, and the first Scottish Text Society edition was produced by James Moir in the 1880s. But Hugh Miller, the Cromarty stonemason, recalls in his 1858 autobiography reading what he called a 'common-stall edition' as a child, before the scholars got hold of it. He quotes Lord Hailes's view that it was 'the bible of the Scotch people'.[7] Barbour's *Bruce* was also reprinted between the sixteenth and nineteenth centuries but much less frequently than Hary's *Wallace*. Although two editions of *The Wallace* were published by the Scottish Text Society in the twentieth century – a facsimile of the 1570 print and Matthew McDiarmid's edition of 1968–69 – by the late 1980s Marinell Ash could argue that Wallace and the Bruce had been killed off as part of national culture by the anglicisation of school history syllabuses. She could not have foreseen the *Braveheart* effect: Randall Wallace's script of the film derives from the Hamilton of Gilbertfield version of Hary's *Wallace*.[8]

One obvious question the poem poses is, why was it located so firmly in popular culture for so long? By popular culture I mean a culture that uni-fies, however temporarily and illusorily, and includes both learned and unlearned, young and old, urban and rural. We know that reading a ver-sion of Hary's *Wallace* sent a 'Scottish prejudice' coursing through the veins of the young Burns, and Hugh Miller says:

> I was intoxicated with the fiery narratives of the blind minstrel, with his fierce breathings of hot, intolerant patriotism, and his stories of astonish-ing prowess, and, glorying in being a Scot, and the countryman of Wallace, I longed for a war with the Southron, that the wrongs and suf-ferings of those noble heroes might be avenged.[9]

For both these boys, reading about Wallace provided them with a fierce sense of Scottish identity, part of which stems from the anti-Englishness I have already emphasised and part from the pathos of the mythical narra-tive of 'the wrongs and sufferings of those noble heroes'. Nevertheless, Scottishness in Hary's *Wallace* is geographical as well as historical. It is not only about autonomy but has to do with being part of Scotland as an imag-ined community: Hary's *Wallace* creates a geography of the mind.

In the late 1990s the Scottish Tourist Board ran an advertisement on English television that began, *Braveheart*-style, with magnificent pictures of Highland scenery. A young couple were seen walking through this land-scape, with 'Let us go, lassie, go' as a voice-over. Then it moved into a pic-ture of the poet Norman MacCaig, in profile, speaking a couple of his own lines: 'Only men's minds could ever have unmapped / Into abstraction such a territory'. These lines come from an early poem, 'Celtic Cross'.[10] What a stone cross asks, says MacCaig, is

> Something that is not mirrored by nor trapped
> In webs of water nor bag-nets of cloud;
> The tangled mesh of weed
> > lets it go by.
> Only men's minds could ever have unmapped
> Into abstraction such a territory.

'Unmapping into abstraction such a territory' seems to me to be a good way of describing what is going on in *The Wallace*: the mythical geography of nationhood that also lies behind our commemoration of the battle of Stirling Bridge. Let me first discuss mapping, though, before I get on to unmapping.

The endpapers of Matthew McDiarmid's Scottish Text Society edition of Hary's *Wallace* consist of two maps of southern and northern Scotland, showing the many locations that are mentioned in the poem. I do not know

ABOVE. Niddrie
Marischal portrait of
William Wallace,
1661/1720. *Stirling Smith
Art Gallery and Museum*

LEFT. Guthrie Castle
portrait, seventeenth
century, now in Torosay
Castle, Isle of Mull.
*Stirling Smith Art Gallery
and Museum / SCRAN*

TOP. Medal, 1797, commissioned by Colonel
William Fullerton (1754–1808), MP for Ayrshire.
Stirling Smith Art Gallery and Museum

ABOVE. The Wallace seal casts.
Mitchell Library, Glasgow

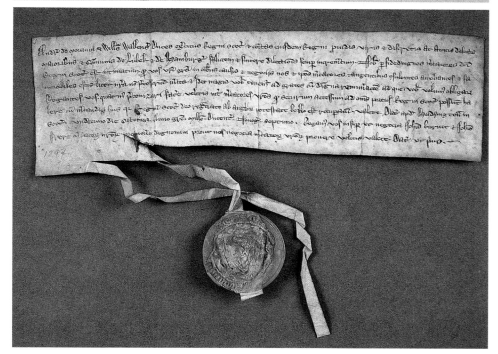

Dryburgh statue, 1814, sculpted by John Smith of Darnick
and commissioned by David Steuart Erskine, Earl of Buchan.

Reproduced courtesy of Graeme Peacock (www.graeme-peacock.com)

Wallace by
Andrew Munro
of Brooklyn.
Watercolour
1908. *Stirling
Smith Art Gallery
and Museum*

The Proposed Wallace Memorial at Elderslie

The Kitchen Fireplace, "Wallace's House." The walls of
the house are three feet thick

"Wallace's House." Popular tradition has it that in this house,
situated in the village of Elderslie, Wallace was born

TOP. Wallace's birthplace, Elderslie.
Watercolour 1908 by Andrew Munro
of Brooklyn. *Stirling Smith Art Gallery
and Museum*

ABOVE. Wallace birthplace. Report
in Scots Pictorial 1909, prior to the
planning of the Elderslie Monument,
1912. *Stirling Smith Art Gallery and
Museum*

Robert the Bruce receiving the Wallace
Sword from the Spirit of Scotland in the
guise of the Lady of the Lake, at Stirling,
on the eve of Bannockburn. Painting at a
time when our ancient freedoms were
under threat from Nazism and Fascism,
1943. Oil on canvas by Stewart
Carmichael (1867–1950). *Stirling Smith
Art Gallery and Museum*

LEFT. Wallace Oak, c.1815. Oil on canvas, by the Reverend John Thomson RSA (1778–1840). *Stirling Smith Art Gallery and Museum*

BELOW. Letters of the European Liberators framed in the Wallace Oak of Elderslie, secured by fundraiser John McAdam (1806–1883) for the National Wallace Movement. *Stirling Smith Art Gallery and Museum*

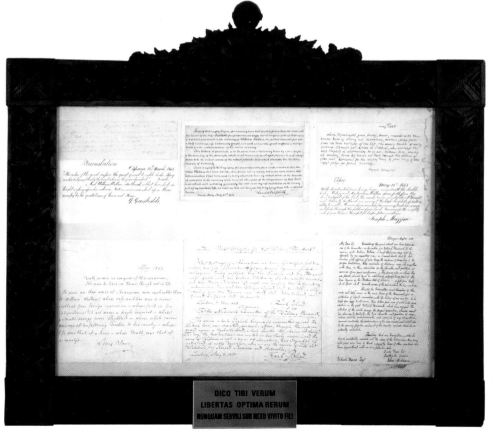

ABOVE. Polaroid photograph, Wallace Sword in captivity, 1972. *Stirling Smith Art Gallery and Museum*

RIGHT. Wallace Sword. *Stirling Council*

THE
WALLACE
SWORD

Wallace Statue, Ballarat, Victoria, Australia. Sculpted by Percival Ball of
Melbourne, unveiled 24 May 1889. The model was Scottish World
Champion athlete, Donald Dinnie (1837–1916) who also modelled for
Barr's Irn Bru. Statue funded by James Russell Thomson and the
Caledonian Society of Australia. *Stirling Smith Art Gallery and Museum*

1955 brochure issued for the 650th anniversary of the death of Wallace by Roland E. Muirhead of the Scottish Secretariat. The Ballarat statue features on the cover. *Stirling Smith Art Gallery and Museum*

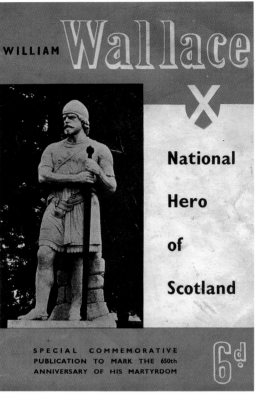

WILLIAM **Wallace**

X

National

Hero

of

Scotland

SPECIAL COMMEMORATIVE
PUBLICATION TO MARK THE 650th
ANNIVERSARY OF HIS MARTYRDOM

6d.

Wallace statue, David Park, Baltimore, and the Caledonian Society, 24 August 1997. The statue is a copy of the D. W. Stevenson statue erected on the façade of the National Wallace Monument in Stirling, 1887. The Baltimore statue, gifted by Scots-born Wallace Spence, was unveiled on St Andrew's Day 1893. Annual commemorations in honour of Wallace take place here. *Stirling Smith Art Gallery and Museum*

Architect's drawing for the National Wallace Monument, 1859, entered in the competition under the title 'Nothing on Earth remains bot faime' by J.T. Rochead (1814–1878). *Stirling Smith Art Gallery and Museum*

OPPOSITE. Wallace Monument. The stone for the Monument was quarried on site from the Abbey Craig. The water which filled the quarry was later drained. Photograph by Sergeant McKenzie, c. 1880. *Stirling Smith Art Gallery and Museum*

ABOVE LEFT. John Thomas Rochead (1814–1878), architect of the National Wallace Monument. *Stirling Smith Art Gallery and Museum*

ABOVE RIGHT. Reverend Charles Rogers (1825–1890), fundraiser and promoter of the National Wallace Monument. *Stirling Smith Art Gallery and Museum*

LEFT. Blind Harry by Alexander Stoddart. Plaster, 1996. *Stirling Smith Art Gallery and Museum*

Battle of Stirling Bridge
by Andrew Hillhouse.
*Stirling Smith Art Gallery
and Museum*

of any other medieval poem, Scots or English, that has so many place names in it. The historical Wallace's family originated in the southwest, and in the poem a certain amount of the action takes place in Ayrshire, but by no means all. McDiarmid points out that Hary himself probably came from the 'area comprising North-East Stirlingshire . . . South-East Perthshire, with the adjoining parts of North-West Fife and South-West Angus'. This may be why he gives Wallace uncles in Dunipace, Kilspindie and Elcho, sends him to school in Dundee, and has his mother seek sanctuary at Dunfermline Abbey. Nevertheless, the effect is to make Wallace, on the run, rallying support or ejecting the English, a more than local hero. He not only rescues Scotland three times, as Thomas the Rhymer prophesied he would in Book II, but his exploits map the country. Real places are mentioned again and again throughout the poem. These are places that had perhaps never before reached the written word, except in documents, and certainly not all together: Blackford, Airth, Leckie, Gargunnock, Drip Ford, Gask, Dalreoch, Ardargan, Kenmore, Murthly. A striking difference between Hary's *Wallace* and *Braveheart* is that in the latter Wallace has been turned into a Highlander. The film uses very few different settings: Wallace's Highland glen features quite a lot; there are fields labelled 'Stirling' and 'Falkirk'; a home-made-looking Edinburgh and an equally rickety York. By contrast, Wallace in Hary's poem is constantly on the move all around Scotland, particularly Lowland Scotland, although he does go into the Highlands as well. His farthest-north point is Hugh Miller's Cromarty:

> Into Bowchane Wallace maid him to ryd,
> Quhar lord Bewmound was ordand him for to bid . . .
> Quhen he wist weill that Wallace cummand was,
> He left the land and couth to Slanys pas
> And syne be schip in Ingland fled agayne.
> Wallace raid throw the north-land in-to playne.
> At Crummade feill Inglismen thai slew.
> The worthy Scots till him thus couth persew;
> Raturnd agayne and come til Abirdeyn
> With his blith ost apon the Lammas ewyn;
> Stablyt the land as thocht him best suld be,
> Syne with an ost he passit to Dunde. (VII.1077–8; 81–90)

This short passage illustrates well the restless movement of the hero, whose actions and those of his cowardly antagonist, Beaumont, who turns tail and flees, are used to map the northeast: Buchan, Slains Castle, Cromarty, Aberdeen, Dundee. Hary says he 'stablyt the land', which is both a matter of stabilising it politically and fixing its geography. The nation that is brought into being as an imagined entity, traversed and connected by the hero's journeys, is not centred on Edinburgh, or even on Glasgow. Edinburgh is mentioned only four times in the whole poem, much less frequently than Ayr, St Johnstoun (Perth), Dundee or Stirling. That is, part of the effect of the mapping of Scotland in *The Wallace* is to shift the axis, or at least the focus of attention, away from the traditional centres of power and status. Hary's geography is partly a geography of castles but also of small towns, woodlands, rivers, hills and, of course, a bridge.

Let me invoke another of Hary's fifteenth-century contemporaries: this is an English chronicler called John Hardyng, who completed the second version of a chronicle of English history some time in the mid-1460s, only ten years or so before Hary's *Wallace* was written.[11] Hardyng was as obsessively anti-Scots as Hary was anti-English; he wrote to encourage first Henry VI and then Edward IV to make war on Scotland and reclaim what he was convinced was England's rightful heritage. Like Hary, although for opposite reasons, he loathed any policy of peace with Scotland. His version of 'British' and then English history is skewed throughout to support the rightfulness of the English claim to Scottish overlordship, and he actually forged a number of documents to support this point of view, which he presented to Henry VI. Hardyng was a Northumbrian, a follower of Robert Umfreville whose family had been deprived of their Scottish titles in the 1330s; he was an old soldier who had fought at Agincourt and he had a Borderer's bitter understanding of the relations between Scotland and England. My point in introducing Hardyng, however, is that he was another contemporary mapper of Scotland. At the end of his chronicle he appends a handy invasion route for the royal army to take, with distances between the major Scottish towns: 'Fro Haddington to Seton iiii m. Fro Seton to Musselburgh vii m. Fro Musselburgh to Edenburgh wher the castell stondeth upon an high roche of stone and a goode merchaunte town with an abbaie of Haly Rodehouse wher your flete may come to lie be you in the Scottish see that is called the water of forth vii m.' Having got the army to Edinburgh, he then shifts into what passes for verse, addressing the English king:

> And if your wille and noble high corage
> Thynketh this is ouer litill to your puissaunce
> When you have brente with all your baronage
> Edenbourgh Toune and ther doon your plesaunce
> And haue that castell at your obeissaunce
> And it please you ferther for your comforte
> To your highness the waie I will reporte.[12]

He then goes on to describe what we might call the burning, raping and looting route through central Scotland, via Stirling to Glasgow and thence to the coast, 'wher a flete of the west see myght mete you at Dunbarton and at Ayr'. In some manuscripts of Hardyng's chronicle there are even diagrammatic maps in case the English army should get lost. Hardyng's map of Scotland is a place of grand castles dominated by Berwick, Edinburgh, Falkland, Andirstoun (St Andrews), St Johnstoun (Perth) and Dumbarton, with a much smaller castle representing Stirling. The northern boundary of the kingdom is bordered by 'Styx the ynfernall flode', which separates Scotland from the palace where Pluto, king of Hell, lives. It is hardly surprising, given these attitudes, that Hary should be so anti-English. But my point is that while Hardyng's Scotland is a place of military targets and sources of booty, as Edward IV must have found when he invaded in 1482, Hary's is a place of sites memorialised – like Stirling Bridge – by heroic deeds and the pathos of suffering.

Hary's *Wallace* maps Scotland, then, but at the same time unmaps it into abstraction as well. What I have not emphasised so far is the extent to which the story Hary tells is simply untrue. Unlike Barbour's *Bruce*, which is treated with some respect as a historical source (if only because, as already suggested, Barbour seems to have had informants who were close to the events in question), Hary's *Wallace* has generally provoked derision among historians. Very little documentary evidence survives about the historical Wallace, except for the period in 1297 when he was Guardian of Scotland. Hary claims that he drew on a Latin life of Wallace written by John Blair and Thomas Gray, two priests who knew him all his life. Although Sir William Craigie was inclined to allow that such a text might have existed, I think that most modern scholars assume this was merely a ploy to lend authority to a largely fictitious narrative. I have already suggested that its general contours fall into a mythic pattern, but the poem does more than this: it creates a mythical geography of nationhood, a Scotland of the mind. This is the sense in which I use MacCaig's phrase: he unmaps the territory into abstraction, into the idea of a nation.

Hary's Scotland is a place of sites memorialised by heroic deeds, many of which never took place. There was no atrocity committed by the English in the 'Barns of Ayr'; Wallace never fought a battle at Loudoun Hill; he did not attack the English camp at Biggar, putting the king to flight and killing 7,000 Englishmen; nor did he receive a visitation from Edward's queen as far south as St Albans, suing for peace; or encounter Robert the Bruce on the banks of the Carron after the battle of Falkirk; or rout Edward's army at Linlithgow the next day. He did not do these things, and yet the story of his doing them and the places he did them in could be said to have created the idea of a nation. Whether or not Hary really did consult a Latin source, the fact that he emphasises that it was in Latin, the pan-European language of learning, draws attention to the vernacularity and particularity of his own Scots. And as the poem went into edition after edition in the seventeenth and eighteenth centuries, it must have become the most widely read work in Scotland after the Bible: the *Wallace* belongs to the era of print. The most important difference, perhaps, between a manuscript and a printed book is that every manuscript is unique, while printed books are produced in hundreds at a time. The reader of the printed book understands this, however unconsciously; we know that the very act of reading constitutes us members of a reading community. So we can see all those readers of Hary's *Wallace*, over four hundred years, as connected through print, forming, as Benedict Anderson puts it, 'a secular, particular, visible invisibility, the embryo of the nationally imagined community', recognising their Scottishness in the pathos of its heroism and its tragically mythical geography.[13] However modernised, however anglicised the language became, Hary's *Wallace* 'unmapped into abstraction / Such a territory'.

8

The Material Culture of William Wallace

Elspeth King

When the long-anticipated Museum of Scotland opened its doors to the public on St Andrew's Day 1998, the hero who saved Scotland from annihilation, who secured the great victory for Scotland at the Battle of Stirling Bridge and whose bravery had been an inspiration to generation after generation of patriotic Scots – not to mention those of other nationalities fighting for their own concept of freedom – was noticeably absent. William Wallace was nowhere featured in the displays of the new Museum of Scotland. Public anger was vented in the media, and the subject occupied the news and correspondence columns of Scottish newspapers for weeks on end. For many people, Wallace and Scotland were one and the same. Robert Bontine Cunninghame Graham perhaps expressed this best when (in 1920) he wrote:

> Wallace made Scotland. He is Scotland; he is the symbol of all that is best and purest and truest and most heroic in our national life. You cannot figure to yourself Scotland without Wallace. So long as grass grows green, or water runs, or whilst the mist curls through the corries of the hills, the name of Wallace will live.[1]

In the public mind, Wallace and Scotland were synonymous. This had been strongly reinforced by a number of events in the previous three years. The film *Braveheart* was launched in 1995 and was an instant success, projecting the story of Wallace and the fight for Scottish independence into cinemas worldwide. It was entertaining, epic, inspirational and got Scottish matters discussed on a global level. At a national level, it reinforced interest in Scottish history and national identity. The Secretary of State for Scotland, Michael Forsyth, took a particular interest, and on St Andrew's Day 1996 the Stone of Destiny was returned to Scotland with great ceremony. Five months later, his government was voted out. On 11 September 1997, the 700th anniversary of Wallace's victory at Stirling Bridge,[2] there was a resounding 74 per cent vote in favour of re-establishment of a Scottish parliament. Confidence in things Scottish was heady and high.

The first elections to the Scottish Parliament were planned for 1999, and when the Museum of Scotland opened in November 1998, there was an unarticulated assumption that Wallace, in one form or another, would be represented. In many other ways, the opening of the Museum of Scotland was a coming of age. The new building by Benson and Forsyth was stylish and well designed; it had its own main entrance, instead of being subsumed into that of the Royal Museum as originally planned, and the building made a distinctive but complementary statement in the surrounding cityscape. Fearing the contentious nature of the Wallace story, the curators and director had taken refuge in the Unionist cloak of a professorial triumvirate of historical advisers. Professors Michael Lynch, Christopher Smout and Tom Devine advised that since there were no 'real' artefacts associated with Wallace extant from the time of Wallace (*c.* 1270–1305) there was no need to deal with or even mention Wallace in the displays of the new museum.[3]

At the same time, the Museum of Scotland curators had created public-relations problems for themselves by abdicating their responsibility to interpret twentieth-century history. They invited various individuals to contribute a twentieth-century artefact that had had an impact on their lives and had significance in social terms. The combination of the absence of Wallace and the presence of a wide variety of twentieth-century consumer goods, many of them not Scottish, was explosive.

Many thought that the shadow had been cast by the contemporary 'father' of the Scottish Parliament, Donald Dewar, who had an infamous dislike for 'nationalist shibboleths'. In the public mind, as expressed in letters to the press, there was a belief that there had been political intervention in the work of the museum. A correspondent in the *Courier*, one of the first to raise the question of the letter sent by Wallace and Murray to Lübeck in 1297, was displeased at the exclusion of Wallace and the inclusion of Tony Blair's guitar. 'There is a stench of politics here, and the naughty school boys responsible should be brought to the front of the class.'[4] Other naughty boys, like Alex Salmond, leader of the Scottish National Party, tried to have Wallace included by donating his *Braveheart* poster to the museum. There was a gloomy acceptance on the part of some nationalists as to the political agenda at work in Scotland's cultural affairs.

The learned professorial advisers were technically correct in maintaining that there were no artefacts or personalia of Wallace available for exhibition. Edward I did a very thorough job in 1305 in destroying his body and possessions. It was perhaps disingenuous to exclude him from the Museum of Scotland altogether on those grounds, although, interestingly enough, the entire output of the *Scottish Historical Review* pre-*Braveheart* is likewise an almost Wallace-free zone. The interest of the professional historian in Wallace is a relatively recent phenomenon.

An enterprising journalist claimed 'discovery' of the 1297 letter of Wallace and Murray to Lübeck and used it to discredit the stand that the Museum of Scotland had taken. As the Keeper of the Records made clear, the Lübeck letter had not been lost.[5] However, sustained press excitement over the 'discovery' forced the museum to borrow the letter from the Lübeck archive for a temporary display, even although the museum director had made clear that objects, rather than archival material, were the museum's main interest.

If there are no 'authentic' artefacts relating to Wallace, is there any point in discussing material culture in relation to him? Should every museum follow the example of the Museum of Scotland and ignore Wallace because there is nothing from his times? Will an exploration of Wallace-related objects serve any purpose amidst academic discourses that focus on the perceived negative effects of the Wallace story? In this chapter I want to look at the dichotomy of material culture and archive-based history and how the latter seeks to invalidate and eliminate the former. I also want to look at the source of material culture in relation to Wallace and the various classes of it – his body, his weapons, furniture, portraits, trees and natural features, the monuments that succeeded them, the domestic ornaments and tourist souvenirs, the artistic interpretations and the groups who continue to commemorate his name in the twenty-first century.

Museums are the repositories of material culture and, at present, Scottish museums are engaged in a fight for survival on every front – financial, cultural, intellectual. Seriously underfunded, and at a local government level competing within the arts, culture and sports sector for a share of shrinking resources, they are an optional facility. In contrast to the provision of library services, which is mandatory, no local authority is obliged to maintain a museum. A series of cultural commissions and a national audit of museums (2001) have failed to deliver any extra finance or even hope.

The plight of Scotland's museums is not unconnected to the long-running academic discourses on the 'manufacture' of Scottish history, the making of Scottish heritage and the creation of cultural identity. There is no space to review the extensive literature on the subject here,[6] but the thrust of it is that Scotland is swamped by histories and heritage presentations that are bogus and informed by myths that require to be deconstructed at length and debunked. Some of these discourses are simplistic and include a whole new mythology about Scotland having too many museums.[7] Added to this is the sneering contempt of academics who characterise the commemoration of Wallace by others as 'karaoke history'[8] and parenthesise and belittle the studies of others as 'Wallaciana'.[9] The overall impression given is that the only acceptable 'authentic' history is written by historians working in universities and published in book form. The history presented in museums is of a lesser variety and not for those who wish to engage with it on a professional level. This is why the Museum of Scotland curators have advisers in academia to tell them that the history of Wallace can be omitted from the museum's presentation. These advisers are the intellectual successors of Lord Hailes (1726–92), 'the father of national history' (according to Sir Walter Scott), who founded the discipline on the study of documents. Two hundred years after his death, his successors, when discussing the future, were still claiming that 'there was so much myth and ignorance about the Scottish past that careful archive-based empiricism probably had to be the *sine qua non* of any mature development of the subject'.[10] This was at a time when the Museum of Scotland's future was by no means assured. Material culture has always been irrelevant to the document-obsessed professional Scottish historian and, in view of the many assertions about the illiteracy of the Scottish people at every level of society over the last millennium, it is interesting to reflect on the reality these document-focused histories claim to portray.

The present-day process of discrediting historical artefacts 'expertly revealed as inauthentic' by the modern discipline of history is well illustrated by the sidelining of the Borestone on the National Trust for Scotland's property at Bannockburn and its replacement by an historical interpretation that ends with the Union of the Crowns. Thus, 'history prevails over myth'.[11] Although Bannockburn was a major battle, with heavy casualties and losses on the English side, virtually no finds are extant. Some pointed stakes, excavated in 1922 from one of the camouflaged pits on the battlefield area[12] and owned by the Stirling Smith Museum, were proved by 'experts' to be tree roots and therefore not authentic.[13] Another myth debunked, and another museum discredited, and all on national television. The debunkers are not new on the scene. Writing in the *Stirling Observer* in 1887, a commentator urged:

> It is high time that we Scots should acquaint ourselves and make our bairns acquainted with all about Bannockburn. All the more so, should we ever fall under the pawky regime of a London Education Board. Nothing is more likely than in the school histories it sanctions, Wallace and Bruce will be turned into rogues or myths, and discreetly left out or thrown into the shade.[14]

So prescient a writer should have been aware of the parcel-of-rogues factor in Scottish history and have anticipated that we would one day have many historians and archaeologists working within Scotland and willing to traduce Wallace and Bruce without leaving it to Londoners. After decades of silence on the subject, it now seems that any study of Wallace in particular has to be prefaced with caveats about the lack of authentic source material, condemnation of '*Braveheart* Blunders' and a thorough discrediting of Blind Hary's *Wallace*.

BLIND HARY'S *WALLACE*

As much of the rich material culture relating to Wallace is inspired by Blind Hary's work, it is appropriate to briefly summarise the circumstances of its composition and publication, and to assess its value. We owe its survival to a single manuscript copied by John Ramsay in 1488 from an original that its modern editor, Matthew McDiarmid, using internal textual evidence, has dated to 1478. It was one of the first printed books in Scotland and was continuously in print until the eighteenth century. In 1722 it was translated into modern English by William Hamilton of Gilbertfield (*c.* 1665–1751). This translation went through many editions and was a source of inspiration to Burns, Wordsworth, Southey, Thomson and Byron, to name but a few writers. Randall Wallace, who used it as a source for the novel and film *Braveheart*, thought that if Blind Hary was 'making it all up, he was a more inventive writer than Shakespeare', echoing Matthew McDiarmid's estimation[15] that 'if we are to look for a parallel to Hary's dramatic creation we must look forward to the tragic figures of the Elizabethan stage'.

Blind Hary's great epic poem on Wallace is the longest work in medieval Scots, with 11,877 stanzas divided into twelve books. It is exciting, entertaining, inspirational and touches every aspect of the human condition. It is a great work of literature, geography and history, drawing strongly on very specific local traditions. These localities are so tied to the landscape of Scotland that no fewer than 83 Wallace place names can still be found on modern Ordnance Survey maps. No other Scottish historical figure is embedded in the landscape in the way that William Wallace is. It is my belief that the story of Wallace was kept alive through people associating his deeds with geographical features, trees and woods to compensate for the historical deficit, the absence of Wallace from the official historical record, and that Blind Hary's work is a reflection of this rather than an invention.[16]

For a major work of national literature, Blind Hary's poem has remained relatively unknown in the past hundred years. The work was not recognised when it appeared in the form of the *Braveheart* film in 1995; there is still a widespread belief that *Braveheart* is 'Hollywood history' and owes nothing to Hary's medieval epic. An accessible edition of the medieval text was produced only in 2003,[17] and even in 1997, the anniversary year of the battle of Stirling Bridge, it was thought that there would be no market for such a publication.

In spite of the public's neglect of Blind Hary's *Wallace*, its text has been the subject of forensic scrutiny and has been found wanting by the majority of Scottish historians, past and present. There is a veritable Greek chorus of condemnation of every aspect of the work: it is unreliable, full of error and exaggeration, anti-English, and so worthless in historical terms that it is pointless to even investigate the identity of the author. To this has been added the anachronistic charge of plagiarism and the oft-repeated suggestion that it was written for the political purposes of the Duke of Albany, brother of James III, to create an anti-English climate and undermine royal policy.[18] How this was to be achieved in a pre-printing-press era and with a less than literate population has yet to be answered.

To dismiss the work wholesale is both to misunderstand its nature as a gathering-in of Wallace stories that are place-specific and to overlook the truths that it contains. Blind Hary claims that his work is based on a Latin book commissioned by Bishop William Sinclair to send to the Pope to appraise him of the truth.[19] Most critics have identified the Latin book as a literary device, but in a country where major manuscripts have survived by chance rather than design, it is premature to dismiss it as fiction. William Sinclair (died 1337) is certainly very real. His defaced tomb effigy survives in Dunkeld Cathedral. Elected to the bishopric of Dunkeld in 1309, he had a three-year fight for his see at the papal court against an English incumbent.[20] He personally took up arms to repel an English invasion of the coast of Fife in 1317 and was referred to by Robert Bruce as 'my bishop',[21] such was his patriotism and loyalty. Commissioning a piece on Wallace as part of the war of words that was being waged between Scotland and England at the papal court would have been in keeping. The cause in which it might have been done is not hard to find. Bishop Robert Wishart of Glasgow (*c.*1240–1316), captured by the English in 1306, had been the first to challenge Edward I, face to face, in 1291. Wyntoun has him address Edward in these terms:

'Excellent prince,' he said, 'and king,
Ye ask ws ane vnlefull thing
That is superiorite;
We ken rycht noucht quhat that suld be,
That is to say, of our kinrik,
The quhilk is in all fredome like
Till ony realme that is mast fre
In till all the Cristianite,
Wnder the sone is na kingdome,
Than is Scotland, of mare fredome.
Off Scotland our king held ever his stait
Off God him self immediat

And of nane other meyne personne.
Thare is nane erdly king with crovne,
That ourelard till oure king suld be
In till superiorite.'[22]

The English were in no doubt that Wishart, who had given full support to Wallace, was the source of the trouble in Scotland. The case was stated boldly in a letter of rebuke from Pope Boniface VIII in 1302:

> I have heard with astonishment that you, as a rock of offence and a stone of stumbling, have been the prime instigator and promoter of the fatal disputes which prevail between the Scottish nation and Edward, King of England, my dearly beloved son in Christ, to the displeasing of the divine majesty and to the hazard of your own honour and salvation . . . It befits you to repent . . . to strive to obtain forgiveness.[23]

Wishart was a pragmatic patriot who broke no fewer than six oaths of fealty to Edward I. After his capture, he was transferred as far south as possible, to Porchester Castle, and Edward II wrote in strong terms to Pope Clement V 'concerning the horrible crimes of the Bishop of Glasgow'.[24]

Only fragments of the special pleading that went on between Scotland and England have survived, but bearing in mind the demonisation of Wallace by the English, it is not unlikely that a cleric like Sinclair might have commissioned a defence of Wallace by way of supporting the cause of a fellow bishop. Wishart, Glasgow's longest-serving bishop, Guardian of the Realm, defender of the rights of the Scots, the man who absolved Bruce for murder and aided his coronation, is one of the great patriots of Scotland. After Bannockburn, his release was secured in exchange for the Earl of Hereford. His damaged tomb effigy lies in anonymity in Glasgow Cathedral,[25] and its contents were desecrated by the youthful Archibald McLellan (1795–1854) who grew up to demolish the western towers of the Cathedral by way of 'improvement' and to bequeath an art collection that was the foundation of the Glasgow Art Galleries.[26]

According to Napoleon Bonaparte, 'History is the version of past events that people have decided to agree upon.' Similarly, people can also elect to choose their cultural heritage, as in the case of Glasgow, trampling upon and destroying the past to embrace and sustain a purchased culture of European art. Yet when an attempt is made to investigate and creatively interpret that past, it is regarded as dishonest fabrication. Even the Victorian interpretation of it is untouchable. The large painting on leather by Thomas Dudgeon, illustrating Wallace's battle of the Bell o' the Brae, which hung above the doorway of Provand's Lordship, *c.* 1840–1900,[27] to remind Glaswegians of the Wallace connection, has remained untreated and in museum storage throughout the twentieth century.

There is likewise an Establishment agreement to discredit or ignore Blind Hary's work. This is why the sculptor Alexander Stoddart elected to create a portrait of Hary,[28] throwing the challenge 'Quham "thowis" thow, Scot?' ('Who is it that you are speaking of in the familiar, Scot?') to his country-men, demanding that we study and respect his work. It seems that this will never come easily.

PERSONAL OBJECTS RELATING TO WILLIAM WALLACE

Tombs and burial sites were the focal points for the development of the cults of saints and associated pilgrimages in the Middle Ages. As part of the desire to discredit, destroy and eliminate the memory of Wallace, the English took care to dishonour and destroy his body, using the parts by way of example to terrorise any like-minded people. A couple of generations later, they burned Joan of Arc, for the same reason. Local stories in Aberdeen persist about one of Wallace's arms being buried there.[29] A cross on the perimeter wall of St Machar's Cathedral is said to memorialise this, while the congregation of St Fittick's Church at Torry claim to have rescued the arm from the Justice Port of Aberdeen and buried it in the southeast corner of the churchyard.[30]

In 1998, many people were keen to point out that Wallace and Murray would not have written the letters sent to Lübeck and Hamburg themselves. Military historian Ashby McGowan wanted to investigate further and checked the facsimile of the Lübeck letter made during the 1911 Scottish Exhibition,[31] which was deposited in Glasgow's Mitchell Library. He found something that had escaped previous notice. There was a distinctive seal attached, showing on one side the royal arms and, on the other, a hand holding a bow and arrow. From this, and using the evidence from Blind Hary, he concluded that Wallace was, by training, an archer and that was his seal.[32] His findings show the benefits of always looking beyond the written word to the object.

The Wallace Sword, housed in the National Wallace Monument, Stirling, since 1888, is well known but its authenticity is as much questioned as any episode in Blind Hary. It was kept at Dumbarton Castle, ostensibly since the imprisonment of Wallace there in 1305, and was refurbished on the order of James IV in 1505. Why such a weapon should be mistaken after a peri-od of only 200 years is open to question. The pikes and halberds taken from the participants of the Radical Rising in 1820 were still in Stirling Castle in the 1950s and were probably discarded only after the army left in 1964. Weapons are always taken as evidence and as a symbol of triumph of the victorious party of whatever cause to be kept as trophies. The Wallace

Sword was one of five swords connected with the War of Independence that were exhibited at the laying of the foundation stone of the National Wallace Monument in 1861. Over the years, it has been a focal point for political discontent. Its case was smashed by suffragette Ethel Moorehead in 1912,[33] and it was stolen in 1936 and 1972 by nationalists.[34]

Another object that has claims to be associated (albeit briefly) with Wallace is the knocking stane from Longforgan in the collection of the McManus Galleries, Dundee. Hollow with a stone cover, it is like any other knocking stane and could serve both for grinding barley and as a seat. In the 1840s it was still in the possession of the descendants of the family who had sheltered Wallace:

> A respectable family of the name of Smith in the village of Longforgan is in possession of a stone which is looked upon with great veneration. . . . The circumstances that make it valuable and venerable in the eyes of its possessors and visitors is the universally believed fact, that it is the stone upon which the youthful hero rested himself in his flight from Dundee to the castle of Kilspindie, in the carse, the seat of his maternal uncle. There is also a universally received tradition, that the good woman of the house, to whom the stone belonged, refreshed the exhausted Wallace with a meal of bread and milk, and that the stone has been handed down from father to son, as an heirloom, during a period of five centuries and a half.[35]

There are also some pieces of furniture associated with Wallace from Lamington Tower, near Biggar, by tradition the home of Marion Braidfoot, Wallace's wife. One now owned by Biggar Museum Trust is seventeenth century in date.[36] Thanks to a family and property amalgamation, the oldest surviving 'Wallace's chair', a structure made of pine and covered in deerskin, is at Balnagowan Castle, Ross-shire, together with a portrait of Wallace. It has been there since 1833. During the Second World War, the Ross family removed the chair temporarily to America for safekeeping.[37]

Blind Hary places a lot of events in Biggar, including the massive battle of Biggar, re-enacted for the townspeople by the famous equestrian Thomas Ord in an amphitheatre built there in 1844.[38] The local lore concerning Wallace is well known by those who live there, and Biggar was virtually the last place in Scotland where children performed the ancient Scottish Galatians or Seguiser's Play, featuring William Wallace.[39] This ritual was probably the last manifestation of the oral tradition, reaching back to the time of Wallace himself. When the poet Hugh MacDiarmid opened Biggar's first museum on 25 May 1968, the platform was adorned by an original Reform Bill banner proclaiming *Lamington, the Land of Wallace. The Battle's done. The Day is Won. 16 July 1832*. The ability of people to see the story of Wallace as a positive, unbroken force, a continuum of Scottish history that enhances and enriches, was manifest on that occasion.[40] In many other places in Scotland, the same connections are made when the story of Wallace is remembered, and the thought that Wallace underpins the history of Scotland is strong and undiminished.

PORTRAITS OF WALLACE

Sir James Fergusson likened the writing of Wallace's biography to the act of restoring a very old family portrait that several painters have tried to improve but which has been very much overpainted, embellished and distorted.[40] The story of the portraiture of Wallace is much the same. It is more a guide to the social and political aspirations of those who commissioned and owned them rather than any likeness of Wallace. It is no less significant for that.

The pencil-sketch portrait of Wallace in the Scottish National Portrait Gallery by David Steuart Erskine, eleventh Earl of Buchan, was reputedly based on a medieval original. Buchan did more than anyone else in his time to draw together the historical portraits of Scotland. It was he who funded John Pinkerton's *Iconographia Scotica*. Buchan, himself a student of three Scottish universities, also drew and made engravings at the Foulis Academy in Glasgow in the 1750s. He founded the Society of Antiquaries of Scotland in 1780[41] and was its benefactor for many years. It was his idea of a Caledonian Temple of Fame that was the begetter of the Scottish National Portrait Gallery. If there were any early images of Wallace, Buchan would have known them.

Buchan's portrait of Wallace takes the form of a bearded warrior with a dragon on top of his helmet, perhaps an iconographic reference to the name 'Wallace', also meaning 'Of Wales'. This image was used to represent Wallace throughout the eighteenth and nineteenth centuries. It was engraved as the frontispiece of Morison of Perth's 1790 edition of Blind Hary (also funded by Buchan), used for the features of the colossal Wallace statue sponsored by Buchan at Dryburgh in 1814 and is well established by the time the mid-nineteenth-century portrait of Wallace in the Smith collection in Stirling was painted. It is also similar in content to the portrait of Wallace painted by George Jamesone in 1633 for the coronation celebrations of Charles I in Edinburgh. The dragon helmet, beard, cloak and brooch are common to all four images. Various unknown artists adopted this particular image, ranging from the medal engraver who produced a Wallace token for Colonel William Fullerton in 1797 to the Montrose stonemason of the 1840s who carved a Wallace image on a 770-millimetre piece of sandstone in high relief, backed with an oriental-looking Scottish lion and embellished with thistles.

There are several Wallace portraits painted in the seventeenth century or earlier, and it is regrettable that so few are in public collections. The Balnagowan Castle portrait is of some antiquity but is not accessible. The Wallace portrait in Torosay Castle, Isle of Mull, is probably of the same time (seventeenth century) and originated at Guthrie Castle, seven miles north of Arbroath in Angus. The label affixed to the frame gives its background:

In the year 1299 the Northern Lords of Scotland sent Squire Guthrie to France to desire the return to Scotland of Sir William Wallace. Guthrie embarked at Arbroath and landed at Sluys from where he conveyed Wallace back to Montrose.

'Squier Guthre' and his journey are in Book IX of Blind Hary,[42] but as Matthew McDiarmid points out, the Guthries are contemporaries of Blind Hary rather than Wallace.[43]

A seventeenth-century portrait that can be documented and dated is one from the house of the Wauchopes of Niddrie Marischal, Edinburgh, purchased in 2004 for the Smith collection in Stirling. The central oval shape dates to 1661 and was part of a decorative scheme commissioned by Sir John Wauchope in 1661 in honour of the restoration of Charles II.[44] In a restructuring of the house in the 1720s, the portrait was set within a surrounding trophy to enlarge it to fit the panel above the fireplace in the new dining room. In 1858, Paterson's *Wallace and His Times* (1858) included an engraving of the image, and it became widely known in the nineteenth century.[45] Photographs show the scheme and the painting *in situ* before the demolition of Niddrie Marischal in December 1957.[46]

The Jamesone portrait and the Niddrie Marischal portrait were both commissioned for coronations, albeit twenty-seven years apart. It was not uncommon for aristocratic families to commission portraits of Wallace or Bruce for their collections. A good eighteenth-century example is the oval-shaped portrait of Wallace in the Smith collection in Stirling by the artist William Robertson, dating to the 1740s.[47] Robertson visited several houses (mainly those of Jacobite sympathisers) in Stirlingshire and Perthshire, painting portraits to order. This is the kind of portrait subject that would have appealed to a disaffected Jacobite laird.

The portrait of Wallace engraved by John Kay of Edinburgh in 1819 was likewise a portrait for its time and political constituency. Kay shows him as 'General and Governor of Scotland'. Wallace was the firm hero of the radical movement; he appeared on a radical banner slaying a beast of tyranny.[48] When the Paisley magistrates jailed an entire band for playing 'Scots Wha Hae Wi Wallace Bled' in 1819, the tune became almost a national anthem within weeks as people took to singing and whistling it in defiance.

The spirit of Wallace continues to inspire present-day artists. Some, like Andrew Hillhouse, spend much of their creative time imagining their own way into the past, and recreating episodes and battle scenes. Others think symbolically, often in terms of regeneration. Alan Reid's *Wallace* (1996, Caithness stone, Pictish symbols and chains) shows a headless Wallace rising to step over a Stone of Destiny writhing with treacherous snakes, the rusty chains of his captivity turning to the silver chain of governance. Richard Price's large ceramic piece (1996, 'Rise and be a Nation Again') shows a thorn-crowned Wallace emerging from the earth, carrying the head of Edward I on his back and about to redress his brutal execution by drawing his sword in Scotland's cause.

Wallace has been given many faces over the centuries, from elaborate paintings in oils to crude sketches for chapbooks. An interesting image of Wallace, purporting to be from the sixteenth century, is conjured up by the chapman Dougal Graham in *The Witty and Entertaining Exploits of George Buchanan* (Stirling, 1799). Graham lived long enough in Stirling to pick up the local lore and legends concerning Buchanan, who was tutor to King James VI, and tells the following tale:

> A young nobleman fell a jocking of George, in saying, he would be as famous a champion for Scotland as Sir William Wallace was. Ay ay says George, William Wallace was a brave man in his time. True indeed says the other, but when he came to London, we did him all manner of justice, and for the honour of the Scots, we have his effigy in the shite-houses to this very day. And do you know the reason of that says George? No I don't, says he. Well, I'll tell you, says George, he was such a terror to the Englishmen when he was alive, that the sight of him yet makes them to beshite themselves. The English took this as a great affront, and forth with caused Wallace's picture to be taken out of that place.[49]

WALLACE IN THE LANDSCAPE

In many places in Scotland, people remembered Wallace by associating his name and deeds with particular trees or landscape features, so rather than one place of remembrance, there are dozens of them. William Wordsworth, who had a deep respect for Hamilton of Gilbertfield's translation of Blind Hary's *Wallace* and aspired to compose a similar epic, had it in mind when describing:

> How Wallace fought for Scotland; left the name
> Of 'Wallace' to be found, like a wild flower

All over his dear country; left the deeds
Of Wallace, like a family of ghosts
To people the steep rocks and river banks
Her natural sanctuaries, with a local soul
Of independence and stern liberty!

Similarly, Burns, who had a copy of the Hamilton translation as his constant companion and subscribed to the 1790 edition produced by Morison's of Perth for the Earl of Buchan,[50] was excited by the landscape narrative produced by Hary and wanted to emulate it:

We'll sing auld Coila's plains and fells,
Her moors red-brown wi' heather bells,
Her banks an' braes, her dens and dells,
    Where glorious WALLACE
Aft bure the gree, as story tells
    Frae Suthron billies.

At WALLACE' name, what Scottish blood
But boils up in a spring-tide flood!
Oft have our fearless fathers strode
    By Wallace side
Still pressing onward, red-wat-shod,
    Or glorious dy'd!

The gory metaphor of our ancestors running through the battlefields of Scotland, their footwear soaked in blood, comes straight from the pages of Blind Hary, reprised by Burns. Again, when Burns's muse comes to him in the form of young Coila, in his poem 'The Vision', her cloak is a shimmering, skinkling moving map of Kyle upon which Wallace – 'His COUNTRY'S SAVIOUR, mark him well!' – is prominent. Burns used Blind Hary virtually as a guidebook to Wallace sites. Moreover, Wallace, allegedly derided by his detractors as a mere 'King of Kyle', was regarded by the lad who was born in Kyle as a kinsman as well as a hero. Guidebooks were printed to reinforce the connection. George McMichael's *Notes on the way through Ayrshire, the land of Burns, Wallace, Henry the Minstrel and Covenant Martyrs* (Ayr, n/d *c.* 1882) examines every detail.

Other parts of Scotland, courtesy of Blind Hary, were able to make similar claims. Edward I, although destroying Wallace's body, splashed him over so many places in Scotland as to make him the national hero. Those places associated with Wallace were actively cherished and are the earliest sources of memorabilia. In Stirlingshire, the Torr Wood is mentioned by Hary as a place frequented by Wallace. Until the last of its roots were used in the 1820s, Torwood was well known for its Wallace Oak, the site of which has been located by Colin Forrester, using Roy's Military Survey.[51] John Harrison, looking at the history of the management of the woodland through the contracts between proprietors and felling contractors, has shown how the oak was specifically protected in agreements of 1687 and 1787, confirming the eighteenth-century assertion that the 'Wallace tree is ever excepted from cutting when the wood is sold'.[52] Lindsay Corbett has pulled together the notes of local historians listing all the known artefacts that were made from the dead oak, from a small quaich to a sideboard.[53]

The importance of the present-day Wallacebank Wood is widely recognised in terms of its local and natural history. It is owned by Glenbervie Golf Club, and there is an agreement with the Scottish Wildlife Trust to manage the wood as a wildlife reserve. Teams of volunteers have cleared the woodland of invasive species, and records are kept of the wildlife and plants.[54] Thus, the name of Wallace continues to be respected even after 700 years. The various Wallace trees in Scotland are the earliest liberty trees, and their memory and presence have outlasted those of the French Revolutionary period.[55]

The earliest souvenir from the Wallace Oak noted to date is a silver-rimmed quaich of 1689 exhibited at the 1911 Scottish Exhibition and loaned by Lord Lamington.[56] It has disappeared within living memory. Another quaich of 1795, also exhibited in 1911, was inscribed: 'This cup is part of the oak tree in the Torwood, which was often an asylum to the immortal Wallace. Drink of this and mark the footsteps of a hero.'[57] The dead oak was depleted and fashioned into such souvenirs between 1689 and 1822, when a snuffbox was made for presentation to George IV during his visit to Edinburgh. An engraving of a drawing by Alexander Nasmyth (1771) shows two stumps of the trunk of the tree,[58] reduced to one by the time John Thomson of Duddingston painted his *Blasted Oak* (now in the Smith collection, Stirling) in the early 1800s.

The Wallace Oak was depleted well before the souvenir woodware of the Mauchline industry was in production. The desire to have such souvenirs is well documented:

> In the neighbourhood of the town, Wallace Oak in the Torwood and the Yew Tree at Grahamston, where fell the gallant Graham, have, within the period of human recollection, been victims to the knives of the curious, and the hammers of the same parties have unwarrantably destroyed a large portion of the Bore Stone at Bannockburn, the Gathering Stone at Sherrifmuir and the whole stone on the Wallace Ridge, where the great Scottish Chief witnessed the approach of Edward's army on the eve of the Battle of Falkirk.[59]

The Wallace Oak of Elderslie on the Spiers Estate in Renfrew furnished an elaborate frame, commissioned by John McAdam in 1867, to contain letters on the hero from contemporary Wallaces (Garibaldi, Mazzini, Kossuth, Blind and Blanc). The aim was to provide a point of attraction in the National Wallace Monument on its inauguration in 1869, the beginning of a Scottish national history collection for the monument and a source of funds through sales of photographs of the piece.[60] Only a few pieces of this oak were turned into Mauchline-ware souvenirs.[61]

MASS-PRODUCTION WALLACE SOUVENIRS

The Mauchline-ware industry, which developed out of snuffbox-making and the Scotch, or hidden, hinge, was geared to production for the mass-tourism market, and the woods favoured were sycamore or plane, for their light colour. The Smith family of Mauchline, in business from 1810 to 1939, were the major producers. They harvested 'wood which grew on the Abbey Craig site of the National Wallace Monument' for several decades, turning it into small articles (card cases, boxes, letter openers, sewing requisites) of souvenir ware with transfer images of the National Wallace Monument. Within this worldwide industry, Wallace-themed pieces are relatively few. Collectors in the field have noted that, as regards Scottish subjects in Mauchline ware, Sir Walter Scott tops the league, followed by Burns.[62] A census of books in Mauchline-ware boards reveals 98 editions of Scott's works and 21 editions of Burns's poems.[63] Books on Wallace in Mauchline boards by comparison are relatively rare.[64]

There was an obvious market for mementoes or ornaments of Wallace, probably fuelled by the erection of local and national Wallace monuments throughout the nineteenth century. The Staffordshire potteries produced various cheap flat-backed chimney ornaments of Wallace. Interestingly, although John McAdam, proprietor of the Glasgow Hyde Park Pottery and a main promoter of the National Wallace Monument, manufactured Garibaldi jugs, neither his nor any other of the Scottish potteries seems to have produced Wallace figures. The expensive and well-made Parian ware figures of Wallace and Bruce of the mid-nineteenth century are also Staffordshire productions.[65] Some are similar in appearance to the silver-plated and copper figures of Wallace and Bruce produced by the art studio of Elkington of Birmingham in 1887–88.[66] All these figures are reminiscent of the design and artwork of Sir Joseph Noel Paton (1821–1901) who had a lifelong interest in Wallace, Bruce and the Wars of Independence.

Smaller, cheaper and cruder copies of Wallace and Bruce figures were made both in spelter and in cast iron for the mass market. Typical of these were the spelter figures kept on the living-room mantelpiece of the Scott family, at 57 Wallace Street, Stirling, 1888–1970. The Scotts had a great deal of admiration for Wallace, as relatives who had a farm in Stirling provided the straw that thatched the top of the Wallace Monument when it was lying incomplete in the period 1865–69.[67]

Hundreds of families who had no direct connection felt the same kind of patriotism as the Scotts, and had Wallace and Bruce at either side of their mantelpiece, the heart of the home in the nineteenth century. From their marriage in 1847 onwards, this was the experience of Dr Robert Pairman of Biggar and his wife: 'There were few ornaments in the apartment, but cast iron figures of Wallace and Bruce, burnished with black lead, adorned each end of the mantelpiece and attested our loyalty to Scotland's greatest heroes.'[68] The Carron Iron Company made a larger two-dimensional image of Wallace (*c.* 1870) that is either found in plaque form or as the back support for an umbrella stand. The company also made Bonnie Prince Charlie in this form. The manufacture of such goods was stimulated by the building of the National Wallace Monument, 1861–69, and there are numerous cast souvenir ornaments of the monument itself, from cast-brass door knockers to German Parian ware.

Wallace was sometimes the subject of longcase clocks. These for much of the nineteenth century were expensive items in any Scottish household and were made to order by local clockmakers. There is no census of subjects for Scottish clocks, but the iconography of extant examples is notable. One by Hendrie Ogg of Dunfermline (1781–1850) has Wallace in the dial arch, the supporting figures in the four corners being Douglas, Bruce, Randolph and Graham.[69] Another of the same date by David Mackay of Arbroath also has Wallace in the arch, flanked by Lady Liberty, holding a red cap of Liberty on a pole, and by Dame Scotia. In the corners are the more traditional four seasons.[70] Having Wallace to mark the hours or keep the letters on the mantelpiece must have been a common experience in thousands of family homes in the nineteenth century.

DAVID STEUART ERSKINE, ELEVENTH EARL OF BUCHAN

David Steuart Erskine (1742–1829) did more than any other individual to celebrate and promote the cause of Wallace as the liberator of Scotland. Mention has been made of his foundation of the Society of Antiquaries, the establishment of the iconography of his Wallace portrait, the sponsorship of the 1790 edition of *Wallace* and the erection of the colossal Wallace statue at Dryburgh in 1814. He was a remarkably talented man, with a deep love of Scotland as well as a great compassion for, and understanding of, his fellow human beings, both women and men. Although a member of one of the oldest aristocratic families, he became a passionate radical who supported the principle of women's education, the fledgling United States of America, the revolutionary government in France and revolution at home. As he explained to Joseph Priestley (who dedicated a book to him), he had no desire to uphold the prejudices of the class into which he had been born:

> I called a General Convention as it were of all my rational powers and deliberated with them in the Senate of my Understanding. I resolved instead of cobbling and patching the Constitution of my Moral Philosophy to dissolve the whole Fabric and erect a new one upon the eternal principles of human reason and Justice.

The promotion of the story of Wallace was part and parcel of that revolutionary outlook. Like Burns, who made the connection in his 'Ode for General Washington's Birthday', he saw Washington, first President of the United States, as the new Wallace and presented to him a box made of the Torwood Wallace Oak, fashioned by the Edinburgh Goldsmiths Company.

On his estate at Kirkhill and Almondell in Midlothian he had stones commemorating Wallace and, believing in liberty for his tenant farmers, granted them leases of nineteen and even thirty-eight years, which was exceptional. In 1786 he acquired the estate of Dryburgh in the Borders, including its ruined abbey where his ancestors had been commendators. He purchased it from the Haliburtons, who were relatives of Sir Walter Scott, and this was undoubtedly the source of Scott's resentment of and contempt for Buchan in later life, concealed behind the mask of friendship. Scott's Toryism was also the polar opposite of Buchan's revolutionary outlook, and this goes some way to explaining why Scott never tackled the subject of Wallace or the War of Independence in any of his historical novels.[71] Scott hated Buchan's monumental Wallace statue at Dryburgh so much that he recorded in his diary the desire to blow it apart with dynamite so that not one fragment of it would remain.[72]

With the clampdown on the revolutionary movement in the early 1790s, Buchan was politically isolated and he retired to Dryburgh. State trials saw the sentencing of Thomas Muir, curator of Buchan's Society of Antiquaries, to transportation to Australia along with Skirving, Gerrard, Margarot and Fyshe-Palmer. Buchan's status as an earl no doubt shielded him from the political witch-hunt of the times. When, after eighteen years, the political climate eased and with a whole generation of reformers exiled, it was Buchan who again lit the beacon of public freedom by promoting the celebrations for the 500th anniversary of Bannockburn, through the inauguration of his Wallace statue, in 1814.

It is not surprising that the radicals of the 1820 rising invoked the name of Wallace, as did their successors in the struggle for political reform. The Scottish colliers, technically in serfdom until the Act of 1799, did likewise, and their successors, the Sir William Wallace Grand Lodge of Free Colliers of Scotland, continue to march every first Saturday in August to this day.

COMMEMORATING WILLIAM WALLACE TODAY

In the nineteenth century, when it seemed that the old Wallace landmarks were being lost or overlooked, more formal monuments and statues were erected to reinforce the memorialisation process. Thus, in 1810, the Wallacestone Pillar was erected in the village of Wallacestone, Falkirk. The monument is carefully maintained. In 1999, the Provost of Falkirk personally renewed the paintwork. Every year, the Free Colliers bid for the privilege of carrying the banners on the annual ten-mile march, the money going to charity. The march is one of the most colourful spectacles to be seen in Scotland, and its aim is to honour Wallace. Other groups are similarly involved. In Aberdeen, the Wallace 700 group, established in 2002, organises an elaborate annual civic pageant centred on the Wallace statue by D. W. Stevenson. In Lanark, the Wallace 700 group, established in 1996, maintains its own ceremonials. At Avoch, Andrew Murray's rising in the north is commemorated every year by a group that describes itself as 'a voluntary sustainable tourism project which aims to promote knowledge about the place of Andrew de Moray and his family in the history of Scotland's wars of independence'.[73] In Dunfermline, Wallace's mother's grave is tended by Dunfermline Heritage Trust members, who raised a new Wallace monument nearby in the grounds of Abbot House in 1995. At Robroyston, the betrayal of Wallace is remembered at the Robroyston Wallace monument every year.

The Society of William Wallace, who held a major event in London in 2005, organises its annual Wallace Day commemoration at the Wallace Monument, Elderslie, on the Sunday nearest to 23 August, the day of Wallace's death. The society has done this ever since the political nationalists found it no longer expedient to remember Wallace in this way. It also organises the Robroyston commemoration every year on the Saturday nearest to 5 August, the day of the betrayal of Wallace. In their convener, David Ross, they have an articulate and charismatic activist who speaks, writes and publishes on Scottish history, and the story of Wallace in particular.

Many people who have had cause to identify with Wallace over the centuries have nurtured or produced objects that are expressions of that inspiration. Museums, misled by false notions of authenticity, have not always paid attention to the rich material culture of the subject. With only three small objects pertaining to Wallace in the Stirling Smith collection in 1995, and a major exhibition to mount in 1997, the gallery hosted a contemporary art exhibition in 1996 to generate some material. The response was strong, many of the 140 artists who exhibited taking their inspiration from the words of Blind Hary or Burns.[74] Nevertheless, once the subject was flagged up, historical material was also offered from places throughout Scotland, and in the space of three years the Stirling Smith had built up a significant collection.[75] With interest in Wallace undiminished, the material culture will continue to grow and develop, artists will continue to create representations, and groups will continue to build new memorials.

For those who find it hard to grasp the patriotism that inspires such engagement with the story of Wallace, the words of the journalist William Power (1873–1951), guest speaker at Elderslie in August 1936, may help:

> Only a noble conception of Scotland could have inspired the noble sac-rifice made by Wallace. It was not for the Scotland of a day that he fought and died, but for the Scotland of all future time. We are Wallace's betrayers if we lose our national spirit, and waste or renounce our national heritage.
>
> If certain sycophantic historians have belittled Wallace, it was because they perceived that he stood for a Scotland which was real, independent, active, progressive and democratic, a Scotland of the Scottish people. For that he stands immortally . . . [it is up to us to] . . . win for Scotland that place among the free nations that was marked for her by the patriotic martyr who gave mankind the ideal of true nationhood.[76]

9

The English Cult of Wallace and the Blending of Nineteenth-Century Britain

Colin Kidd

In today's Scotland most invocations of the name of William Wallace are directed towards nationalist ends or, at the very least, towards unambiguously Scottish causes. As often as not, appeals to the national memory of Wallace and his achievements carry with them an anglophobic resonance. While Scots celebrate Wallace as a nationalist icon, they remember him quite specifically as an uncompromising foe of English imperial pretension. To their credit, Scottish historians have questioned the historical longevity of this nationalist pedigree. In particular, they have shown that, while for most of Scotland's history, Scots have considered Wallace an emblem of national freedom, things were very different during the nineteenth century when Wallace became identified with a particular interpretation of the Union. 'Unionist-nationalism', in Graeme Morton's catchy formulation, involved a strict construction of the Union – the notion that Scotland and England were equal partners in a common enterprise freely entered into by sovereign nations in 1707. Unionist-nationalists read into Scotland's medieval War of Independence the lesson that England had never succeeded in conquering Scotland; amalgamation had come about centuries after the War of Independence only through negotiated union. Thus, commemorations of the deeds of Wallace and Bruce served as a reminder to an oblivious England that the Union was an association of sovereign equals. However, the nineteenth-century Scottish cult of Wallace, which led to the construction of various Wallace statues and towers, including the National Monument on the Abbey Craig, near Stirling, was predicated not only on denial that Scotland was a mere province of England but also on an acceptance by Scots of the Union of 1707. Wallace's nationalist significance was sublimated in a deeper unionism. For mid-nineteenth-century unionist-nationalists ultimately did nothing to challenge the legitimacy of the United Kingdom and a common British parliament.[1]

'Unionist-nationalism', however, while an adequate description of some manifestations of the Wallace cult during the nineteenth century, does not quite capture the texture of Anglo-Scottish relations during this period, nor some of the more surprising features of the Wallace phenomenon. For example, Wallace's name did not only serve to forward unionist-nationalist causes; Wallace was also pressed into the service of outright anglicisation. *The Shade of Wallace* is a poem that argues the Anglo-British case for importing into Scots law the English form of civil jury.[2] Rather than enlisting Wallace's patronage in defence of Scots legal distinctiveness, as might be expected in this instance, the anonymous poet deploys Wallace, somewhat misleadingly, for the anglicisation of the Scottish legal system. The poet claims, however, that medieval Scotland, like her southern neighbour, had in fact enjoyed the benefits of civil jury as part of its Gothic constitution until James V introduced the illiberal Franco-Roman College of Justice:

> Juries, that shall with truth decide,
> Will o'er the Tweed in triumph glide,
> Transmitted down, Old England's pride,
> From Saxon times,
> Across the mountains stride
> To Northern climes.
>
> Shall not a wise judicious race
> This glorious privilege embrace
> That once did Caledonia grace
> Shone bright as moon
> Till James the Fifth did quite deface
> The heavenly boon.[3]

In this instance the cause of anglicisation involved a restoration of traditional medieval rights that Scotland had lost but that had been preserved in England.[4] The association of Wallace's name with the campaign for a civil jury was, if surprising and apparently ironic, far from preposterous.

Similarly, and on a much larger scale, the association of Wallace with the Union also had an obverse English dimension. Politically, there was a growing English identification with Scotland as an increasingly trusted and reliable partner in the Union. This was mirrored in cultural developments. From around the end of the eighteenth century, English poets, novelists and historians began to take a sympathetic interest in the history and literature of Scotland. One curious aspect of this phenomenon was the emergence of Wallace as a genuinely pan-British icon of liberty. Nineteenth-century England – on a lesser scale, of course – would enjoy its own unionist cult of Wallace.

This apparently eccentric phenomenon becomes more readily comprehensible when aligned with current thinking about the nature of nineteenth-century British identities. British patriotism of this era involved pride in a family of sister kingdoms and encouraged expressions of sisterly sentiment and sympathy. As a result, the nineteenth century witnessed reciprocal explorations of English and Scottish nationality from both sides of the border, conducted in a spirit of mutual understanding and sympathy. In particular, Keith Robbins has argued that the bonds of British society were strengthened during the nineteenth century not by a straightforward process of anglicisation or of assimilation to a dominant English norm; rather, he suggests, there was a 'blending of Britain'. 'Scotland and Wales were not absorbed by England in any simple fashion,' Robbins contends, nor was cohesiveness of British society attained 'by the simple imposition' of English culture and norms upon these territories. Britishness was a 'complicated affair', involving the coexistence of multiple identities beneath an overarching common loyalty to the British state.[5] British integration continued apace but was not accompanied by any drive for cultural uniformity or demands for homogeneity; instead, Britishness was marked by broad-based sympathies and a pan-British pluralism. Some of the superficial peculiarities associated with the English cult of Wallace appear rather to be plausible reflections of the deeper cultural trends that Robbins identifies.

Romanticism assisted in the blending of Britain, in part through the recognition that Scotland possessed an intriguing 'otherness' for an English audience. The exotic, the peripheral, the picturesque and the remote – all of which applied in varying degrees to the English perception of Scotland – were themes that exerted a powerful pull on romantic authors. The ploughman poet Robert Burns and his quaint Scots dialect, together with the poetry, and then, later, the novels of Sir Walter Scott, exercised a compelling charm on English readers. Moreover, the appeal of Scotland in particular to English romantic sensibilities was heightened by the duration of the Revolutionary and Napoleonic Wars, when Scotland became an attractive yet safe site for the enjoyment and consumption of 'otherness' while Continental Europe remained out of bounds and Ireland dangerously associated with the rebellion of 1798.[6] Tourism enhanced the appeal of romantic Scotland. The cultural blending of the romantic era was far from a simple process of Anglo-Scottish reconciliation, however. In recent years scholars working in the field of 'English romantic literature' have broken with that subject's traditional Anglocentricity to explore the richer textures of a 'four nations' literary history, one that investigates the various interactions of Scottish, Welsh, Irish and English cultures in the making of British romantic literature. Literary historians have drawn attention to various 'Anglo-Celtic dialogues' between the English heartland and her imagined 'Celtic' provinces. Anglo-Scottish cultural relations constituted only one strand in a complex web of influences.[7]

Indeed, an Anglo-Irish model provided significant inspiration for the mediation of Scottish history to an English audience. The first decades of the nineteenth century saw the emergence of the 'national tale'. This new genre was conceived initially as a way of explaining Ireland – which had joined the United Kingdom in the Union of 1800–1 – to England. The principal begetters of the new genre were Maria Edgeworth, whose novels include *Castle Rackrent, an Hibernian Tale taken from facts and from the manners of the Irish squires before the year 1782* (1800) and *The Absentee* (1812), and Sydney Owenson, Lady Morgan, the author of a number of influential novels, including *The Wild Irish Girl: a national tale* (1806) and *The O'Briens and the O'Flahertys: a national tale* (1827). The national tale was further developed by the Irish Gothic writer Charles Maturin, author of *The Wild Irish Boy* (1809) and *The Milesian Chief* (1812). Writers of 'national tales' celebrated Britishness as an overarching unity in diversity. In particular, Anglo-Irish novelists saw the potential in the national tale to explain their unfamiliar society to the English. A common theme involved the return of an absentee landlord unacquainted with his native soil and tenantry. Acculturation and familiarisation stood at the centre of such plots.[8]

Scottish writers also saw the potential in the romantic national tale – and variants on the genre such as the historical novel – to introduce an English readership to Scotland and its history. Early examples of the Scottish national tale include Scott's *Waverley* (1814) and Christian Isobel Johnstone's *Clan-Albin: A National Tale* (1815).[9] *Waverley*, which revolves around a young Englishman's visit to Scotland during the Jacobite rebellion of 1745, follows the contours of the national tale and adds a significant new dimension to the genre. Scott was no great fan of Owenson but acknowledged his debt to Maria Edgeworth in the 'General Preface' to the Waverley Novels, noting that her:

> Irish characters have gone so far to make the English familiar with the character of their gay and kind-hearted neighbours of Ireland, that she may be truly said to have done more towards completing the Union, than perhaps all the legislative enactments by which it has been followed up.

The Union in question was, of course, the British-Irish Union of 1800–01, but Scott saw the potential to use the national tale as a means of strengthening the bonds of the Anglo-Scottish Union of 1707:

> I felt that something might be attempted for my own country, of the same kind which Miss Edgeworth so fortunately achieved for Ireland – something which might introduce her natives to those of the sister kingdom, in a more favourable light than they had been placed hitherto, and tend to procure sympathy for their virtues and indulgence for their foibles.[10]

The national tale and historical novel stood at the centre of a rich network of cultural and historical cross-appropriation. In Scotland during the second half of the eighteenth century, both the philosophic historians of the Scottish Enlightenment and members of the radical movement urged Scots to treat English constitutional history as their own.[11] To all intents and purposes, they seemed to suggest, through the incorporating Union of 1707, the glorious heritage of English liberty stretching back to the days of the Anglo-Saxons had become the common property of North as well as South Britons. Scottish historians such as David Hume and John Millar, however, also played a major role in revising and modifying some of the central narrative features in that history. Scots were not only laying claim to English history but also trying to rewrite it in their own terms.[12] In his own way, Scott continued this process. Scott himself produced the definitive myth of English medieval nation-building. His novel *Ivanhoe* (1819) explored the twelfth-century origins of English nationhood, providing an influential account of Saxon-Norman struggle followed by eventual reconciliation. The Normans had conquered Anglo-Saxon England in 1066. *Ivanhoe* picks up the story of Saxon-Norman relations just over a century later, during the reign of Richard I. At this period Saxons and Normans still constitute distinct ethnic groups as well as social strata in an unstable Anglo-Norman country. John Sutherland even contends that *Ivanhoe* was 'the main popularizer' of the Norman Yoke myth 'among the English at large' during the nineteenth century.[13] Indeed, John Burrow argues that the popularity of Scott's *Ivanhoe* inspired a literary enthusiasm in England for its Anglo-Saxon heritage that manifested itself in such works as Bulwer Lytton's *Harold, Last of the Saxon Kings* (1848) and Charles Kingsley's *Hereward the Wake* (1866).[14] Nor did Scott confine himself to the twelfth century. He followed *Ivanhoe* with other novels on English historical themes: *Kenilworth* (1821) was a tale of merry England during the Tudor age and *Woodstock* (1826) a novel of the English Civil Wars. On the other hand, Scott's major contribution to British culture lay in the opposite direction, in the wider dissemination of Scottish history and culture to an English audience, with the aim of winning over English readers to the notion that the Scottish past was part of their own British heritage, not least by presenting it as picturesque, firmly in the past and, hence, unthreatening.[15] Quite apart from the bare statistics of Scott's sales as a bestselling novelist[16] – in spite or because of his primary reliance on Scottish historical subject matter – there is also oblique testimony to his success in promoting English identification with North Britain.

Sarah Green's light comic romance *Scotch Novel Reading; or Modern quackery* (1824) provides compelling evidence that the contemporary English fascination with Scotland's history and literature was sufficiently modish to attract satirical attention. Indeed, the novel's principal subject matter is the

Caledonian fever brought on by reading too many Scotch novels, particularly those of Scott. As one character complains, "'nothing now goes down but Scotch stories; and Scotch dialect, by the way a very unpleasant one, is thrust upon us, as if there was not another country under the sun worth hearing of than poor, miserable little Scotland'". The novel is largely set in London where our comic heroine, Alice Fennel, has developed, under the influence of Scott but also through exposure to the works of the Ettrick Shepherd and other Scotch novelists and bards, an obsessional identification with all things Scottish. According to Mr Fennel, Scottish literature has gone to his foolish daughter's head:

> We have been now, for some years, inundated with showers of Scotch novels, thicker than the snow you now see falling; and Alice, who is now in her nineteenth year, has read them all, or rather skimmed them over . . . without understanding one half of what she has perused, and scarce comprehending one word of a dialect with which they abound, but which she affects to use on all occasions.

Indeed, Alice, Mr Fennel reports, had fallen into floods of tears on discovering that the romantic Ettrick Shepherd had the very unromantic name of Hogg. When we first encounter Alice herself – a Londoner born and bred without a trace of Scottish ancestry – she interrupts her father's anxieties about his daughter's 'Caledonian mania' to summon him to his dinner of calf's liver and bacon: "'Why should ye fash yoursel so, feyther?" said Alice . . . "I was ainly aboot to tell ye, that it were beest ye ganged into the deening parlour, for the haggis will be there directly.'" Alice affects a thick Scottish brogue for most of the novel and a vocabulary in which the words 'muckle', 'bonnie', 'fash', 'hoot' and 'chiel' are somewhat overused. Moreover, Alice not only sounds like her idea of a Scotswoman, she also dresses the part. She wears a handsome Highland cap with large black plumes, while her coats are 'kiltit', her arms and back are left bare, and her bust is likewise, although modesty makes her 'twitch the true tartan scarf, that hung in drapery over her form, across her bosom'. The Fennel household is 'littered with *Blackwood's Magazine*, and the *Edinburgh Review* etc, wherein she found the puff direct, or collateral, given in surfeiting abundance to her favourite novel writers of North Britain'.

The novel recounts our romantic heroine's 'awakening' from her 'airy' fancies of 'Scotch perfection'. Alice is freed from her ridiculous delusions only through meeting some real Scots – the Macbane family – and being vigorously wooed by a rough-and-ready pantomime jock, Captain Duncan Macgregor, who turns out to be her English lover in disguise. Although *Scotch Novel Reading* provides only a highly exaggerated version of a contemporary trend, it is nevertheless suggestive of a milieu in which an English cult of Wallace might seem less of a paradox.[17]

For this contradiction in terms was a visible – albeit minor – feature of English literary culture during the first decades of the nineteenth century. From the end of the eighteenth century several English writers, poets especially, became entranced with the topic of Wallace's achievements, defeat and martyrdom. In 1798 Robert Southey composed a short poem, entitled 'The Death of Wallace', that used a lament for Wallace largely as a vehicle for the condemnation of tyranny, in this case Plantagenet:

> Go, Edward, triumph now!
> Cambria is fallen, and Scotland's strength is crush'd;
> On Wallace, on Llewellyn's mangled limbs,
> The fowls of Heaven have fed.
>
> Go, Edward, full of glory to thy grave!
> The weight of patriot blood upon thy soul.[18]

John Stoddart, an English tourist who came to Scotland in 1799 and 1800, was struck by the popularity of the Wallace cult in Lowland Scotland and issued a recommendation to the readers of his *Remarks on Local Scenery and Manners in Scotland* (1801) that Wallace would provide a wonderful subject with a universal appeal for a Miltonic-style epic:

> If, indeed, any man were really possessed with the spirit-stirring enthusiasm, of the true epic (the same, which worked, from youth to age, in the breast of Milton), he could no where find a more noble subject than the life of this patriot warrior. From the materials afforded by record, and tradition, by the historian, and the poet, might be drawn a character, interesting every powerful sentiment in the human heart, exciting the sympathies of domestic affection, and public virtue, calling forth applause for his valour, exultation in his triumphs, contempt of his base betrayer, indignation at his tyrannical punishment; noble tears over his fall, and more noble joy in his imperishable fame. This is a whole, which Shakespeare might have conceived by the power of genius alone; but for which another poet needs other aids.[19]

Stoddart's friend, the great English poet William Wordsworth, who would also tour Scotland, in 1803, produced a poetic echo of such sentiments. In his thirteen-book 1805 version of his great work on the mental formation of the poet, *The Prelude*, Wordsworth recounts how he had contemplated the composition of an epic poem on the theme of how Wallace fought for Scotland, leaving his name on the landscape.[20]

Less dreamily, albeit in a more pedestrian fashion, a stream of lesser English writers realised Wordsworth's yearnings to engage with this promising subject. In 1809 Miss Margaret Holford (1778–1852), a Cheshire lady, published *Wallace, or the Fight of Falkirk*. Miss Holford's poetic 'Dedication' to her compatriot, Miss Gertrude Louisa Allen, which precedes *Wallace* expresses a proud English patriotism, couched as an apology for her apparently unpatriotic choice of subject:

> And deem not, jealous for our native land,
> With alien step I sought the billowy Forth,
> Whence led a pilgrim by the Muse's hand,
> I climb'd the rude hills of the stormy north,
> And sung her songs – their hardihood and worth!
> No! as I turn again my truant eyes,
> To mark the pleasant land which gave us birth,
> Quick in my soul what rushing crowds arise,
> Heart-cheering visions of all native sympathies!

Despite her celebration of a Scottish hero, England remained, to Miss Holford, she insisted, the 'gem and glory of the west'.[21]

The next year saw the publication of *the* Wallace sensation of the nineteenth century, a novel written not by a Scot but by an Englishwoman. Jane Porter's five-volume novel, *The Scottish Chiefs*, took the world by storm. Porter (1776–1850) was born in Durham, spent her early years in Edinburgh, and then moved to London in 1803. *The Scottish Chiefs* was published in London in 1810, and by 1816 was already in its third edition. Between 1816 and 1882 the novel was reprinted nine times. It was also published in the United States, where it enjoyed tremendous success, and was translated into French, German and Russian. In short, *The Scottish Chiefs* was a literary sensation. Porter's novel, to take but one curious example, appears to have haunted the peculiar imagination of the radical English poet and artist William Blake, who experienced his own personal vision of Wallace.[22] Indeed, the very success of *The Scottish Chiefs* explains in part why Scott – who ranged otherwise across the whole gamut of Scottish history in his novels – should neglect the story of Wallace as matter for his historical fiction. Only in his very last work, *Castle Dangerous* (1832), did Scott even touch upon the wider subject of the Scottish Wars of Independence. Porter's introductory apparatus acknowledges the novel's provenance in a new British patriotism, a fusion of the old historic allegiances to rival Scottish and English nations. Declaring herself in favour of 'an honest pride in ancestry', Porter contends that at a time when Britain is threatened by Napoleonic France there is a place in the new order for the spirit that had once animated the old Border feuds:

respect for noble progenitors cannot be wrong, for it proceeds from the same source – the principle of kindred, of inheritance, and of virtue. Let the race of Douglas, or the brave line of Percy, bear witness whether the name they hold be not as a mirror to show them what they ought to be, and to kindle in their hearts the flame which burnt in their fathers. Happy is it for this realm that the destiny which now unites the once contending arms of those brave families has also consolidated their rival nations into one, and by planting the heir of Plantagenet and of Bruce upon one throne, hath redeemed the peace of Britain, and fixed it on lasting foundations.[23]

The Scottish Chiefs provided an important point of entry to the Wallace story for generations of English readers. More immediately, enthusiastic immersion in *The Scottish Chiefs* helped to provide an unlikely English winner for the literary competition on the subject of Wallace held in 1818–19.

In December 1818 a competition was announced in *Blackwood's Edinburgh Magazine*. An anonymous benefactor had offered to donate fifty pounds to be divided into three prizes of twenty-five, fifteen and ten pounds 'for the best lines, in verse or prose, on the subject of Sir William Wallace inviting Bruce to the Scottish throne'. This alluded to the long-standing tradition that Wallace and Bruce had found themselves in one another's company – although on opposite sides of the River Carron – in the confused aftermath of Wallace's defeat at Falkirk. Conversing across the river, Wallace called on Bruce to cast off his demeaning vassalage to Edward I, inviting him to assert his right to the Scottish throne. The benefactor, a native of Edinburgh who had left the city at the age of twelve and was now a member of the Highland Society of London, also promised to make a much larger donation of a thousand pounds were a project to be mounted to erect a statue to the memory of Wallace on Arthur's Seat or Salisbury Crags. Nevertheless, despite his manifest patriotism and obsession with Wallace, the shadowy philanthropist desired that the literary efforts submitted to his competition should be expressed in such a way 'as not to give offence to our brethren south of the Tweed'.[24]

Submissions for the prize were to be made to the booksellers Manners and Miller by 1 May 1819. In the end, the competition appears to have attracted fifty-seven entries, including one that was reported to have been as long as *Paradise Lost*.[25] First prize went to an Englishwoman, Mrs Felicia Hemans (1793–1835), a poet best remembered today for her poem 'Casabianca' (1829), which opens with the memorable lines, 'The boy stood on the burning deck / Whence all but he had fled'. In the apparatus that accompanied the published version of her prize poem, 'Wallace's Invocation to Bruce', Hemans alludes to Wallace's growing reputation in England:

'It is a noble feature in the character of a generous and enlightened people, that, in England, the memory of the patriots and martyrs of Scotland has long excited an interest not exceeded in strength by that which prevails in the country which boasts their birth, their deeds and their sufferings.'[26] Indeed, her own upbringing and literary formation encapsulate the blending of Britain. Born in Liverpool to a Venetian-German mother and an Irish father, she moved with her family to Denbighshire and later Flintshire.[27] As a result, she maintained a broad range of sympathies for the peoples and cultures of Britain. Not only did she compose a series of Welsh melodies celebrating the culture of her adopted Wales, but she would also add to 'Wallace's Invocation to Bruce' a shorter piece entitled 'The Heart of Bruce in Melrose Abbey'.[28] Moreover, she was a fan of Jane Porter and had clearly caught the Wallace bug long before the competition was announced. Writing back in 1811 to Matthew Nicholson, a Manchester cotton merchant who had retired to Liverpool, the then Miss Felicia Browne confessed to lapsing into some light reading:

> Will you assume a very good grave mentorial face, and give me a long lecture, when I tell you I have also been guilty of reading a romance? It is *The Scottish Chiefs* by Miss Porter, and though I am by no means an advocate for historical novels, as they bewilder our ideas, by confounding truth with fiction, yet this animated authoress has painted her hero, the patriot William Wallace, in such glowing colours, that you cannot avoid catching a spark of her own enthusiasm, as you follow him through the incidents of the narrative.[29]

In the course of her victory in the competition of 1818–19 Hemans had triumphed over one of Scotland's finest writers, James Hogg. Hogg was a gallant loser and was happy to cede the prize to Hemans: 'Had I been constituted the judge myself, I would have given hers the preference by many degrees'. Moreover, Hogg was won over by the fact that this was an English celebration of Wallace: 'I estimated [the poem] the more highly as coming from one of the people that were the hero's foes, oppressors, and destroyers.'[30] Not all Scots shared Hogg's graciousness on this topic of vital patriotic significance. Another loser, the female author of 'Wallace and Bruce, a Vision', commented that 'the far-famed interview of our patriot heroes ought not to be left entirely to English celebration' and puffed instead her own composition as 'a simple strain of genuine Scottish feeling, flowing from a mind that owns no other muse but the *amor patriae*'.[31]

Nevertheless, the general run of opinion in Scotland tended to a generous appreciation of English acknowledgement of Wallace's achievements. In fact, the *Edinburgh Monthly Review* reported that several competitors came from 'the other side of the Tweed'. Nor was this a problem, rather a matter for congratulation. Indeed, according to the journal, English participation in the competition seemed indicative of the transition in both England and Scotland towards a more pluralist patriotism, towards a Britishness that invited celebration of the best elements in its different constituent parts:

> That a Scottish prize for a poem on a subject purely, proudly Scottish, has been adjudged to an English candidate, is a proof at once of the perfect fairness of the award, and of the merit of the poem. It further demonstrates the disappearance of those jealousies which, not a hundred years ago, would have denied to such a candidate any thing like a fair chance with a native – if we can suppose any poet in the south then dreaming of making the trial, or viewing Wallace in any other light than that of an enemy, and a rebel against the paramount supremacy of England. We delight in every gleam of high feeling which warms the two nations alike, and ripens yet more that confidence and empathy which bind them together in one great family. We hail every fresh proof of a generous community of worth, which entitles each people to adopt the other's moral ornaments; and to look upon their respective great names as a common patrimony – a sum of British genius, virtue, and glory, which stands unequalled in the world.[32]

The *Scots Magazine* also responded positively to the 'poetical magic' of Hemans' triumph by reflecting how in recent years the process of British integration had moved up a gear with the emergence of a sympathetic development of English interest in Scottish history and culture:

> We live now in very cordial union with our south country friends, and the benefits of that union which we so much detested, and they so much despised, at the time it took place, are now found to be mutual and important. One peculiar benefit is only of late occurrence, yet, perhaps, full as much valued as any of the others; it is that our southern neighbours have learned (though late) to appreciate the Scottish character, and to discern and taste Scottish genius even in the disguise of our national language.

The causes of this transformation, the *Scots Magazine* believed, were not hard to find: the phenomena of Burns and Scott and the great impression they made on English literary circles.[33]

During the course of the nineteenth century, the blending processes of British integration continued apace. By the mid-nineteenth century, moreover, there was a large Scots diaspora in England, evidenced by the huge number of dinners held throughout England to commemorate the centenary of Burns's birthday in 1859. This Scots presence in England helped to reinforce Anglo-Scottish cultural connections. At the Burns centenary meeting in Carlisle it was remarked that 'the sympathies of the two countries have become interwoven and consolidated'.[34] Burns and Scott were, of course, central to this extension of sympathy,[35] but so too was Wallace. Nineteenth-century Scots not only celebrated Wallace as the champion of a Union of equal partners, they also acknowledged the English celebration of Wallace and pondered the particular reasons why the English should have become so captivated by the history of the Scottish national hero.

The principal reason Scots adduced for this unusual phenomenon was that the English had come to view Wallace as a symbol of resistance to a threatened Plantagenet absolutism the realisation of which might have diverted the beneficent course of English history. In particular, nineteenth-century commentators held the view that the conflicts of Wallace's epoch were not only – or even primarily – Anglo-Scottish but also involved the common, if then unrecognised, interests of the British nations of Scotland and England in the face of an alien (French) and imperialist Norman-Plantagenet monarchy. Wallace stood as an exemplar of British freedom in the face of the ambitions of the Plantagenet monarchy not only to a pan-British empire but also to a despotic form of government within England itself. Thus, the story of Wallace, it seemed, had become intertwined with the history of English liberty. Joanna Baillie, who included Wallace as a subject of one of her *Metrical Legends*, asserted that 'England as well as Scotland, under Divine Providence, may owe its liberty to [Wallace]: for, had the English crown, at so early a period, acquired such an accession of power, it would probably, like the other great crowns of Europe, have established for itself a despotism which could not have been shaken'.[36] Scottish patriots happily conceded that Wallace was an Anglo-Scottish icon who had made a positive contribution to English as well as Scottish history. Even the Scottish nationalist historian William Burns recognised the significance of Wallace in English history. Scotland, Burns contended, was:

(unconsciously, perhaps) the means of securing the liberties of England. Every student of history knows that the Plantagenet race of kings were systematically bent on acquiring despotic power; and that it was long a very critical question, whether England was to become a despotism, or a constitutional monarchy. Had Scotland succumbed to Edward I, she would assuredly have been made the ready tool for enslaving that king's English subjects. But Scotland resisted, and by that very means enabled the English to wring from their unwilling tyrant the privileges they never afterwards lost. In fact, paradoxical as it may, at first sight, appear, Wallace, the arch enemy of England, was indirectly, one of her greatest benefactors. The national independence of Scotland, and the political and civil liberties of England, at that time, trembled in the same scale. The life, and much more, the death of Wallace, turned that scale.[37]

A similiar line also appeared in the unsuccessful proposal of 1859 for a national monument to Wallace and Bruce in Edinburgh: 'Intelligent Englishmen also know that their countrymen from Wallace's day . . . not only had no sympathy with the feudal despotism of the Norman kings, but mourned for the Scottish patriot as the forlorn hope against the "common oppressors of both countries".'[38] Without Wallace, it seemed, the civil and political liberties enjoyed by modern Britons might not have been achieved.

Actually, Wallace's liberal appeal in England was of two kinds. Not only did Wallace stand out as a significant figure in the history of British liberty, but he also belonged to an international pantheon of liberal-democratic heroes. When Chartists gathered at Ashton-under-Lyne in November 1839 to celebrate the birthday of Orator Hunt, they toasted:

> The immortal memory of Thomas Paine, William Cobbett, Major Cartwright, Robert Emmett, John Knight, Julian Hibbert, Hampden, Wat Tyler, Sidney, Thomas Hardy, Horne Tooke, Volney, Voltaire, Elihu Palmer, Mirabeau, Robespierre, William Tell, Andreas Hofer, Washington, Wallace, and all the illustrious dead of every nation, who by their acts and deeds have contributed to the cause of liberty.[39]

Wallace's international fame as a champion of freedom helped to reinforce his local celebrity as a champion of specifically British freedoms. In addition, nineteenth-century theories of racial difference accentuated Wallace's appeal, for the story of Wallace meshed neatly with the Norman Yoke theory of English history, the notion that the commoners had been libertarian Saxons conquered in the eleventh century by an aristocratic caste of Normans, until the former regained their historic freedoms.[40] In a sense, the Saxon commons of twelfth- and thirteenth-century England had shared a virtuous political cause with the Scots commoners led by Wallace. Both had been the victims of alien Norman-Plantagenet oppression. Moreover, during the nineteenth century Wallace tended to be depicted – even by Scots – as the champion of the Saxon Lowland 'race' within Scotland.[41] These various factors – along with a contemporary Victorian obsession with the medieval past, which also embraced other folk heroes, including King Arthur and, more pertinently, Robin Hood[42] – combined to raise Wallace's profile in the English historical memory.

This was as much a feature of popular as of high culture. In his inaugural lecture as professor of history at the University of Glasgow, Richard Lodge, an English incomer who regarded the Forth–Clyde line rather than the Tweed–Solway border as the real racial frontier in Britain, assured his audience that

> English boys are taught both in prose and in poetry to regard Wallace and Bruce as the heroic champions of a just cause, and to attribute to them perhaps greater purity of motive than they can justly claim. I cannot remember that one ever acquired the habit of regarding Bannockburn as a great English disaster and disgrace . . .[43]

Jane Porter's *The Scottish Chiefs* had an important role in the formation of this English boyhood cult of Wallace. So too did G. A. Henty, the popular English writer of historical adventures for schoolboys, who produced a novel of Wallace and Bruce, *In Freedom's Cause* (1885). Henty's novel views events from a Scottish rather than an English angle. To be strictly accurate, however, the perspective of the novel is not so much anti-English as anti-Norman. The invaders of Scotland are described as oppressive Normans throughout, that is, the same Normans who had earlier trampled on the liberties of the Anglo-Saxons.[44]

On a more elevated level, Wallace also came to occupy an important niche in the narrative framework of English Whig history, which told a progressive story of the unfolding of liberty. Historians perceived that Wallace had championed a kind of popular liberty that transcended the rigid social demarcations of feudal society. In his popular *History of the English People*, J. R. Green commends 'the instinct of the Scotch people' which:

> guided it aright in choosing Wallace for its national hero. He was the first to sweep aside the technicalities of feudal law and to assert freedom as a national birthright. Amidst the despair of nobles and priests he called the people itself to arms, and his discovery of the military value of the stout peasant footman, who had till then been scorned by baronage and knighthood – a discovery copied by the burghers of Flanders, and repeated in the victories of the Swiss – gave a deathblow to the system of feudalism and changed in the end the face of Europe.[45]

Wallace was a similar hero to the last of the great English Whig historians, George Macaulay Trevelyan. In his *History of England* (1926) Trevelyan celebrates Wallace as the founder of a new brand of politics:

> This unknown knight, with little but his great name to identify him in history, had lit a fire which nothing since has ever put out. Here, in Scotland, a few years before the very similar doings in Switzerland, a new ideal and tradition of wonderful potency was brought into the world; it had no name, but now we should call it democratic patriotism.

149

Trevelyan reckoned 'Wallace's amazing appeal to the Scottish democracy to save the Scottish nation' to be 'abnormal' in its day, for in thirteenth-century Christendom, society was divided 'horizontally into feudal strata' rather than into discrete national units. Wallace called into being a nation of 'burghers and peasants, led by the lairds or small gentry' of whom he himself was one, which defied not only the might of England but also Scotland's cross-border Anglo-Norman ruling elite who had been 'excusably lukewarm in their Scottish patriotism'.[46]

From the 1930s the Whig tradition of history came under sustained assault from historians, beginning with Herbert Butterfield in his classic book, *The Whig Interpretation of History*. Unionism in Scotland followed a similar trajectory of decline from the 1960s, while in England, too, a sense of shared Britishness has yielded in recent decades to a less comprehensive Little Englandism (unconscious as well as overt) that conveys scant sympathy for the non-English peoples of the United Kingdom except, on occasions, in the special case of Northern Ireland. In these circumstances, it is unsurprising that the English cult of Wallace which prevailed in the nineteenth century has disappeared. The film *Braveheart* (1995) rearticulated the 'international' version of Wallace as a universal icon of freedom, but the specifically 'British' appeal of Wallace that once exercised the English historical imagination is now literally unimaginable except to historians prepared to reconceptualise the nineteenth-century blending of Britain. Today, Wallace has become a symbol of otherness. He now represents a line of division between Scotland and England, and stands as an icon of historic enmity. Nevertheless, the nineteenth-century English cult of Wallace stands as a reminder to those trapped in the mindset of the present that the historic configuration of Anglo-Scottish relations is rich in unexpected ambivalences on both sides of the border.[47]

10

Unionist-Nationalism in Stone? The National Wallace Monument and the Hazards of Commemoration in Victorian Scotland

James Coleman[1]

The National Wallace Monument on the Abbey Craig near Stirling is one of the most enduring testimonials to the glorification of that most potent of Scottish heroes, William Wallace; yet the circumstances of the monument's construction and the ideology that it was originally intended to convey have been obscured by subsequent views of what Wallace means to Scotland.[2] The early twenty-first-century significance of the National Wallace Monument is markedly different from that intended by its 'authors', those Victorian gentlemen who raised the funds for its construction, chose the design, and faced the slings and arrows of the monument's critics.[3] Our purpose here is to shrug off this post-*Braveheart* image of William Wallace and its associations with modern Scottish political nationalism in an attempt to recover the Wallace of the nineteenth century, a Wallace whose monument was intended both to mark the patriot-hero's achievement of independence for Scotland and to commemorate what he had done for the Union and the Empire. This requires the consideration of two complementary ideas.

First, consideration of commemorative monuments involves the idea of cultural nationalism as an expression of a nation's sense of self, its national identity or, to use a term that occurs often in the rhetoric of the nineteenth-century Wallace cult, its 'nationality'. Historiographical examinations of nineteenth-century Scotland have tended to view Scottish cultural nationalist discourse and practices as being poor substitutes for the kind of nationalism that Scotland conspicuously did not have: political nationalism.[4] Alternatively, the commemoration of the Scottish past through the construction of such monuments as the National Wallace Monument, and the worship of the national hero that these symbols represent, has been presented as signifying a lack of a proper national historiography.[5] These reductionist views have been countered somewhat by Graeme Morton's resonant term, 'unionist-nationalism'.

Derived from an examination of the civil and political autonomy of Scottish Lowland civil society, unionist-nationalism represents the operation and expression of a distinct Scottish national identity within the overarching ideal of Great Britain and Empire; that is, to be self-consciously and loyally British did not involve the renunciation of one's Scottishness. Quite the opposite, in fact, as unionist-nationalist Scots held fast to their identity as Scots, viewing their Scottishness as an essential component of their Britishness.[6] The identification of unionist-nationalism in nineteenth-century Scotland provides an alternative to the view of Scotland as turning up late for the nationalist party. In control of the apparatus of civil society, Scots felt no need for political nationalism as there was no significant groundswell of political grievance. In cultural terms, unionist-nationalism was articulated through the contribution of Scots to the greatness of Britain and the successes of the imperial project, whether these Scots were scientists, economists, historical novelists or, looking to national memory, thundering reformers or patriot-heroes. Unionist-nationalism permitted Scottish national self-expression within the cultural sphere.[7] The construction of cultural nationalist symbols, such as the Wallace Monument, was not a surrogate for something more potent – i.e. something political – but a form of nationalist expression seen as being every bit as legitimate as calls for constitutional change. Although the vast majority of Victorian Scots felt no need for political nationalism, this did not mean that their cultural-nationalist practices suffered. Victorian Scots were particularly skilful at expressing their Scottishness, as distinct from, yet complementary to, their Britishness. There was an active, articulate and popular Scottish nationalism in the nineteenth century – it was cultural nationalism, and we should not underestimate its potency simply because it had no political correlative.

This leads us to the second component, that of the role of commemorative practice as cultural-nationalist expression, a practice that defines the role of the National Wallace Monument for nineteenth-century Scotland. Like all symbols that have been formed with the intent to communicate a specific idea or concept, commemorative monuments involve a paradox between intention and interpretation, where the intention is to fix some idea of the nation in stone and to present that conception of the nation to subsequent generations as a means of nurturing national identity.[8] These structures are meant to inspire, to fill those who gaze upon them with a sense of their nation's greatness in the past, present and future, emphasising the nation's historic legitimacy by veneration of heroic precedents. Yet, regardless of any meaning the monument was intended to transmit, ultimately it is the 'reader' rather than the 'author' who decides what the monument signifies. Each new generation of viewers brings its own set of cultural and historical assumptions to the monument, feeding a constant flow of interpretation and re-interpretation of the person or event being commemorated. In other words, a monument does not project meanings – it operates as a screen on to which meaning is projected by the viewer.[9] It is this process that has led to the original meaning of the National Wallace Monument disappearing; the balance between unionist and nationalist readings of Wallace has been lost, as the Victorian unionist counterweight weakened and the scales tipped in favour of the nationalist reading.

To tell the story of the National Wallace Monument, from its first proposal to the close of the nineteenth century, would take an entire book in itself, so this chapter will not attempt to tell that story in any detail, although a brief summary of the most significant dates is necessary. Further to proposals in the Glasgow press and through the zeal of the Rev. Dr Charles Rogers of Stirling, the movement to erect the monument was launched at a 'Great Public Meeting', held on the anniversary of the battle of Bannockburn in June 1856, after which a committee of management was elected. Five years later, the foundation stone of the monument was laid, again on the anniversary of Bannockburn, yet, despite the enthusiasm of the fundraisers, subscriptions sufficient to complete the monument were not forthcoming, and it would be another eight years before the completed monument was handed over to Stirling Town Council, this time on 11 September, the anniversary of the battle of Stirling Bridge. On another Bannockburn anniversary, in 1887, a statue of William Wallace was added to the front of the monument, with the so-called 'Wallace Sword' being transferred to the monument from Dumbarton the following November. Over the years, numerous busts of Scottish men deemed sufficiently illustrious by the monument's custodians were placed in the monument's 'Hall of Heroes', beginning with Robert Burns in September 1886 and John Knox, George Buchanan and Sir Walter Scott in September 1887. Further busts were added over the following twenty years, including those of the geologist and journalist Hugh Miller, the Enlightenment economist Adam Smith and the weaver poet Robert Tannahill. The monument's entrance hall also contains busts of two men who had become synonymous with the difficult movement to have the monument erected: the aforementioned antiquarian, historian and genealogist, the Rev. Dr Charles Rogers, and the Glasgow lawyer, historian and pamphleteer, William Burns.[10] As we shall see, these men represent two opposing faces of Scottish cultural nationalism in the nineteenth century. Charles Rogers was a particularly crucial figure in the fundraising and in the construction of the monument, having had a remarkable ability for arranging the erection of Scottish historical monuments. In his time Rogers was responsible for the erection of statues to James Hogg at St Mary's Loch, to Wallace and to the Covenanting martyr

James Guthrie in Stirling, as well as participating in numerous other 'national' endeavours, many of which failed to gain much momentum, possibly because of Rogers' 'persecution complex'.[11] His most lasting legacy – certainly for those examining the nineteenth-century mania for monuments – is his two-volume *Monuments and Monumental Inscriptions in Scotland* from 1871, as well as the equally monumental *Book of Wallace*, published in 1889 by the Grampian Club, which Rogers founded. Much of what we know about the progress of the Wallace Monument's fundraising and construction comes from Rogers' numerous writings, biased and full of puffing self-justification though they are.

Constructing a monumental shrine in honour of a national hero like William Wallace was by no means unique to Scotland. The worship of national heroes as secular saints was commonplace throughout Europe and North America in the nineteenth century, as monuments and colossal statues were erected with the intention of commemorating the deeds of those heroes sustaining the national virtues they were supposed to represent.[12] Through the selection of some element from the nation's character or memory and the commemoration of that element in material form, monuments could be a potent way of reminding the members of the national community about the essential characteristics of the nation to which they belonged. This element might be drawn from the past or from the present; it might be an event, a person, or an ideology; it might be given form by direct representation of the commemorated individual, or reflected through architecture or images from the realm of allegory. Yet, regardless of the form, the intention was to take this element of the nation and give it an enduring definition. National monuments were an expression of what Ernest Renan described in 'What Is a Nation?' as:

> the social capital upon which one bases a national idea. To have common glories in the past and to have a common will in the present; to have performed great deeds together, to wish to perform still more – these are the essential conditions for being a people.[13]

The role of the national monument was to establish precisely what these 'common glories' were. Once fixed in place, the monument was supposed to transmit the meaning of the commemorated subject in order that members of the national community could look upon the monument and receive suitably patriotic inspiration. As nations were formed and sustained through a communicated sense of shared experience, across geographical space and 'calendrical' time, national monuments were intended to act as expressions of this collective sense of self, this consciousness, this *nationality*.[14] The virtues of the nation could be embodied in the hero thus signified, a single, resonant figure acting as a correlative of national virtue, most commonly perhaps in the hero's patriotic love of liberty. This passion was shared by the members of the modern nation: the Swiss possessed an ever-evolving cult of William Tell, the French venerated Joan of Arc or the Gauls, while the Germans, among numerous other national monuments, erected the *Hermannsdenkmal* to Arminius the Cheruskan, conqueror of the Roman legions, a monument that shares many of the qualities of the Wallace Monument. All these monuments were intended as 'a mirror image of national tradition'.[15] The Wallace Monument fits neatly into this nineteenth-century vogue for erecting assertively national monuments, being constructed as a symbol of the Scottish nation and of that nation's virtues, personalised in the patriot-hero William Wallace. The cult of William Wallace shows the Scots were just as adept at playing culturally nationalist games as their European counterparts who may have indulged in 'proper' political nationalism.

If the meaning of the past is so vital to the meaning of the present, and to the legitimacy of the nation to which these memories belong, control of that past becomes of great significance; to be able to claim the national hero as one's own is to hold the rights to one of the defining symbols of the national consciousness – Renan's 'social capital'. To possess Wallace was to possess one of the most powerful precedents from the Scottish national past, and his memory was co-opted by numerous disparate bodies – there were as many William Wallaces as there were causes seeking to deal in his social capital: Wallace the Chartist, Wallace the Liberal, Temperance Wallace, Proletarian Wallace and, eventually, Wallace the proto-Nationalist.[16] These deployments of Wallace all tended to share certain key components, principally Wallace's role as a champion of liberty, whether that liberty was national, constitutional, personal or social. Wallace, the 'great liberator', had freed Scotland from the tyrannical yoke of the Plantagenets and, in so doing, forged the Scottish nation, giving it the necessary historical legitimacy that a nineteenth-century nation required. At the same time, Wallace had been a 'man of the people'; by not being a member of the aristocracy he had the advantage, in terms of his cultural capital, of not being aided in his exertions by any inherited privilege.[17] By combining Wallace the liberator and Wallace as 'one of us', the hero could be made to represent extension of the electoral franchise, free-trade liberalism or simply the Victorian values of hard work and self-improvement.

In part, it was the role of the National Wallace Monument to act as a focus for representations of the patriot-hero, and the conception of Wallace outlined above appeared again and again in the rhetoric of the speeches delivered in aid of raising the monument. The National Wallace Monument saw Wallace deployed as Scotland's national hero, not just within the Scottish context but transmitting Wallace's patriotism across a burgeoning international network of nations, heroes and monuments. It was necessary for Wallace to take his place in the pantheon of great national heroes, as powerful as the heroes celebrated by other nations. One speaker at Bannockburn in 1870 suggested that the Swiss national hero, William Tell, was the closest any other nation might get to a hero of Wallace's quality, 'but,' he added, significantly, 'some said that William Tell was a myth'.[18] Wallace's historic reality legitimised him as a more 'efficacious' symbol of the nation, one of the 'great men', not only of the Scottish past but of the history of all nations. Speaking at the 600th anniversary of the battle of Stirling Bridge, held at the Wallace Monument in 1897, the Liberal peer Lord Rosebery placed Wallace in his pantheon of great men:

> It is the same whether you call it Caesar or Luther or Washington or Mirabeau or Cavour. Crisis is a travail, and the birth of the man ends or assuages it. (Cheers.) We recognise in Wallace one of these men – the man of fate given to Scotland in the storms of the thirteenth century.[19]

Comparison with the great men of history is a recurrent theme in the deployment of Wallace: part of the inscription on another Wallace monument, a baronial tower erected at Barnweill in Ayrshire in 1859, likens Wallace to, again, George Washington and also to Leonidas, the victor of the battle of Thermopylae, as being 'names which shall remain through all time the Watchwords and Beacons of Liberty'.[20] William Wallace is exalted in terms of his contribution to ideals that transcend national boundaries yet are still held to be definitive of the Scottish national character, specifically in his role as the great liberator. In bequeathing these qualities to Scotland, Wallace not only rendered it a distinct nation with its own laws, institutions and character but also ensured that the Scots had no need for political nationalism. At the laying of the National Wallace Monument's foundation stone in 1861, the author, James Dodds, who provided a constitutional reading of the Scottish past, reminded the assembled multitude that had it not been for Wallace's victory at Stirling Bridge, 'instead of coming here with your peaceful banner and the insignia of social triumph, you would have been engaged in the same awful and terrible contest in which Poland, Italy, and Hungary are now engaged'.[21]

Dodds, like Charles Rogers, represented the voice of the moderate unionist-nationalist who had not necessarily attained any great social rank, having achieved his popularity as a writer and public speaker. His articulation of Wallace's legacy, one commonplace in invocations of the patriot-hero during this period and coming from various levels of Scottish civil society, acts as a counter to the twentieth-century accusation that Scotland did not express any 'proper' political nationalism. The worship of Wallace involved a significant element of gratitude for the fact that Wallace ensured, at Stirling Bridge in 1297, that political or constitutional struggle was neither necessary nor desirable – rather than being deficient in not requiring profound constitutional change, the discourse of the Wallace Monument indicates that those unionist-nationalist Scots who found a platform at the monument saw it as a decidedly good thing that they were not in the same position as Italy, Hungary or Poland. This cultural nationalist rhetoric expressed the nation's historic identity but also the superfluity of its political counterpart.

The ability to claim possession of such a vital symbol as Wallace was of exceptional importance in nineteenth-century Scotland and, as a result, control of the National Wallace Monument inevitably entailed control of one of the most significant symbols of the patriot-hero – to dictate the meaning of the monument would be to direct the resonance of the patriot's historic achievement. The debates and controversies concerning the monument's construction point to the importance of the Wallace myth to Victorian Scots yet also to the difficulty of erecting a monument to such a major figure in the *mythistoire* of the Scottish nation and, of much more profound significance for Wallace's unionist-nationalist acolytes, celebrating a potentially disruptive figure, one who was most famous for defeating the army of an English king. One of the initial objections to the monument was that no physical memorial of Wallace was necessary, as his true monument was the free and independent Scottish people: 'Wallace required no monument as he lived in the hearts of his countrymen.'[22] Critics claimed that such structures were simply a waste of time and money, requiring justification from the very beginning. In a pamphlet printed in 1860, intended for circulation in aid of the Wallace Monument movement, the Rev. Dr Charles Rogers argued the case for the defence against 'the absurd cry of the utilitarian', stating that regardless of the passing of the centuries, nothing could 'detract from the approbation due to heroic and patriotic deeds'. In thus promoting the monument, in which he had a fairly serious concern, Rogers outlined the role of the monument as a necessary symbol of the national existence, saying that monuments 'evidence national merit and national gratitude – merit in those who are commemorated, gratitude in those who delight thus to do honour to the meritorious'.[23] Despite the eager harangues of Rogers and others, and support from every corner of the Empire, sufficient funds were not forthcoming. By the time the foundation stone was due to be laid, still only half the necessary funds had been raised, although Rogers had attempted to receive assurances from some wealthy donors that the slack would soon be taken up.[24] This lack of momentum in gathering subscriptions would ultimately contribute to Rogers' ejection as secretary and principal fundraiser.

Although the 'utilitarians' caused some difficulties, probably the most significant obstacle facing the organisers of the movement to erect the monument was the taint of anti-Englishness. In 1856, as the National Wallace Monument movement was first beginning to gain some momentum, *The Times* printed an editorial on the subject of these Scottish attempts to articulate their national consciousness, referring to Wallace as 'the merest myth' and going on to accuse the Scots of 'exclusiveness' and 'provincialism', proclaiming 'the more Scotland has striven to be a nation, the more she has sunk to be a province'.[25] *The Times'* thundering charted the stormy waters that the fundraisers for the Wallace Monument would have to navigate, by asserting the commitment of the English to 'the conception of the United Kingdom; nay, more, of a British Empire', and accusing the Scots of being un-British. Association with such anti-Union sentiment was an ever-present threat, as the historian Archibald Alison identified prior to assuming the chair at the banquet held to celebrate the laying of the monument's foundation stone. Alison wrote in his autobiography of how easy it would have been to have 'wound the audience up to the highest pitch of enthusiasm by praise of the Scotch and abuse of the English, for they were to a man intensely national, and highly excited'.[26]

Instead, and fully aware of the perils of Anglophobia hanging over the entire project, Alison

> endeavoured to present a view of the achievements of Wallace which, while it should do justice to the memory of that illustrious patriot, should at the same time exhibit clearly the immense advantages which Scotland, in common with every other part of the empire, derived from union with England.[27]

The necessity of talking up the union was a defining theme of the Wallace Monument movement, featuring time after time in speeches delivered throughout the monument's development. If the extracts reproduced by Charles Rogers in his *Book of Wallace* are to be viewed as representative, almost every meeting held by the likes of Rogers and James Dodds to raise interest and subscriptions was characterised by their attempts to respond to objections that the monument was intended to be 'a demonstration of hostility against England', with the sole purpose of reviving 'ancient prejudice and animosities'.[28] Yet, just as Wallace could be summoned to fight for extension of the franchise or the satisfactions of a temperate life, so he could be deployed as a champion of British nationalism – Constitutionalist Wallace, a truly unionist-nationalist hero.

One of the fundamental aspects of the Wallace cult in the nineteenth century, not merely deployed in an attempt to appear self-consciously British but applied almost universally when robing Wallace in any form of nationalist garb, was that his patriotic struggle represented the triumph of Scottish liberty over Plantagenet tyranny, the forging of a national independence that had allowed the Scottish nation to grow and achieve its distinct character. Wallace was literally credited with forming the Scottish nation. Sir John Melville, Lord Provost of Edinburgh, spoke at the 1856 'Great Public Meeting' of Scotland as owing its national existence to 'the prowess of Wallace and the indomitable spirit of resistance which he manifested'.[29] Over forty years later, the same was being said by Lord Rosebery: in his speech at the 600th anniversary of the battle of Stirling Bridge, he projected Wallace as the one who had 'asserted Scotland as an independent country, who made or remade the Scots as a nation', receiving loud cheers in response.[30]

At Stirling Bridge, and through the example of a life lived within the sacred spirit of patriotism, Wallace bequeathed to Scotland a legacy of personal and national liberty, forging the Scots into a proudly historic nation that would go on to make its contribution to Union and Empire. The idea that, had the Scots under Wallace not won at Stirling Bridge, and had Wallace not left this legacy of national independence, the Union of 1707 could not have taken place as a union of equals, is one of the defining characteristics of unionist-nationalist discourse in Victorian Scotland.[31] Speaking at the ceremony to mark the handing over of the Wallace Sword to the National Wallace Monument in 1888, Provost Yellowlees of Stirling said:

> The sword would not lie in the monument as a symbol of strife and hate and bloodshed, but as a reminder of the weary and long-continued struggle for liberty and national independence. It would be a symbol of that struggle which culminated in the consummation of the Union between Scotland, not as a servile and conquered race, but as a free and independent nationality, on the one hand, and its richer and more populous neighbour on the south, a union entered into on equally free and independent terms, and which had been fraught with untold blessings to both nationalities. (Applause.)[32]

In this way, Wallace could be made to play a fundamental role in the formation of Great Britain, for the patriot was as much a British hero as a Scottish one, not only a champion of the historic independence of Scotland but of the constitutional government that made Britain and its Empire so great. By defeating a tyrannical, and therefore unconstitutional, monarch,

Wallace had taught the English a lesson in the meaning of what it was to be British.[33] An article on the 1856 'Great Public Meeting' in the radical *Tait's Magazine* stated that Wallace's 'value to English liberty was equal to his efforts for Scottish independence', or in the words of the more moderate Charles Rogers:

> Thanks to Wallace that we have not been irritated by feelings of national degradation; and by him, too, taught the lesson that it was our privilege and our duty to battle for the right, to rally round the throne, and fight manfully for the constitution. And well, too, we may claim the privilege of saying that if we derived, as we certainly did, many national benefits from our union with England, we, too, conferred on the south reciprocal advantages; the rose of England never bloomed so fair as when entwined and enfolded by the thistle of Scotland.[34]

Not only had Wallace won Scotland's historic independence, he had also fought – whether he knew it or not – in the name of the constitution. Just as the Scots were making their own contribution to the Union and the Empire in the nineteenth century, so too their hero had participated in the development of the British nation in the late thirteenth century. To commemorate Wallace's victories was not only profoundly Scottish but was also to celebrate what it was to be British, dovetailing both Scottish and British national identity into a definitive statement of unionist-nationalist pride. This was supremely deft cultural nationalism, a carefully constructed image of the patriot-hero that was ably deployed by those who sought to promote the movement for the National Wallace Monument, providing a route through the dangerous waters of Anglophobia.

It was not all plain sailing, however. Accusations of anti-Englishness did not come from nothing – they had been born of an association, in the eyes of the press and no small proportion of the public, with an earlier Scottish national movement that had had as its focus the redress of certain perceived imbalances in the operation of the Union: the National Association for the Vindication of Scottish Rights. The NAVSR, or Scottish Rights Society, is often viewed as a forerunner of the Wallace Monument movement, and, although connections between the two bodies have been overstated, it is true that some of those involved in the NAVSR went on to play a role in the collection of subscriptions for the National Wallace Monument.[35] What both the NAVSR and the Wallace Monument committee undoubtedly did share was a clash of attitudes between moderate and radical nationalists. The moderate nationalists such as Charles Rogers or Archibald Alison looked upon the Wallace Monument as both honouring the deeds of the patriot and symbolising the distinctiveness of Scottish nationality in a firm and unquestioningly unionist context.[36] For these moderates, who, if Charles Rogers is to be believed, represented the majority on the monument committee, there was never any questioning of the Union, no subtext of constitutional dissatisfaction implicit in the intended meaning of the monument. Ranged against these moderate unionist-nationalists were those former members of the NAVSR who became involved in the Wallace Monument movement as a direct result of their – Rogers claims, anti-English – grievances and who sought to make the erection of the monument a focus for nationalist dissent. This body's most vocal spokesman was William Burns, who represents the more radical face of Victorian Scottish cultural-nationalism. No enemy of the Union *per se*, Burns was a proponent of – at times quite virulent – anti-Englishness, derived from his perception of the ever more problematic anglicisation of Scotland allied with a neglect of Scottish matters in the imperial parliament and within British culture more generally. To this end, Burns was an early advocate of constitutional change, his objections to the status quo being expressed in printed letters and pamphlets bearing titles such as *Scotland and her Calumniators: her past, her present and her future*, although he is perhaps best remembered for his two-volume history, *The Scottish War of Independence*, and his hatred of the term 'Scotch' when denoting 'Scots' or 'Scottish'.[37]

Much to the detriment of the monument's progress and to its profile in the press, William Burns and Charles Rogers clashed continually throughout the period that both men were on the Wallace Monument committee. According to Rogers, the moderate members of the committee had constantly to deny the charge that the movement was merely the NAVSR under a different name and hence associated with anti-Union sentiment.[38] Writing of the establishment of the NAVSR in *The Serpent's Track*, a pamphlet he composed with the sole purpose of describing 'twenty-two years of persecution', Rogers accuses William Burns of being the most 'conspicuous' of these former NAVSR 'malcontents – persons disposed whether to gratify a puerile vanity or to re-awaken international dissension'.[39] Rogers argues that it was as a result of the involvement of William Burns and others that the Wallace Monument movement had encountered resistance from those who did not wish to contribute financially to a movement so wholly associated with the NAVSR. For instance, the presence of Burns's 'malcontents' caused difficulties in finding a suitable noble figurehead for the movement, as without noble patronage the monument would not possess the required cachet.[40] Archibald Alison, who was involved in both the NAVSR and the Wallace Monument movement, had 'perceived elements of a dangerous character' in the NAVSR, and agreed with Lord Eglinton to 'abide firmly by the Union, and utter nothing which could shake the general attachment to it', wholly disapproving of those elements in the NAVSR who were espousing dissolution of the Union.[41] Eglinton's experience with Burns and his colleagues in the NAVSR appears to have discouraged him from participating in the Wallace Monument movement; he remarked, according to Rogers, that 'already he had been "burned"'.[42] The Earl of Elgin's acceptance of the chairmanship of the monument committee seems to have been partly because he was out of the country during the NAVSR's period of notoriety.[43] Ultimately, it was deemed necessary that assurances must be received from any former NAVSR firebrands that they would not attempt to hijack the monument for their own ends, with William Burns being allowed on to the committee only after he had made 'a distinct promise' not to reintroduce any Anglophobic sentiments.[44] Both the moderate unionist-nationalists, such as Rogers, Dodds and Alison, and radical promoters of Scottish rights, such as William Burns, understood the importance of the monument and its role in fixing the meaning of the patriot-hero Wallace, and in this way the schisms within the monument committee represent a struggle for ownership of the past: whoever controlled the monument could control the kind of Wallace, and so the kind of Scotland, that the structure would transmit to its viewers. In the ideological deployment of Wallace, the difference between the moderate unionist-nationalist reading and the more radical view of the Burns nationalists finds its definition not in 1297, or in 1305, or even 1314: the historical moment that divides these two views of Wallace is 1707 – it is their attitudes to the Union that distinguish one from the other. For the moderate, holding the archetypal unionist-nationalist view, Wallace's victories allowed the Union of 1707 to take place between two proudly historic nations engaging in an equally historic and constitutional partnership; for radical Victorian nationalists, 1707 was the moment when the Scots squandered the magnificent legacy of national independence that Wallace had bequeathed to his nation – not a union of equals but the submission of one nation to another.

These two conflicting readings provided the basis for one of the most rancorous and divisive episodes in the story of the monument's construction – the choice of a design. Since the physical form of the monument would inevitably be the most enduring method of transmitting its meaning, choosing a design that reflected the kind of Wallace that the monument's progenitors preferred was of profound importance. Considering that the committee was split between the moderate and radical views of how Wallace's legacy ought to be signified, there was always going to be trouble. The first design to be chosen by the monument committee was, according to Rogers, selected practically single-handedly by William Burns and his former NAVSR cronies in the convenient absence of a sufficient number of moderate committee members. Designed by the artist J. Noel Paton, the proposed colossal structure was entitled 'Lion and Typhon', being 'a symbolical group of a lion with a broken chain overthrowing a crowned Typhon', intended to represent the moment when 'the lion of Scotland breaks from his fetters and overcomes tyranny'. Rogers, representing the voice of the moderates, took a more unkind view, describing the proposal as 'Scotland as a lion throttling "the English monster"'.[45] That Paton's design might actually be constructed appears to have been the cause of some alarm: in a letter to Charles Baillie, the chairman of the National Wallace Monument committee, William Stirling of Keir, MP for Perthshire, expressed his confusion over the precise meaning of 'Lion and Typhon':

> How does the composition symbolise the great career and touching story of Wallace? We have a comely lion standing upon the body of an ill-favoured king with thighs twisting and wriggling themselves into serpents, of which the heads form his inconvenient feet. . . . What do these two figures mean? What does the lion represent? Is he Wallace or is he Scotland?[46]

Even taking into account Charles Rogers' evident dislike of both the design and its proponent, it seems that he was accurate in observing that 'dissatisfaction was universal', and the 'Lion and Typhon' was rejected at a second committee meeting held in June 1859.[47] This controversy is symptomatic of the differences that existed between the moderate and radical members of the Wallace Monument committee. By extracting as fair a reading as possible from amongst Rogers' propaganda, it would appear that William Burns was intent on rendering the monument as a statement of political intent as much as a symbol of Scottish cultural distinctiveness – despite any ambiguity in its significance, the 'Lion and Typhon' was undoubtedly an image of struggle and mastery rather than of tranquil repose in the Union.

After Paton's design was dropped, new designs were called for consideration, the submissions being put on public display in Edinburgh, Glasgow and Stirling in order that members of the public could voice an opinion on which design was best suited to the monument's purpose. If Charles Rogers is to be believed, J. T. Rochead's Scotch-baronial tower was the popular choice. Describing his preferred mode for the proposed monument during the 'Lion and Typhon' débâcle, William Stirling had suggested 'a tall and stately tower of our early national architecture, suggestive of the manners and history of the time' – Stirling's reference to '*our* early *national* architecture' representing the cultural-nationalist concern with projection of the existence of the nation into the past from the present.[48] According to Rogers, Rochead had read a printed copy of this letter and had adopted its suggestions when working on the design, his proposal differing from Keir's only in being topped by an 'Imperial Crown'. At the committee meeting called to make the final decision on the monument's design, Rochead's was chosen 'by acclamation' following a proposal by Sheriff Henry Glassford Bell, who would go on to describe the design as being 'simple, national, and appropriate'.[49] It was still not universally popular: the architect J. J. Stevenson, apparently no great fan of Scotch baronial, claimed that 'the design seems to aim at being wild'; a retrospective on J. Noel Paton in the *Art Journal* refers to the Wallace Monument, perhaps unsurprisingly considering the rejection of Paton's early design, as 'conventional and utterly barbarous'; while, in 1870, the *Scotsman* called it 'a tower of questionable elegance and unquestionable pettiness'.[50]

Despite such disapproval, however, the Scotch-baronial style was wholly appropriate in fulfilling its intended purpose – the National Wallace Monument is unionist-nationalism in stone, a metaphor for the William Wallace that moderate Victorian cultural unionist-nationalists intended the monument to signify. The ultimate choice of a Scotch-baronial design indicates the success of the moderate nationalism represented by Rogers over the more aggressive deployment of Wallace as promoted by Burns. The rock-faced rubble construction of the superstructure of the tower was intended to represent the historicity of Scotland and its culture, as modern construction methods drew on precedents from the past. At the same time, the 'imperial crown' forming the apex of the monument symbolised the power of the British Empire. In other words, the past supports the present; the legacy of Scottish history is crowned with the achievements of the nineteenth century, all combined into a sturdy and harmonious whole – that whole being both the Wallace Monument and the British Empire.[51] Such a sentiment was explicit in the intentions of those who chose the design and were responsible for raising the funds for the monument's construction.

Although the choice of design for the monument was a battle won by the moderates, Burns and his colleagues could still scent a sort of victory. Shortly after the laying of the foundation stone in 1861, Rogers was either ejected from his role as secretary because of financial irregularities or resigned as a result of being too often persecuted by William Burns.[52] Still keen to be involved in the erection of a monument that he believed was his idea in the first place, Rogers set up a 'supplementary committee' and proceeded to continue his fundraising efforts. The divide between Rogers' 'supplementary' fundraising and the official committee, now in the charge of Burns, seems to have very much retarded construction, with Rogers blaming Burns's extremism and the latter's supporters pointing the finger at Rogers' creative accounting.

One of the most significant events concerning the monument during the Burns ascendancy must be the presentation to the committee in 1868 of 'patriotic sentiments' from the 'celebrity' nationalists Kossuth, Mazzini,

Garibaldi and others, mounted in a frame constructed from pieces of the so-called 'Wallace Oak of Elderslie'.[53] The intention was that copies of these framed testimonials would be circulated in an attempt to raise interest in and funds for the monument.[54] Such a self-conscious association between the unambiguously political nationalism of these European leaders and the commemoration of Wallace emphasises the kind of national hero that the radical cultural-nationalists intended the monument to represent. This was an interpretation symbolised by their preference for the 'Lion and Typhon' and sustained through their promotion of the contributions of Kossuth *et al* – a relic of the historical Wallace surrounds and protects the messages offered in support by the patriot's nineteenth-century counterparts. It is important to emphasise that the committee under Burns's more radical secretaryship appears to have been every bit as successful in raising subscriptions for the monument as it was under Rogers' more politically moderate, if no less zealous, hand.[55]

It would take until 1869 for the monument to be completed, during which time, along with sporadic but strong criticism in the press, the architect died and it was discovered that the price quoted for the construction of the tower had been too conservative. A 'quiet ceremony' was held on 11 September 1869, there not being enough money in the coffers for a large 'demonstration', attended by members of Stirling Town Council and the monument's committee, including William Burns. The inauguration was something of a muted affair, with very little of the celebratory commemoration that had marked both the Great Public Meeting and the laying of the foundation stone.[56] There do not appear to have been any lengthy speeches celebrating Wallace's achievements, nor was there a particularly high attendance. The most significant speech seems to have been made by the secretary of the monument committee at that time, a Mr Morrison, who merely read out the minutes of the last committee meeting, not missing an opportunity to criticise the Rev. Dr Rogers. In a separate event, held later that day in a Stirling hotel, Rogers was presented with a portrait of himself, given in acknowledgement of his labours.[57]

Despite the dominance of the Burns-led committee during the latter part of construction, the moderates would ultimately regain control of the monument's signification. William Burns died in 1876, by which time, according to the autobiography of the partisan John McAdam, those parties deemed 'objectionable' by the Burns party – i.e. Rogers – were once more beginning to assert themselves.[58] For proof of this we need look no further than the next major event to take place at the Wallace Monument after its inauguration: the unveiling of a bust of Robert Burns, donated by Andrew Carnegie, in the Hall of Heroes in September of 1886. There not being enough space within the monument for the 'goodly number of people' who arrived at the Abbey Craig for the event, it was arranged that one of the speakers would 'deliver an "oration" on the patriotism of Burns'. That speaker was none other than the Rev. Dr Charles Rogers, his reappearance marking the shift away from radical control back to that of the moderate unionist-nationalists.[59] Rogers' persistent presence at events subsequent to this emphasises the control exerted by moderate unionist-nationalism in determining the monument's representation of Wallace and his legacy. In 1887, a statue of Wallace, mounted in a niche on the side of the monument, was unveiled by the Marquess of Bute, 'right-wing' Scottish nationalist and one-time member of the Scottish Home Rule Association.[60] Despite his more radical nationalist propensities – radical, certainly, in the context of the monument's moderate unionist-nationalism – it would appear that Bute was asked to unveil this new adornment because of his title and renowned interest in Scottish history. Although certain statements in Bute's speech proved somewhat controversial – he claimed that the difference between Scotsmen and Englishmen was 'scientifically, even physiologically, true' – his rhetoric was replete with the necessary gestures to Wallace as champion of liberty and father of the nation. He stated that 'our country owes its existence to-day quite as much to [Wallace] as to any other', and at no point did he suggest that the nation might have somehow squandered Wallace's glorious legacy.[61] It is also worth noting that Charles Rogers gave a fairly lengthy speech, setting the record straight on the progress of the monument and delivering a eulogy on its architect, J. T. Rochead. Also, in a mild yet uncharacteristically political statement, Rogers made reference to the recently installed Scottish Office in calling the monument's imperial crown 'the watchtower of Dover House'.[62]

The last major event to be held at the National Wallace Monument in the nineteenth century sets the seal on the moderation of the Wallace myth it was intended to convey – the celebration of the 600th anniversary of the battle of Stirling Bridge, with Lord Rosebery as the principal speaker. Closely following the unionist-nationalist script, Rosebery was careful not to strike any Anglophobic chords, delivering a speech replete with all the necessary unionist-nationalist tropes concerning Wallace's place in the formation of a secure and contented Union and a prosperous Empire.[63] The moderate cultural unionist-nationalism that had defined the Wallace Monument practically since its inception continued to provide the significance for both hero and monument that its custodians aimed to project. It is interesting to note that, despite the controversies surrounding the monument's birth and early development, by this stage of its life the archetypal unionist-nationalist reading of Wallace appears to have made itself acceptable beyond Scotland; whereas in 1856 *The Times* had accused the Scots of provincialism, forty-one years later, in commenting on Rosebery's speech, it celebrated the 'deep and lasting impression' that Wallace had made upon the Empire:

> The conflict which WALLACE began, and which was continued through generations, was the seed-time of qualities and tendencies that the Empire could ill spare. We can all heartily unite in commemorating the work that, in the slow ripening of centuries, has produced a noble harvest of intellectual force, high moral aims, and steadiness of character and purpose.[64]

The Times was not alone in endorsing the commemoration of Stirling Bridge and its heroic victor, the *Telegraph* stating that Englishmen and Scotsmen should join together in celebrating the 'shared advantages' and 'yeoman service' that the national independence of Scotland had brought to the Union and the British Empire, while the *Standard* praised the beautiful surroundings of the monument and called Wallace a man of the people.[65] Yet, just as the unionist-nationalist projection of Wallace appears to have gained acceptance by a formerly disapproving English press, the Burns view of Wallace's legacy was alive and well, albeit at a short remove from his monument. On the same day as Rosebery's speech, the Scottish Home Rule Association held its own commemoration of the battle of Stirling Bridge, where, alongside the familiar idea of Wallace as having rendered Scotland a nation of 'free-born men and women', Charles Waddie, the Association's secretary, failed to see any modern Wallaces amongst the representatives of Scotland at Westminster, saying:

> It was in a different spirit that Scotland maintained her independence. If this generation of Scotsmen are not prepared to do the same, let them abstain from celebrating the battles of Stirling Bridge and Bannockburn.[66]

By 1897, the SHRA was no longer enjoying the kind of support it had formerly attracted, and press reaction to its gathering was fairly critical. Still, Waddie's and the SHRA's sentiments resonate with the interpretation of Wallace preferred by the radical nationalists of the Wallace Monument committee, viewing any of the current generation of Scots who were not willing to spend Wallace's legacy in the correct way – in defence of Scotland's rights in an unequal union with England – as akin to those nobles who had failed to stand up for Scotland in the late thirteenth century. Crucially, however, this message was not expressed at the Wallace Monument but at a separate event held on the supposed site of the battle – control of the messages transmitted by the National Wallace Monument remained firmly within the grasp of moderate unionist-nationalism and a rhetoric kept clear of any anti-Union sentiment or Anglophobia.

Scottish cultural unionist-nationalism, while participating in the discourses and practices of European cultural nationalism through the deployment of national heroes and the inauguration of national monuments in their name, emphasised the commitment of Victorian Scots to both the constitution of Great Britain and the distinct national character and virtue of the Scottish nation. For these Scots, William Wallace was a hero of truly international significance, representing the essential ideals of personal and national liberty, able to keep company with the greatest of great men from the histories of all nations. So, too, the Wallace Monument, with its national architecture and Hall of Heroes, represented a significant landmark in the emerging tradition of national monumentation. Yet the intended meaning of that monument was contested from the very beginning by two brands of nationalism, each determined to control the meaning of the monument. Despite the efforts of those in possession of what was generally viewed as a nationalism too far, one that stressed the frittering away of Wallace's legacy of national and personal liberty, for the majority of its public life the National Wallace Monument remained firmly under the control of a moderate unionist-nationalism that saw the patriot-hero as having left Scotland a legacy of independence, allowing the nation to participate in the Union as an equal with England. The National Wallace Monument was the centre for a cultural nationalism that, rather than acting as an inadequate substitute for political nationalism, stressed Wallace's role in ensuring that a peaceful union with England rendered such efforts unnecessary.

Still the paradox remains. Although, as the nineteenth century drew to a close, the unionist-nationalist interpretation of Wallace was still ringing around its walls, it was nevertheless the more nationalistically radical deployment of the Wallace myth that was to attain ascendancy. As the politico-cultural milieu around the monument shifted, particularly as the appeal of Scottish political-nationalism broadened, the image of Wallace became increasingly associated with profound constitutional change, even divorce. Cultural operators such as Charles Rogers may have struggled to retain control of the meaning of their monument, to transmit their intentions to future generations, yet it is the interpretation of the viewer – the tourist, the passing motorist, the nationalist pilgrim – that decides what the symbol means.

11

The Wallace Sword

David H. Caldwell

Big men have big swords. None comes any bigger for the Scots than William Wallace, so it can be no surprise that the sword enshrined in the National Wallace Monument at Stirling is a large weapon, technically a two-handed sword since it was designed for wielding with both hands. It is also appropriately plain and businesslike, reflecting Wallace's 'man of the people' image, and looks as if it has been through the wars. Nobody has doubted that a sword was the weapon for Wallace. While swords were expensive, and may have been relatively rare amongst the rank and file in Wallace's time, someone of his rank and stature could surely not have managed without one.

Hary's *Wallace* is full of descriptions of how Wallace used his sword; for instance:

> Than Wallace selff in-to that felloune throng
> With his gud swerd that hevy was and lang.

The sword in Wallace's hand was obviously capable of wreaking destruction although it was 'a staff of steyll he gryppyt in his hand', that is, a single-handed weapon. There is no suggestion that it was any more than a particularly effective working tool, but in a dream our hero imagined St Andrew giving him a sword with a pommel like a topaz and a hilt and grip glittering like glass.[1]

The Wallace Monument, completed in 1869, clearly needed a relic of the nation's favourite hero to heighten the feeling of awe and reverence amongst visitors. Mementoes and relics of other famous Scots, including Robert Bruce, Mary, Queen of Scots and Bonnie Prince Charles, were conveniently coming to light as more and more interest was being taken in Scotland's past. So why not Wallace? All that appeared to be available was a sword that had already been damned by expert opinion as the wrong thing, but this was the unpromising material that metamorphosed anew into the 'Wallace Sword'.

On 17 November 1888, with due ceremony, the Wallace Sword was presented to the Rev. Charles Rogers in Stirling Castle by Colonel Nightingale, the commander of the garrison, acting on instructions from the Secretary of State for War. It was Rogers who had petitioned for the sword to grace the monument, the realisation of which was largely owing to him. This must have been a considerable moment of triumph for Rogers, the importance of which he was determined should be understood by the populace at large. As is evidenced by contemporary press cuttings in the library of the National Museums of Scotland, he was very successful in having his explanation of the sword and its significance widely reported.[2] It is only fitting that we quote his words at length, from his *The Book of Wallace*, published in 1889:

This sword is associated with a glorious history, for it was wielded by one who, in his age when principle succumbed to expediency, was pure and without reproach; who never yielded allegiance where it was not strictly due; and who resisted oppression to the death. Consequent on two weld-ings the weapon has been reduced from its original length, but it was orig-inally a noble blade, which, in respect of the owner, was, in the poet's words,

'Fit for archangel to wield,
Yet light in his terrible hand.'

Borne by the Patriot at the battle of Stirling Bridge, it signalled the com-mencement of a struggle which was not to terminate until the prostrate spirit of the nation was fully revived, not again to droop or decay till on the field of Bannockburn were repelled the hosts of the invader. When foully captured, as he slept at Robroyston, on the night of the 5th August 1305, Wallace had this great blade resting by his pillow; and when he was hastened to London to meet his cruel death, it was borne to Dunbarton [*sic*] as the prize of its governor, the recreant Scotsman who had betrayed its possessor. At Dunbarton the sword has for six long centuries remained as a protest against treachery and injustice, and now, from the hands of the commander at Dunbarton, it is to become a trophy in our Patriot's monument. As governor of Dunbarton, Sir John Menteith received this sword in August 1305, and two hundred years thereafter, namely, on the 8th December 1505, the accounts of the Lord High Treasurer inform us that, at the command of James IV, the sum of twenty-six shillings, equal to about thirty pounds of our present money, was paid to an armorer for binding a riding sword and a rapier; also for the 'binding of Wallas sword with cords of silk,' and providing it with 'ane new hilt and plomet,' also with a 'new scabbard and a new belt.' And it will be remarked that while the rapier and the riding sword are named as being simply repaired, the Wallace sword is described as adorned with trappings of silk; also as hav-ing been furnished with the specified additions of a new hilt and pommel, a new scabbard and a new belt. Concerning the weapon we learn noth-ing further for three centuries, but in a letter which, in October 1872, I received from the War Office, I was informed that in the year 1825 it was sent for repair to the Tower, when the Duke of Wellington, as Master-General of the Ordnance, submitted it for examination to Dr Meyrick. This gentleman, afterwards Sir Samuel Meyrick, was an authority on ancient swords, but in estimating the age of the Dunbarton weapon, he was guided by its mountings only. Judging from these, he concluded that the sword was not older than a sword in the British Museum, connected with the earldom of Chester, and belonging to the reign of Edward IV. That I may not misinterpret his sentiments, I quote from Sir Samuel's work on 'Ancient Armour', in which, at vol. ii, page 177, when referring to the reign of Edward IV, he writes, 'The two-handed sword, shown at Dunbarton Castle as that of Wallace, is of this period, as will be evident to any one who compares it with that of the earldom of Chester, in the British Museum.' The Chester sword was afterwards examined by Mr George Omerod, of the Society of Antiquaries, who, in the fifth volume of *Vetusta Monumenta*, shows that the weapon was the Sword of State which Edward V had borne before him, when, as Prince of Wales, he, in 1475, made his triumphal entry into Chester Castle. If then the Chester sword belongs to the year 1475, Sir Samuel Meyrick approximated nearly to the date of the mountings of the Wallace sword, which occurred just thirty years later. But the Wallace sword was, in 1505, an old blade, which required a new hilt and pommel, a new scabbard and a new belt. And as the weapon was then so materially shattered, it seems reasonable to conclude that it was decidedly ancient; moreover, that before it was allowed to rest in the Dunbarton armory, it had been subjected to much hard usage. And its being adorned with silk tassels by the King's command leaves us in no doubt as to its being held in special veneration; while in the register the weapon is described as 'Wallas sword', no qualifying word of doubt being expressed as to its genuineness. And apart from the circumstance that by two separate weldings the blade has been shortened, it is otherwise a duplicate of the two-handed blade of Sir Richard Lundin, used at the battle of Stirling, now preserved at Drummond Castle. One blunder leads to another. Consequent upon Sir Samuel Meyrick's judgment, propounded in 1825, the mountings of 1505 were removed, and a common handle of the 15th century substituted. So I was informed in the letter, which, in 1872, I received from the War Office. But now that we have got possession of the sword, we shall be careful that the weapon with which the hero was wont to 'mak great rowme' about him, will be mounted in the fashion in which he nobly grasped it, and we shall retain it as no unimportant addition to the national regalia.[3]

So Rogers' case was that the sword had been misdated by the expert,

Meyrick, to a later era on the basis of a restoration of the weapon that Rogers could now show took place in 1505. Despite his ingenious spin, no serious scholar has in recent times been inclined to give the Wallace Sword any credence as the hero's own. It is generally well known that two-handed swords came into use only long after Wallace's time. The earliest documentary reference to 'twa handit swerdis' in Scotland comes in government instructions for the arming of the lieges, issued weeks after the disaster at Flodden in 1513. It occurs in a list of weapons, perhaps at that time now deemed acceptable for the army as an alternative to pikes.[4] They had probably been around since the late fifteenth century.

There we might be tempted to leave the story of the Wallace Sword, yet another example of a relic of the wrong type and the wrong date. In my opinion, however, it is worth re-examining Rogers' account of the sword and the sword itself, which remarkably seems to have escaped detailed scholarly examination since the time of Samuel Meyrick.

The explanation of why William Wallace's sword should have ended up in Dumbarton Castle is plausible, but mere supposition. It appears that the earliest record of its presence in that stronghold is in an inventory of May 1644 that lists 'ane auld twa handit sward, without a scabbard' in the Wallace Tower.[5] The latter was erected only in 1617, primarily to protect the north entry to the castle.[6] Why this structure should have been named the Wallace Tower is not clear. The general assumption is, of course, that it commemorates Wallace, but we are not aware of any tradition that would associate him directly with the castle. It seems unlikely that the tower should have been named from the sword. The converse has to be considered a distinct possibility.

When William Wordsworth visited Dumbarton Castle with his sister Dorothy in 1803, they were taken into the guardroom and shown 'a large rusty sword, which they called Wallace's Sword'.[7] This appears to be the earliest actual identification of the Dumbarton Castle sword as having belonged to the patriot.

While the two-handed sword in Dumbarton Castle in 1644 might reasonably be the sword delivered to the Wallace Monument in 1888, serious doubts must be entertained as to whether it is the 'Wallas sword', repaired in 1505 with the addition of a new hilt, pommel and other fittings.[8] It is difficult to believe that anyone at the beginning of the sixteenth century would have accepted a two-handed sword as the hero's weapon. The craftsman who worked on it was Robert Selkirk, a cutler in Edinburgh. None of Selkirk's work is known to survive, but payments recorded to him in the *Treasurer's Accounts* indicate that he produced work of the highest quality. He held the position of royal cutler to James IV from 1497 until his death in 1512.[9] There is a certain ambiguity about the use of the word 'hilt', which might mean just the sword handle itself or could include the guard and pommel as well. If we want to believe that the Wallace Sword is indeed the 'Wallas sword', it needs to be understood that the guard, as I will show below, is of a later date than Selkirk.

There are no clues in the *Treasurer's Accounts* as to where Selkirk acquired the sword. It might be supposed it was a royal possession, and possibly it was not a coincidence that it should receive attention on the 200th anniversary of the hero's death. Robert Bruce's sword had been held in such veneration by James IV's father, James III, that he had taken it with him to battle in 1488,[10] ironically meeting defeat and death on almost the same terrain where Bruce achieved his greatest victory, Bannockburn, in 1314.

Samuel Meyrick's lengthy statement is capable of more than one interpretation. Rogers believed that Meyrick was comparing the fittings, especially the pre-1825 grip, to those on the state sword of the Earl of Chester (Edward, Prince of Wales). The latter has the enamelled arms of the prince on its grip and pommel and a simple bar guard. It would surely be amazing if Meyrick, a fine scholar, should have been party to the removal of anything so fine on the Wallace Sword and that no record should be kept of it. It is surely better to interpret Meyrick's statement comparing the two swords as referring solely to their size and proportions. It might also be noted, incidentally, that Meyrick's work was published in 1824, suggesting some inaccuracy in Rogers' account, perhaps deriving from a letter sent to him by the War Office.[11] Bob Savage of the Royal Armouries has confirmed to me that no contemporary papers concerning the sword's trip to the Tower of London are known to survive.

Finally, in dealing with Rogers' case for the Wallace Sword, something should be said about the sword used by Sir Richard Lundin at the battle of Stirling Bridge. This is a claymore – a two-handed sword of the type used by Highlanders in the sixteenth century. An alternative tradition, that it was used by Lundin of that ilk at the Battle of Bannockburn in 1314, was published a few years before Rogers made his comparison.[12] It is still in a private collection, and I studied it a number of years ago. There is no reason to think that any of it is of an earlier date than the sixteenth century.

While the Lundin sword is a Highland weapon, the Wallace Sword is a two-handed sword of Lowland type. The term 'Lowland' has been assigned in recent times by experts on the basis that such weapons are associated with Lowland families. Their main defining feature is their cross-guard, consisting of long rod-like quillons at right angles to the blade. The ends are turned down, or in, and terminate in knobs. Many have open ring-guards on both sides, sometimes with decorative infills. All have langets – reinforcing tongues extending down the blade. They appear to date to the late sixteenth or early seventeenth century.[13]

The Wallace Sword has a blade length of 131.5 centimetres and an over-all length of 168 centimetres. The guard is of iron and of typical Lowland form, with two side rings. One of them has been bent so that its outer portion lies parallel to the blade. A crude strap has been welded on, running from one of the quillons to the bottommost part of this ring. This arrangement is secondary, and unusual. The most likely explanation is that it was done to aid in mounting the sword flat against a wall. The quillons are diamond shaped in cross-section, with faceted and pointed knobs. The guard has a maximum length of 26.7 centimetres, with relatively long langets and quillon terminals well turned in. This may be a late feature in Lowland swords since it seems to mirror the form of quillons on Scottish 'clam shell-lit' swords, first documented in 1583 when Robert Lyell, an Edinburgh lorimer, was required to make such a hilt as part of his essay for admittance as a freeman of the Hammermen.[14] The wooden grip is covered in leather and is presumably of early nineteenth-century date. So, probably, is the solid iron, pointed oval pommel.

Many of the blades on Scottish two-handed swords are clearly German imports, but the blade of the Wallace Sword offers no clues as to its origin. If it ever had any maker's marks – which typically would have been inlaid in copper or brass – they have disappeared through corrosion and over-zealous cleaning. It has a rounded tip and a ricasso – that is, a section adjacent to the hilt that is unsharpened so that it might the more readily be gripped by the user. Apart from the reshaping of the guard, this sword does not appear particularly untypical of the two-handed swords in use in the Lowlands of Scotland in the late sixteenth or early seventeenth centuries. In construction, it appears cruder than many and shows signs of having been mistreated, although there are no obvious nicks on the blade from use in combat.

A close examination of the blade explains Rogers' mention of two weldings. Remarkably, the blade, as we now have it, seems to have been welded together from at least three separate pieces. The obvious conclusion might be that the blade has been put back together after having been snapped in pieces. Rogers, ever anxious to see everything about his hero as big, concluded that this was a side-effect of an even larger blade being made smaller. The opposite could well be the case since at least two of the pieces do not seem to match up well. The bottom 87.7 centimetres has for the most part a flattened diamond section, unlike the flattened profile of the upper portion, and seems to belong to a relatively narrower weapon. The other break approximates to the position of the ricasso. Possibly this amounts to a single-handed blade that has been deliberately enlarged to give it the appearance of a two-handed one. A close date could not be put on such a single-handed blade, but it might well be of thirteenth-century date.

Does this offer just a very faint ray of hope for those who would believe this to be William Wallace's actual weapon?[15]

12

The Wallace Cult in the Twentieth Century: The Making of a Nationalist Icon

Richard J. Finlay

Whatever was valuable in the kingdom was seized upon by its oppressors; even the cause of female virtue was not held sacred under their unhallowed domination; and in short, the whole country was laid under a military despotism of the most unqualified and irresponsible kind. It was at this dark hour of Scotland's history, when the cry of an oppressed people ascended to heaven, and the liberty for which they had so long struggled seemed to have departed forever from them, that Sir William Wallace arose to avenge the wrongs and restore the rights of his country . . . in *less than six months* from the death of her great champion, Scotland, roused to the cause now sealed and made holy by her patriot's blood, shook off the yoke of England, and became once more a free kingdom.
(*A Biographical Dictionary of Eminent Scotsmen*, ed. Thomas Thomson, 1870)

Contestés par les desseins ambitieux de Souverains anglais, les libertés et les droits nationaux de la nation écossaise furent, après longue guerre dévastatrice et sanglante, maintenus avec succès à la celebre bataille de Bannockburn, évènement après lequel l'Angleterre renonça définitivement, par un traité, à ses prétentions d'excercer une supériorité féodale sur l'Ecosse.
(*Petition Nationale de l'Ecosse pour obtenir sa Representation au Congres de la Paix*, 1919)

The case of Wallace is different; he was not a baron, but an outlawed guerrilla leader, skilful and daring, but ruthless in his conduct. He adhered to no rules of chivalry, but waged total war against man, woman, and child. It was as a leader of sedition that he was formidable, but it was cold-blooded murder and incendiarism, which led him to the scaffold after his capture. Had his offences been merely political he would have found the same mercy that Edward's other opponents never sought in vain; but Wallace was not the romantic hero of later legend, but a leader of well-organized criminals in an assault upon society. For 300 years the

Borders suffered cruelly for this one man's misdeeds, and it is strange that the Scots, who were the great sufferers, should have so long idealized their destroyer.

(John Harvey, *The Plantagenets*, London, 1959, 1967 edn, 121)

At the end of the screening of *Braveheart*, audiences throughout Scotland burst into spontaneous applause. In spite of the film's evident popularity, the critical response was less welcoming.[1] *Braveheart* was denounced for its historical inaccuracy, its anti-English sentiment, its right-wing ideological connotations and its overbearing machismo. Hollywood's treatment of Scottish history was likened to a 'western in kilts'. Not everybody was so negative. The Scottish National Party (SNP) believed the film would act as an ideal recruiting tool, and the nationalist leader, Alex Salmond, urged Scots to be 'Bravehearts not Fainthearts'. Undoubtedly, much of the hostility to the film was motivated by the belief that it manipulated Scottish sentiment straight into the hands of the nationalist camp and, worse still, it encouraged the growth of Anglophobia. Yet, the popularity in Scotland of *Braveheart* raised other deeper issues regarding the relationship of the Scots to their culture and history. Why was it, many asked, that most Scots had their introduction to one of the pivotal characters in Scottish history via Hollywood?[2] The issue raised further questions as to the place of Scottish history in the school curriculum, and a gaffe by the newly opened Museum of Scotland that excluded Wallace on account of a lack of 'material artefacts' fuelled suspicions of Unionist interference in the presentation of Scotland's past.[3] Unconsciously or not, all assumed that Wallace was a thirteenth-century warrior for Scottish independence whose relevance to contemporary society was to act as a spur to nationalism, hence the contrast between the SNP's unquestioning approval of *Braveheart* and the marked ambiguity of the Unionist parties. Yet, such a stark representation of Wallace as the total embodiment of Scottish nationalism was not the case in the nineteenth century, nor was it true for a good part of the twentieth century either. It is the aim of this chapter to examine why it was that the story of Wallace came to be most associated with the nationalist movement in the twentieth century and how, as a consequence, Wallace was marginalised to such an extent that the *Braveheart* phenomenon could take Scotland by storm in the early nineties.

All nations need heroes, and political ideologies like to claim exclusive ownership of such heroes as a means of reinforcing their claims to represent the true 'national' interest.[4] It is a way of shoring up the political legitimacy of a particular ideology by making the claim that, if such heroes were alive today, they would be supporters of that particular ideology. William Tell and Joan of Arc are two excellent cases of national saviours whose stories have been modified to accommodate historical change. The canonisation of Joan in 1920 was indicative of an endeavour to claim the martyr of France back to the Catholic right and away from the secular republic.[5] Even the Soviet Union was forced to turn to the bourgeois Russian past during the Second World War and dust off the heroic tale of Alexander Nevsky, the Slav king who defeated the Vikings for Mother Russia. It was perhaps no coincidence that the Nazi invasion of the Soviet Union was named Barbarossa, after King Frederick I who invaded the Russias, and among the Nazi elite Heinrich Himmler created a cult of Heinrich I, not to mention Hitler's obsession with Wagnerian myth. Even the story of Sir Francis Drake underwent a revival during the Second World War as the English nation needed to remind itself of a hero who had stood up to a powerful invasion armada, and won. It is not rare for societies to reinterpret their past and their heroes to suit the specific exigencies of the present. Throughout the nineteenth century, Sir William Wallace belonged to the pantheon of national heroes who were regularly recruited for the promotion of the nation-state. Mazzini, Garibaldi and Kossuth all paid tribute to Wallace's qualities as a defender of national freedom, and he was cited as an inspiration for contemporary nineteenth-century nationalist movements.[6] Even before the advent of *Braveheart*, Wallace had attracted a significant following in the United States of America where the tale of a fight for independence from a tyrannical English monarch by a man of the people had obvious resonances with the history of that republic.[7] In spite of the worldwide appeal of Wallace in the nineteenth century, the 'Great Liberator' found it difficult not only to hold on to his international status but also faced increasing marginalisation at home in the period after the First World War. In order to explain this development, it is necessary to examine how the cult of William Wallace was used by Scottish political movements to bolster and add credibility to their respective ideologies. Historical icons are invariably subject to competing claims of ownership from different political movements as a means of conferring legitimacy on particular interpretations of tradition. By appealing to 'tradition', it is possible for political movements to present themselves as upholding values and beliefs that have had longevity in society and, consequently, claim themselves to be the natural heirs of such traditions.

William Wallace was an ideal icon for nineteenth-century Scottish liberalism. This was a man of the people who rose to a position of eminence in spite of the perfidy of the aristocracy.[8] According to one popular historian, John MacIntosh, 'Wallace belonged to the lower class of Scotch nobles [and] kindled in the heart of the nation an unquenchable spirit of resistance to oppression'.[9] Indeed, it is possible to argue that Wallace was a medieval lad o' pairts. He was held up as an emblem of a meritocratic, individualistic Scotland that chimed in well with notions of laissez faire, hence the frequently cited motto 'Liberty and Freedom', which tended to emblazon his statues. The historical consensus regarding Wallace that emerged during the nineteenth century was that he inspired the national awakening of Scotland. His refusal to submit to English domination at his trial, in which he claimed he could not be a traitor to Edward I because he had never owed him allegiance in the first place, demonstrated an unequivocal commitment to the national cause. This set the template for Bruce's campaign, and the victory at Bannockburn was frequently represented as the culmination of the national effort that Wallace had instigated. Scotland's successful defence of liberty in the fourteenth century meant that union would not come through conquest. According to Thomas Carlyle, 'A heroic Wallace, quartered on the scaffold, cannot hinder that his Scotland become, one day, a part of England; but he does hinder that it become on tyrannous unfair terms part of it. . . . If the Union with England be in fact one of Scotland's chief blessings, we thank Wallace that it was not its chief curse.'[10]

Without Wallace there could have been no independent Scotland. Wallace was necessary to build up the Scottish character and identity that would find its historic destiny in the Anglo-Scottish Union. While it was argued that Wallace paved the way for Scotland to grow to maturity in time to capitalise on the Union of 1707 and that at heart he was the embodiment of the Scottish meritocratic culture, most Scots venerated him because he was, without question, a national hero. That in itself was enough.

One intriguing issue is the question of why Wallace was abandoned by the political right after 1918. After all, he was the stuff of right-wing ideology, and certainly the example of contemporary Europe showed that the right was especially adroit when it came to enlisting the support of the national canon of heroes. Furthermore, as the nineteenth century demonstrated, there was no difficulty in casting Wallace as a national hero within a Unionist reading of history. Part of the explanation may lie in the fact that the right in Scotland had been so dominated by the issue of union with Ireland that anything that smacked of nationalism was jettisoned. This was especially the case after the Anglo-Irish War, or the Irish War of Independence. The figure of Wallace was further isolated on the right by the work of a number of Tory historians who downplayed the significance of the Wars of Independence. As Graeme Morton has pointed out, Unionists could use the Anglo-Scottish Wars of the late thirteenth and early fourteenth centuries as a means to make the case that the victory of Scottish independence paved the way for a union of two equals in the eighteenth century rather than an absorption of Scotland into a greater England in the fourteenth century. As such, the maintenance of Scottish freedom would pay dividends when union came about later.

Not all Unionists agreed with this line of thinking, however. The Tory MP for Wigtonshire, Sir Herbert Maxwell, faced opprobrium from his Scottish colleagues in the House of Commons when he dared to suggest that the Scottish victory at Bannockburn had not necessarily been a good thing because it meant centuries of Anglo-Scottish conflict. An English victory, on the other hand, would have brought union centuries earlier.[11] Sir Henry Craik and John Colville were other Scottish Unionists who subscribed to the idea of an earlier union as a missed opportunity in Scottish history.[12] The extent to which the Anglo-Scottish wars were a source of contention in Scottish historical thinking in the late nineteenth and early twentieth centuries has been one that has been downplayed in recent discussions of Scottish historiography.[13] If there were Tory heroes in Scottish history, they increasingly became the Jacobites and the ideal of the loyal clans. The inherent militarism and unthinking obedience associated with Jacobitism had a strong appeal to Unionists.

In the period after the First World War, the Unionists abandoned Wallace to the left and the nationalists. Even with the resurgence of interest in Wallace occasioned by the release of Mel Gibson's *Braveheart*, Scottish Tories struggled to make any capital out of him. This was in spite of the fact that the Lega Norda in Italy and the anti-state right in the United States used Wallace as an icon. Right-wingers all over the world had no problem in seizing the potential qualities of the Great Liberator; only those in his homeland resolutely refused to engage with the myth. The lack of utilisation of the Wallace cult by the Scottish right was one of the great missed opportunities of Scottish political history in the twentieth century. After all, he was the ideal man of action, the touchstone of individualism and meritocracy, and, a real favourite among Tories, a great military leader. As the Duke of Atholl put it:

> Deep humiliation at the hands of Edward I in the time of Balliol, and years of adversity, brought forth Sir William Wallace, and even to-day no song (though written many years later) moves the hearts of Scotsmen more than 'Scots wha hae'. Until that date the courage of the Scots had been squandered in deeds of personal valour, and his loyalty had been misdirected into narrower channels. From that date the magnetic force of Wallace's example, his loyalty to his country, his personal courage, and his ghastly death stirred the people as they had never been stirred before, and imbued the body politic with a national soul.[14]

Perhaps the ambiguities in the Tory relationship with William Wallace can be illustrated by reference to John Buchan. In spite of the obvious dramatic material associated with the Wallace myth, Buchan chose Montrose, probably because of the association with loyalty to the British crown by his Scottish hero: 'I found the Whig historians had dismissed him as at best a bandit of genius, and had beatified the theocrats who opposed him. . . . I came to the conclusion that he was the most balanced and prescient mind in Scotland at the time, as well as the greatest of Scottish soldiers.'[15] The reason why the Unionists abandoned Wallace after the First World War is to be found in the crisis of confidence engendered by the profound social and economic problems experienced during the inter-war period.

Confident pre-war Unionism gave way to one that was dominated by pessimism. The old cliché that the Scots ran the Empire and punched above their weight in the partnership with England gave way to one that stressed Scottish dependency on a more powerful southern neighbour.[16] Effectively, this invalidated the previous notion that Wallace was the initiator of the Wars of Independence that kept Scotland free until it had reached the historical maturity necessary for the 1707 Union of equals. Although much of the negativity emanating from Unionism was driven by economic arguments, it inevitably spilled over into the cultural arena and affected how Scots perceived their history. Indeed, a number of historians actively set out to reverse such pessimistic views of the past, driven, it ought to be remembered, by the need to counteract the belief that prior to 1707 the Scots did not have a history worth celebrating.[17] Furthermore, Unionism was dead set against nationalism and the prospect of Scottish home rule; and the fact that nationalists and socialists were using the legacy of Wallace further distanced Tory association with the Wars of Independence. Home-rulers hit back at the fact that the Scottish establishment issued a declaration against nationalism in 1932 by referring to it as the 'Ragman's Roll': a sardonic reference to the declaration of loyalty by the Scottish aristocracy to Edward I.[18]

The period after the Second World War, likewise, witnessed no serious engagement by the Unionists with the cult of Wallace. Paradoxically, as the party modernised its social composition in the inter-war period by attracting more middle-class businessmen, the post-war period witnessed an aristocraticisation of the party to a greater extent than south of the border. By such time, the idea of Wallace as a man of the people was unlikely to cut much ice within a party that was not only increasingly aristocratic but also largely English-educated.[19] Yet, the potential of Wallace as an icon of the right is revealed by the activities of the shadowy 1320 Club, an extreme nationalist association among whose adherents was Nicholas Fairbairn, the future Conservative MP for Perth and Kinross.[20] A key argument put forward by Scottish Tories in the late sixties and early seventies in opposition to the rise of the SNP was the claim that nationalism could lead to Anglo-Scottish conflict and that the Union had brought all this to an end. A frequently cited term of derision was the expression 'latter-day William Wallaces who want to turn the clock back to the bad old days'. The Tory view of the pre-Union Scottish past was one that tended to revolve exclusively around anti-English sentiment and, as such, could offer no useful pointers for the future.[21] Even when the Scottish Tories, somewhat belatedly, came to accept the legitimacy of Scottish national sentiment within the context of a Unionist settlement, Scotland's great national leader could find no place within Tory hearts. Ian Lang, a former Scottish Secretary of State, argued that Bannockburn and Robert the Bruce were more significant than Wallace on the grounds that Bruce was a winner and Wallace was a loser. Lang went on to bemoan the fact that, when it came to history, the Scots seemed to prefer glorious defeat to victory.[22] Yet, more than anything, Tory ambiguity over Wallace followed from the fact that Unionism during the twentieth century had a blind spot with regard to Scottish history and had effectively abandoned the notion that the Scots took anything of advantage from their history to the Union with England in 1707. It is almost true to say that, in the race to capture the iconic status of Wallace for political purposes, the Conservatives were non-starters.

Both the left and the nationalists used Wallace in the twenties and, for the most part, neither believed it to be a question of exclusive ownership. Until the Labour Party began to have second thoughts over its championship of home rule in the latter part of the decade, nationalism and the left had had a fairly symbiotic relationship. In part, this can be explained by the inheritance of the radical tradition where home rule was part and parcel of a Scottish political culture that also included other Liberal staples such as land reform, temperance and the like. As with other Liberal icons, such as Robert Burns, Wallace was absorbed into a new pantheon of the left. Wallace was 'The great Scottish patriot and lover of liberty who played a very important role in bursting the chains of feudalism and paved the way for the democratic principle in government'.[23] Thomas Johnston, arguably Scotland's most important Labour leader of the first half of the twentieth century, used Wallace as an emblem of the nation's supposed democratic and egalitarian ethos. Wallace was recast as a proletarian leader who sought to break the shackles of feudalism. The battle of Bannockburn, Johnston claimed, was won by the Scottish working class, but it was in vain because Bruce, as his previous machinations proved, was a self-seeking member of the aristocracy:

If at bottom Wallace's revolt was not a last effort to cast off feudalism from Scotland, why did the Scoto-Norman nobles hate him so? It could scarcely have been that they esteemed themselves more 'highly born' than he, for well they knew, most of them, that they were but one or two removes from nondescript barbarism. Yet, that they did hate him is undoubted, and even the two possibly genuine nationalists and English haters among them, Sir Wm. Douglas and Bishop Wishart of Glasgow, ran in haste to meet the English general, Warenne, with the assurance that 'they were no party to the rising of William Wallace'. And when, after success had come failure, was Wallace not deserted 'by all men who had property at stake'? In truth, the 'good king Robert' of our school-books played a most despicable, vacillating, and traitorous part in the by no means clearly defined drama of the times.[24]

Johnston was echoing an increasingly Marxist account of Scottish history that had been promoted in some socialist circles before the First World War. There was opposition to the celebration of the battle of Bannockburn by socialists on school boards who challenged the conventional accounts of Bruce in school textbooks, and John Maclean argued that the battle of 1314 was one fought by serfs for the benefit of a few barons.[25] Labour support for home rule in the early twenties conditioned a promotion of Wallace as a nationalist proletarian hero that was shorn of the difficulties of venerating a feudal magnate in the shape of the Bruce. In the inter-war period other Labour MPs reiterated the view of Wallace as the unambiguous leader of the common folk of Scotland. Speaking during a debate on education in the House of Commons in 1936, James Barr said:

> Why should we speak of William Wallace? I would have every text-book tell of the indictment of Wallace, when he was tried in Westminster Hall on 23 August, 1305. It is no legend that his head was fixed on London Bridge. But I would not have these things taught to bring any animus against England. I would rather have the teacher show that when you behead a man you turn him into a patriot, and you weld his nation together, as was done in that case. The character of Robert the Bruce is a little more dubious in some ways.[26]

Indeed, Barr was known to stop at the tablet in Westminster Hall where the trial of Wallace is supposed to have taken place and ask the Scots to kneel and do homage to Scotland's greatest patriot. On his election as the first SNP Member of Parliament, Robert McIntyre described Westminster as the place where 'they judiciously murdered William Wallace'.

The link with home rule was the most important feature of the venera-tion of Wallace among members of the Labour Party. In 1924, the Scottish Home Rule Association (SHRA), an organisation dominated by the Labour

Party and the Scottish Trades Union Congress, made the anniversary of Wallace's death its most important date in the calendar and gathered at Elderslie to celebrate his life.[27] Among the many speakers who turned out at the annual event were Thomas Johnston, William Adamson (the first Labour Scottish Secretary) and the veteran socialist campaigner R. B. Cunninghame Graham. During the demonstration, the same annual resolution was read out:

> This meeting of the Scottish people – assembled here at Elderslie, the birthplace of Sir William Wallace, Scotland's greatest fighter for national freedom, to commemorate his martyrdom on this . . . Anniversary – pledges itself individually and collectively, to work steadily for National Self-government, until the Scottish people regain full control of their own affairs.[28]

The early Scottish Home Rule demonstrations at Elderslie were fairly anodyne, with most of the day taken up with demonstrations of country dancing, marching pipe bands and choral music, with only a couple of speeches by political figures, most of whom paid tribute to the memory of Wallace but usually in a fairly uncontroversial way. As the Scottish Home Rule Association began to splinter between Labour loyalists and those who demanded a more aggressive policy, the figure of Wallace was increasingly used by those of a more nationalist persuasion. The growing moderation of Labour, together with its increasing equivocation on home rule, meant that the figure of Wallace, quite an uncompromising one, could no longer be safely endorsed. Also, the intellectual drift within the party was one that emphasised centralised economic planning focused on the present.[29] Furthermore, the growth of fascism and nationalism in mainland Europe meant that such associations at home should be denounced on account of their bourgeois sensibilities.[30] Almost by default, the icon of Wallace fell into the hands of the nationalists, dropped by an increasingly timid and centrist Labour Party.

The nationalists had no such ambiguity regarding Wallace. He featured in the early propaganda and literature of the National Party of Scotland (NPS), which was formed in 1928. Also, the NPS took over the Elderslie demonstrations, and these became increasingly politicised as the spirit of Wallace was enthusiastically enlisted for the nationalist cause. At the North Midlothian by-election in February 1929, Lewis Spence, the nationalist candidate, used a poster designed by Wendy Wood, featuring the candidate standing beside the ghost of Wallace with the words 'To the English Parties! Go back to your English masters and tell them we are not here to treat but to FIGHT FOR THE FREEDOM OF SCOTLAND'. Unfortunately, the poster misattributed the words to Wallace before the battle of Falkirk, not Stirling Bridge.[31] The June gathering to celebrate the victory at Bannockburn was the most important event in the nationalist calendar, but due deference was paid to Wallace. The Bannockburn demonstration was baptised 'Scotland's Day' and did not commemorate the battle as Bruce's achievement but rather sought to represent it as a combined national effort. In June 1930, the NPS issued a 'New Covenant' to outline the party's objectives. According to R. B. Cunninghame Graham, arguably the NPS's star speaker:

> We Scottish nationalists are in one thing more fortunate than the Nationalists of other countries. We have for our very own the patriot who has inspired all their movement for Liberty. The real liberator of Scotland was not Bruce. Scottish liberty was not won at Bannockburn. The real liberator was Wallace twenty years earlier, because he liberated the minds of the people from the acceptance of superior force. He liberated them from the alien feudal system in which a succession of Anglicised monarchs had tried to enmesh them. We are the heirs of Wallace. The fight that we are fighting is the same fight that Wallace fought – the fight against the domination from Westminster, even though Scottish representatives were to sit there. Have we too, not to seek to liberate the minds of our fellow-countrymen, aye, and our own minds, from the effects of Anglicised education? For 300 years – because the trouble stems from the Union of the Crowns, when we lost control of our foreign policy, when it went with the king to London.[32]

By 1931, the NPS had added a demonstration in August at the Wallace statue at Robroyston on the Saturday nearest the anniversary of 'the base betrayal of Scotland's national hero'.[33] The NPS used Wallace to promote key political messages and, as such, adapted the Wallace story for its own political ends. The relatively moderate and anodyne Wallace who was a feature of the Labour Party and the Home Rule Association was replaced by one who was altogether much more uncompromising in his quest for independence.

A reprint of an article that first appeared in *Scottish Home Rule* was worked over for inclusion in the *Scots Independent* and had the following paragraph inserted:

1. Wallace was a Nationalist Extremist
There were many half-hearted and fair-weather nationalists in the Scotland of his day, men professing loyalty to the Nationalist cause but ready to desert it in the hour of danger or some poor temptation. Wallace was uncompromising, not afraid of being called extremist, as he doubtless

185

often was. He was for the complete independence of his country and never in the slightest degree trimmed his faith or weakened his purpose. So be it with us. The charge of extremism need not dismay us. It is a tribute of our consistency and courage and vision as it was in the case of Wallace. There are always plenty of men to advise what they call moderation, but moderation is often a moral betrayal of the spiritual vision.[34]

Along with other choice insertions, what the article demonstrates is the way in which the story of Wallace was radicalised in order to suit the political interests of the nationalists. Moderates and waverers were denounced as weak-willed, and the establishment of the day was described as self-serving and venial. The message was clear: that the Scottish enemies of Wallace were the same type of people as the enemies of the NPS. The National Party was predominantly made up of former Labour home-rulers and nationalists of a fundamentalist persuasion who were strongly influenced by the example of Irish nationalism and the ideas of pan-Celticism. Leftist and racialist ideas were combined in their reading of the Scottish past. The theme of betrayal was a favourite one in their reading of history:

> The nobility and gentry were fickle and unreliable, ready to make terms to save their estates and material interests. At Irvine only Sir Andrew Moray of the leading men stood by Wallace; all the rest deserted him. It was the same in 1707; Scotland was betrayed by the titled ones, and Andrew Fletcher carried on the work of Wallace. To-day it is just the same. The great ones stand aloof, because of economic entanglements with England or merely commercial considerations too narrowly regarded.[35]

The comparison of the betrayal of Wallace and the Union of 1707 was a common theme for speakers at Elderslie. R. B. Cunninghame Graham claimed that Elderslie symbolised 'the death of Wallace and the awaking of Scotland to the realisation that she is a separate entity, a separate nation. Fraud and cowardice brought about the Union of 1707'.[36] The Union was represented as a betrayal of the work of Wallace: the same factors that had led to Wallace's betrayal were at work in the nation during the Union negotiations. Furthermore, this group of people in Scottish society was still active, and it was the 'establishment' who were the leading opponents of nationalism as epitomised by the 'Ragman's Roll'. The fact that Scotland's leading aristocrats, nobles and members of the elite had signed a declaration opposing Scottish nationalism was an ideal propaganda weapon for the NPS, who were keen on drawing historic parallels with the time of Wallace. In this way the NPS constructed a view of Scottish history in which the same self-serving aristocrats who put personal gain above national interest undermined the template of Wallace's achievement. In short, to undo the Union of 1707 would be to finish the work of Wallace.

Reflecting a wider debate within nationalist circles, racial notions filtered into the debate regarding Wallace. For one scholar, the racial and ethnic divisions of Scotland were a factor in inhibiting the development of a coherent nationalist movement in the sense that the Scots were divided between Teutons and Celts. Not surprisingly, given that the example of Ireland loomed large in nationalist discourse, with many believing that a racial dimension was a critical factor in Scottish nationalism, efforts were made to Celticise Wallace. This was especially the case among left-wing Celtic nationalists in the early twenties:

> The community will be the ruling power and on the sane and stable foundations of Celtic culture and Celtic communism, from which Wallace drew his inspiration, we who share his convictions and speak his tongue, will use both to work out freedom for our beloved land.[37]

According to H. C. MacNeacail: 'His name shows his Celtic descent. . . . From a passage in "Blind Hary", we may probably infer that Wallace spoke the Celtic tongue then still living in Strathclyde, and from another we know that he wore the Celtic dress.'[38] Celtic nationalists sought to de-Saxonise Wallace, although there is little evidence that racial notions had much impact in the creation of Wallace as a nationalist icon, with most accepting that Scottish ideas of nationalism outweighed the racial combination of the Scots. Indeed, part of Wallace's achievement was the promotion of the idea of a nationalism that could overcome ethnic and racial differences. In a BBC broadcast on 5 November 1929, Compton MacKenzie railed against the division of Scotland into Teutonic and Celtic parts:

> Circumstance and climate may have fostered the development of the two types we recognise as Highlander and Lowlander, but racially the stock is the same. The blood of the Norseman has blended with the Gael and the Pict, even in the outermost islands of the west and that blend modified and preserved by climate and conditions has produced as obstinately characteristic a strain as any in Europe.[39]

Yet, for MacNeacail and some others who wanted to promote the notion of a Celtic Scotland, Wallace could be brought into a Celtic pantheon of heroes who fought Teutonic imperialism:

> With his statesman's vision, he may have also seen the baleful effects of the spread of the Teutonic language in Scotland, and, if he had lived, he might have done much to restore his native Celtic speech to its rightful

place in the lowlands. . . . England, the enemy of all the small nationalities in her path, the enemy of Wales and Ireland as well as Scotland, saw
to that. She sent Wallace off to a shameful death before his work was finished. England has oftimes slain, and even murdered, the patriots. We
think not only of Wallace, but also of Llywelyn and Owain Lawgoch, of
Aedh Ruadh and Padriac MacPiarais, of Jeanne M'Arc and many another.[40]

The image of a kilt-wearing Wallace was not just a latter-day invention
by the film *Braveheart*. The youth wing of the NPS, Clan Scotland, even
went so far as to claim that Wallace wore the kilt and that it was the insults
of the anglicised nobility when he adopted feudal costume that drove him
to fury and back to traditional Celtic garb.[41] Yet, the most important Celtic
comparison was that with the Irish myths that had acted as such a font of
inspiration for Sinn Fein:

As Cuchulain, single-handed, defended the marches of ancient Uladh, so
Wallace, also almost single-handed at times, defended his native land. As
in the case of the great epic hero just mentioned, it might have been said
that the tales of his high deeds shall be told forever, but he shall be short-
lived and fleeting. As with Cuchulain, so with Wallace, a prophet might
have foretold that 'the men of Eire and Alba shall hear that name and the
mouths of the men of Eire and Alba shall be full of that name'.[42]

Too much should not be read into this, however. The most frequent assertion made regarding Wallace's racial origins was that he was of a mixed
background, as was the case with most Scots. William Power, a frequent
speaker at Wallace Day demonstrations, denounced endeavours to divide
the Scots on the basis of racial characteristics. Indeed, the nationalists made
continuous efforts to disregard racial notions and used, after Andrew Lang,
the idea of the nation as the most important component in their construction of Wallace's nationalism. This trend was further confirmed by the publication of Evan Barron's *Scottish War of Independence* in 1934, which put
forward the argument that Scottish nationalism in the thirteenth and
fourteenth centuries embraced both the Highlands and Lowlands. The fact
that Barron was both a Unionist and a Highlander helped his case in the
sense that, as a Gael, he did not try to Celticise the whole of the nation and,
as a Unionist, he applauded the partnership of Celt and Teuton.

The leftist radicalism of the NPS was also reflected in the Wallace
demonstrations. As has been discussed, the motif of aristocratic treachery
was one that not only served as a warning against the dangers of anglicisation but also had undertones of class conflict. This was especially promi-

nent among those who had been former members of the Labour Party and still maintained their socialist credentials. R. B. Cunninghame Graham used his Spanish connections to enlist the support of the Spanish ambassador of the newly created republic at the Elderslie demonstration in 1933. The image of Wallace was closely related to the internal politics of the nationalist movement, and the pro-left and hardline independence stance of the early NPS was reflected in the veneration of the Great Liberator. Moderate nationalism began to assert itself in the leadership of the NPS in the early thirties, largely in response to the emergence of the pro-devolutionist and right-wing Scottish Party in 1932.[43] Moderates in the NPS believed that fundamentalists within the party were putting off the electorate, making a merger with the Scottish Party more difficult. In response, the leadership began a series of purges designed to rid the party of its wilder elements. When the two organisations merged in 1934 to form the Scottish National Party (SNP), moderates were in charge, with official policy on independence watered down to a form of devolution.

Obviously, such a change in political direction had consequences for the image of Wallace within nationalist circles. Could the uncompromising defender of Scottish liberty be recast as a devolutionist? The Elderslie and Robroyston demonstrations continued and still attracted those of a more fundamentalist persuasion, but the coverage given to the Wallace demonstrations dried up in the pages of the party's newspaper, the *Scots Independent*. No mention of the event occurred after the formation of the SNP in 1934. Much of the criticism of the nationalist movement – that it was Anglophobic and backward-looking – had stung, and increasingly the party sought to escape from its '1314 and all that' image. A drive to present the party as moderate and forward-looking resulted in a focus directed more at contemporary Scotland than at past history. Indeed, an emphasis on the present has been one of the abiding characteristics of the SNP up to the present day, in contrast to other nationalist movements. The anachronistic aspect of Wallace and his association with nationalism was captured by two of Scotland's leading leftist writers, Edwin Muir and Lewis Grassic Gibbon (James Leslie Mitchell). In *Gray Granite*, Gibbon puts forward a conventional leftist line of thinking on the nationalist movement:

> Chris minded back to her days in Segget and said that nationalism was just another plan to do down the common-folk. Only this time twas to be done in kilts and hose, with bagpipes playing and a blether about Wallace, the English to be chased over the border and the Scots to live on brose and baps.[44]

A case can be made that there was an increasing association between nationalism and Wallace in Gibbon's mind from the fact that in one of the previous novels of the trilogy, *Sunset Song*, Wallace is mentioned without comment. Yet, writing in 1935, Gibbon still regarded the victory of Bruce as the victory of a 'shoddy, noble adventurer' and one who brought no benefit to the ordinary Scottish people.[45] Muir linked the veneration of Wallace with the insipid Anglophobia of Scottish society. He recounted the story of an old Glaswegian carter who became more morose the more he drank until he slapped his hand on the table and roared 'Wallace; the hero of Scotland. . . . D'ye ken what the English did to him, the dirty bastards. Libbed him.'[46] Although both Muir and Gibbon cast the Reformation as the villain of Scottish history and idealise pre-industrial medieval society, they stop short of support for the Wars of Independence.[47]

Most nationalist commentaries that dealt with history now began their analyses at 1707. Furthermore, as the decade of the thirties progressed, the party began to disintegrate under a confusion of political strategies and objectives as fundamentalists staged a comeback.[48] With the majority of nationalist critiques directed against the Union of 1707, Andrew Fletcher of Saltoun rose towards the top of the nationalist pantheon.[49] Also, Robert the Competitor began to enjoy something of a comeback. Agnes Muir Mackenzie did much to restore the reputation of the king in the thirties, and in the post-war period the *Ladybird* history and Nigel Tranter put Bruce back at the centre of Scotland's War of Independence in the popular mind. In scholarly terms, the publication of Geoffrey Barrow's *Robert Bruce* in 1965 firmly cast the king as the deliverer of Scottish independence. The nationalists themselves did much to remove Wallace from centre stage. The party's moderation, but also its eschewal of republicanism, meant that there was a greater case to be made for Bruce. In spite of shaky genealogy, it could be claimed that the current monarch was a direct descendent of Robert, and therefore the nationalists could still promote the cause of independence without disloyalty to the Crown, as was formally enshrined in the party's constitution of 1946.[50]

During the Second World War the nationalist movement underwent a period of turmoil in which competing moderate and fundamentalist factions sought to establish control. In 1942, the moderates left and went on to form the genesis of what would become the Scottish National Covenant. Moderate nationalism was problematic for the SNP. The Covenant, although ultimately unsuccessful, demonstrated that there was a considerable residue of support for moderate nationalism. Furthermore, the period of the fifties was one in which support for the monarchy remained high, even though the 'theft' of the Stone of Destiny, the Coronation and Queen Elizabeth's numeral caused offence at the casual indifference to Scotland's royal history.[51] The need to court moderate opinion, the general revulsion at extremist nationalism following the Second World War and the belief that it was best to make the case for independence in terms of contemporary social and economic criteria relegated Wallace in nationalist iconography. It may also be the case that as the SNP was not committed to the creation of a Scottish republic, Bruce, an ancestor of the royal family, began to creep back into favour. In terms of nationalist demonstrations, Bannockburn and the celebration of 1314 overshadowed the Elderslie demonstrations in the post-war era. Even at the time of the SNP's electoral breakthrough in the late sixties and the early seventies, the party made little allusion to Wallace and instead focused on issues of a more contemporary nature, such as 'It's Scotland's Oil'. The performance of Sydney Goodsir Smith's *The Wallace* at the Edinburgh Festival in the late sixties further confirmed the widely held assumption that Wallace was firmly the intellectual property of nationalism, with audiences standing up to sing the Scottish national anthem, 'Scots Wha Hae', at the end of performances. The theft of the sword from the Wallace Monument in the seventies demonstrated that some nationalists still attached a great deal of significance to the Great Liberator, but the promotion of Bannockburn as a tourist site further deflected attention away from Wallace. Finally, the SNP's flirtation with a more overt left-wing stance in the eighties and the existence of organisations such as Siol na Gael increased the association between Wallace and extreme nationalism: a position the party leadership endeavoured to reverse.

In addition to the relegation of Wallace in the ranks of the nationalist heroes, further trends within Scottish society in the latter part of the twentieth century contributed to the alienation of Wallace from the historical mainstream. The fact that Scottish history received scant attention in schools and universities did little to help. The intellectual construction of the case for home rule in the eighties was based on notions of civic society that stretched its historical comparison back to 1690 and excluded the Wars of Independence. When *Braveheart* was released, it coincided with a period of demand for constitutional change and a growing upsurge in Scottish history, as well as a Scottish cultural revival generally, but the position of Wallace had been marginalised in the story of the nation to such an extent that it exploded on popular consciousness in a way that few could have predicted. The increasing popularity of Wallace may also have been helped by the fact that, apart from having the stamp of approval from Hollywood in an increasingly globalised world culture, it also coincided with a period when royalism was firmly in retreat throughout the United Kingdom. As the symbolic power of the monarchy declined in the contemporary world, it can be argued, although not demonstrated empirically, so too did the appeal of monarchy diminish in the historical canon. Thus, in the 1990s, reflecting either a growing republican sentiment, a decline in support for the institution of monarchy, or a combination of the two, Wallace was increasingly seen by many Scots as a more appropriate national icon than Bruce for contemporary Scotland. The man of the people knocked King Robert off the top spot in nationalist iconography once again.[52]

William Wallace: A Select Bibliography

Lizanne Henderson

Alexander, Derek and Alan Steel. *Wallace, Renfrewshire, and the Wars of Independence*. Renfrewshire Local History Forum 1997 (Edinburgh, 1997)

Alexander, G. *Sir William Wallace: the Hero of Scotland. An Historical Romance* (London, 1903)

An appeal to Scots and Friends at Home and Abroad for a London Memorial to Sir William Wallace, Scots Patriot (1954) National Library of Scotland

Anderson, David. *The Martial Achievements of Sir William Wallace; an historical play, in five acts and in verse* (Aberdeen, 1821)

Anderson, Lin. *Braveheart: From Hollywood to Holyrood* (Edinburgh, 2005)

Anon. *The Life of Sir William Wallace, the Scots Patriot* (Edinburgh, 1810)

Armstrong, Peter. *Stirling Bridge and Falkirk, 1297–98* (Oxford, 2003)

——. *The Battles of Stirling Bridge and Falkirk: Heraldry, Armour and Knights* (Keswick, 1998)

Ash, M. 'William Wallace and Robert the Bruce: the life and death of a national myth', in *The Myths We Live By*, ed. R. Samuel and P. Thompson (London, 1990)

Bain, J. and J. Paterson. *The Surroundings of the Wallace Monument as seen from the top* (5th edn, 1920)

Barbour, John. *The Bruce*, ed. A. A. M. Duncan (Edinburgh, 1997)

Barbour, John. *The Bruce and Wallace; published from two ancient manuscripts in the Library of the Faculty of Advocates. With notes, biographical sketches, and a glossary [by John Jamieson]* (Glasgow, 1869)

Barrow, G. W. S. *Robert Bruce and the Community of the Realm of Scotland*, 4th edn (Edinburgh, 1992)

Borland, J. C. *William Wallace. His Birthplace and Family Connections* (n.p., 1999)

Bower, Walter. *Scotichronicon*, 9 vols., ed. D. E. R. Watt (Aberdeen, 1987–97)

Brady, Sean. *Wallace. A drama in two acts* (Glasgow, 1998)

Brown, Chris. *William Wallace: The True Story of Braveheart* (Stroud, 2005)

Brown, J. T. T. 'The Wallace and the Bruce Restudied'. *Bonner Beiträge zur Anglistik* (Bonn, 1900)

Brown, Michael. *The Wars of Scotland, 1214–1371* (Edinburgh, 2004)

Brunsden, G. M. 'Aspects of Scotland's Social, Political and Cultural Scene in the Late Seventeenth and Early Eighteenth Centuries, as Mirrored in the

Wallace and Bruce Traditions', in *The Polar Twins*, eds. Edward J. Cowan and Douglas Gifford (Edinburgh, 1999)

Brunton, Alexander. *Life and Heroic Actions of Sir Willliam Wallace, Knight of Elderslie* (Edinburgh, 1863; Glasgow, 1881; Edinburgh, 1883; Inverkeithing, 1883)

Buchan, *Copy of Earl of Buchan's Letter to General Washington, President of the United States of America, sent enclosed in the box of Wallace's oak, June 25th, 1791; contained in The Earl of Buchan's Address to the Americas at Edinburgh on Washington's Birthday, February 22nd* (1811)

Buchanan, Robert. *Wallace: A Tragedy in Five Acts* (Glasgow, 1856; Edinburgh, 1859)

——. *Tragic dramas from Scottish history: Heselrig, Wallace, James the First of Scotland* (Edinburgh, 1859)

Burns, W. 'Association for the Vindication of Scottish Rights' (*c.*1853)

——. *The Scottish War of Independence. Its Antecedents and Effects*, 2 vols. (Glasgow, 1874)

Bute, John Patrick Crichton-Stuart, 3rd Marquis of. *Early Days of Sir William Wallace* (Paisley, 1876)

Calendar of Documents relating to Scotland (CDS), 5 vols., ed. J. Bain *et al* (London, 1881–1986)

Cant, R. G. 'David Stuart Erskine, 11th Earl of Buchan: Founder of the Society of Antiquaries of Scotland', in *The Scottish Antiquarian Tradition: Essays to mark the bicentenary of the Society of Antiquaries of Scotland, 1780–1980*, ed. A. S. Bell (Edinburgh, 1981)

Carnegie, A. *Autobiography of Andrew Carnegie* (Boston and New York, 1920)

Carrick, John Donald. *Life of Sir William Wallace, Knight of Ellerslie and Guardian of Scotland*, 2 vols. (Glasgow, 1827; Edinburgh, 1830; 3rd edn 1849)

Carruth, J. A. *Heroic Wallace and Bruce* (Norwich, 1986)

Child, F. J. *English and Scottish Popular Ballads*, 5 vols. (Boston, 1882–98)

The Chronicle of Lanercost, 1272–1346, trans. H. Maxwell (Glasgow, 1913)

Cochrane, Mary. *Wallace and Bruce, Heroes of Scotland . . . Illustrated* (London and Edinburgh, 1897)

'Colossal Statue of Sir William Wallace', *Gentleman's Magazine*, vol. lxxxvii (1817)

Conditions Relative to Proposed Public Competition for the Wallace and Bruce Memorial. Captain Reid's Bequest, City of Edinburgh (1882)

Cooper, Anthony. *William Wallace. Robin Hood Revealed* (Greenock, 2000)

Correspondence of the Custodians of the National Wallace Monument. 1936–1938, 29 January 1937, 2 April 1937. Stirling Council Archive

Cowan, Edward J. *'For Freedom Alone': The Declaration of Arbroath, 1320* (East Linton, 2003)

——. 'The Wallace Factor in Scottish History', in *Images of Scotland*, eds.

R. Jackson and S. Wood in *The Journal of Scottish Education Occasional Paper*, No. 1 (Dundee, 1997) 5–17

Craigie, William A. *The Actis and Deidis of Schir William Wallace, 1570* (Edinburgh: Scottish Text Society, 1940; New York, 1940)

Craigie, W. A. 'Barbour and Harry as Literature', *The Scottish Review*, Vol. XXII (1893)

Dalrymple, David, Lord Hailes. *Annals of Scotland From the Accession of Malcolme III to the Accession of the House of Stewart*, 3 vols. (Edinburgh, 1776–79)

Davidson, J. M. *Scotia Rediva: Home Rule for Scotland with the Lives of Sir William Wallace, George Buchanan, Fletcher of Saltoun, and Thomas Spence* (London, 1888; 1890; 1893)

Donaldson, P. *The Life of Sir William Wallace, the Governor General of Scotland and Hero of the Scottish Chiefs. Containing his parentage, adventures, heroic achievements, imprisonment and death; drawn from authentic materials of Scottish History* (Hartford, 1825)

Douglas, George A. H. *Sir William Wallace, and other Poems* (Glasgow, n.d. [*c.*1887])

Duncan, Lesley and Elspeth King, eds., *The Wallace Muse: Poems and Artworks inspired by the Life and Legend of William Wallace* (Edinburgh, 2005)

Edensor, T. 'National Identity and the politics of memory: remembering Bruce and Wallace in symbolic space', *Environment and Planning D: Space and Society*, Vol. 15, No. 2 (1997)

——. 'Reading Braveheart: Representing and Contesting Scottish Identity', *Scottish Affairs*, Vol. 21 (1997)

Fergusson, J. *William Wallace: Guardian of Scotland* (London, 1938; Stirling, 1948)

Finlay, J. *Wallace, or the Vale of Ellerslie, with other poems*, 2nd edn (Glasgow, 1804)

Finlay, Richard J. 'Controlling the Past: Scottish Historiography and Scottish Identity in the nineteenth and twentieth centuries', *Scottish Affairs*, No. 9, Autumn (1994)

Fisher, Andrew. *William Wallace* (Edinburgh, 1986; new edn 2002)

Fleming, Maurice. *The Real MacBeth and other stories from Scottish History* (Edinburgh, 1997)

Forbes, George. *William Wallace: Freedom Fighter* (Glasgow, 1996)

Forrest, M. 'The Wallace Monument and the Scottish National Identity', unpublished BA (Hons.) dissertation, University of Stirling, 1993

Four new songs, and a prophecy: I. A song for joy of our ancient race of Stewarts. II. The Battle of Preston, that was fought by his Royal Highness Prince Charles, the 21st of September 1745. III. On an honourable atchievement of Sir William Wallace, near Falkirk. IV. A song, call'd, The rebellious crew. V. A prophecy by Mr Beakenhead, Song 111 [Chapbook] c. 1750

Fraser, J. '"A Swan from a Raven": William Wallace, Brucean Propaganda, and *Gesta Annalia* II', *Scottish Historical Review*, Vol. 81 (2002), 1–22

Fraser, William Crawford. *Crawford: from the burning of the castle by Sir William Wallace to the visit of King Edward VII* (Crawford, 1909)

Fyfe, W. T. *Wallace, the Hero of Scotland* (Edinburgh, 1920)

L. G. M. G. *Authentic Life of Sir William Wallace; with chapter on Traditional Wallace. Compiled from the best authorities* (Dundee, 1877)

Geddie, W., ed., *A Bibliography of Middle Scots Poets: with an introduction on the history of their reputations*. Scottish Text Society, Vol. 61 (Edinburgh, 1912)

The Generous and Noble Speech of William Wallace . . . at the Battle of Falkirk (n.d. [*c*.1707])

Gentleman, Ebenezer. *Wallace and his times . . . Prize essay which gained the silver medal given by the 'Sir William Wallace Lodge of Free Gardeners', Stirling* (Edinburgh, 1858)

Gibson, R. M. *Freedom is a Noble Thing: Scottish Independence, 1286–1329*. Scottish Record Office (Edinburgh, 1996)

Glass, C. G. *Stray Leaves from Scotch and English History, with the Life of Sir William Wallace, Scotland's Patriot, Hero, and Political Martyr* (Montreal, 1873)

Goldstein, R. J. *The Matter of Scotland. Historical Narrative in Medieval Scotland* (Lincoln and London, 1993)

Gourmand, Paul. *William Wallace. Drame en cinq actes, en vers* (Paris, 1898)

Graham, Henry Grey. *William Wallace: The Scottish Patriot / by the Right Rev. Bishop Graham* (Glasgow, n.d. [*c*. 1900])

Grant, A. *Independence and Nationhood: Scotland, 1306–1469* (London, 1984)

Gray, D. J. *William Wallace: the King's Enemy* (London, 1991; 1995)

The Gude Wallace; to which is added Lord Thomas Stuart (Glasgow, n.d. [c. 1840])

Guide to the National Wallace Monument (n.d.), Stirling Public Library

Guide to the National Wallace Monument. Situated on the Abbey Craig near Stirling containing the Great Sword of Sir William Wallace. The Finest View in Scotland (n.d. [*c*.1964])

Hamilton of Gilbertfield, W. *A New Edition of the Life and Heroick Actions of the Renoun'd Sir William Wallace, General and Governour of Scotland. Wherein the Old obsolete Words are rendered more Intelligible; and adapted to the understanding of such who have not the leisure to study the Meaning, and Import of such Phrases without the help of a Glossary* (Glasgow, 1722)

Hamilton, William. *The History of the Life and Adventures and Heroic Actions of the Renowned Sir William Wallace* (Edinburgh, 1816)

Hamilton, William of Gilbertfield, *Blind Harry's Wallace*. Introduced by Elspeth King. Illustrations by Owain Kirby (Edinburgh, 1998)

Harriston, William. *Wallace; or the knight of Ellerslie; a poem; in three parts; [and Proposal, for publishing by subscription, Sir William Wallace, a tragedy, in five acts; specimen pages]* (Glasgow, 1819)

Hearn, J. *Claiming Scotland: national identity and liberal culture* (Edinburgh, 2000)

Henderson, T. E. *Scottish Vernacular Literature: a succinct history* (London, 1898)

Henry, the Minstrel. *Hary's Wallace (vita nobilissimi defensoris Scotie Wilelmi Wallace militis)*, ed. Matthew P. McDiarmid (Edinburgh, 1968–69)

——. *Sir William Wallace: His Life and Deeds* (Glasgow, 1910)

——. *Sir William Wallace* (Abbotsford Series of the Scottish Poets, 1891)

——. *The Actis and Deidis of the Illustere and Vailyeand Campioun Schir William Wallace, Knicht of Ellerslie*, ed. James Moir. Scottish Text Society (Edinburgh, 1885–89)

——. *The life and heroic achievements of Sir William Wallace . . . and the Life of Robert Bruce, king of Scotland: from the original edition in verse* (Aberdeen, 1794; Aberdeen, 1842)

——. *The history of the life and adventures, and heroic actions, of the renowned Sir William Wallace, general and governor of Scotland / wherein the old obsolete words are rendered more intelligible . . . by William Hamilton; to which is annexed, The life and martial achievements of . . . Robert Bruce, King of Scotland; by John Harvey* (Ayr, 1799; Glasgow, 1802; Edinburgh, 1807; Glasgow, 1811; Edinburgh, 1812; Edinburgh, 1816; Edinburgh, 1819; Edinburgh, 1820; Glasgow, 1822)

——. *A new edition; of the life and heroic actions of the renown'd Sir William Wallace general and governor of Scotland / wherein the old obscure words are rendered more intelligible . . . by William Hamilton* (Aberdeen, 1794)

——. *The metrical history of Sir William Wallace, knight of Ellerslie, by Henry, commonly called Blind Harry: carefully transcribed . . . under the eye of the Earl of Buchan. And now printed for the first time, according to the ancient and true orthography. With notes and dissertations* (Perth, 1790)

——. *A new edition of the life and heroic actions of the renown'd Sir William Wallace . . . Wherein the old obscure words are rendered more intelligible . . . by William Hamilton. To which is annexed, the life . . . of . . . Robert Bruce . . . by John Hervey* (Glasgow, 1722; Glasgow, 1756; Dundee, 1770; Aberdeen, 1786)

——. *The ancient and renown'd history of the surprising life and adventures and heroic actions of Sir William Wallace . . .* (Falkirk, 1785)

——. *The life and surprising adventures and heroic actions of Sir William Wallace, general and governor of Scotland. A new edition. Wherein the old obsolete words are rendered more intelligible* (Aberdeen, 1774; Crieff, 1774)

——. *The acts and deeds of the most famous and valiant champion Sir William Wallace . . . Written by Blind Harry in the year 1361. Together with Arnaldi Blair Relationes* (Edinburgh, 1758)

——. *The life and acts of . . . Sir William Wallace, knight of Ellerslie; maintainer of the liberty of Scotland; with a preface containing a short sum of the history of that time* (Glasgow, 1713; Glasgow, 1736; Glasgow, 1747; Glasgow, 1756)

——. *A new edition of The life and heroick actions of the renoun'd Sir William Wallace, general and governor of Scotland / wherein the old obsolete words are rendered more intelligible . . . [by William Hamilton]* (Glasgow, 1722)

——. *The life and acts of the most famous and valiant champion Sir William Wallace, Knight of Ellerslie . . . With a preface containing a short sum of the history of that time*

(Edinburgh, 1640; Edinburgh, 1661; Glasgow 1665; Glasgow 1685; Glasgow, 1699; Edinburgh, 1701; Edinburgh, 1709)

——. *The lyfe and acts of the most famous and valiant Champion, Sir William Wallace . . . Mayntayner of the Liberties of Scotland* (Aberdeen, 1630)

——. *The life and acts of the most famous and valiant Champion, Syr William Wallace . . .* (Edinburgh, 1620)

——. *The lyfe and actis of the maist illuster and vailzeand campioun William Wallace, knicht of Ellerslie, mainteiner and defender of the libertie of Scotland* (Edinburgh, 1594; Edinburgh, 1601; Edinburgh, 1611)

The heroic exploits of Sir William Wallace and King Robert Bruce . . . [Chapbook] (Falkirk, 1813)

The history of the renowned Sir William Wallace [Chapbook] (Edinburgh, *c.*1850)

The History of the Scottish Patriot, Sir William Wallace (Edinburgh, n.d. [*c.*1850])

History of Sir William Wallace: The renowned Scottish Champion [Chapbook] (Glasgow, *c.*1850)

Holford, Miss. *Wallace; or, the Fight of Falkirk: a Metrical Romance* (London, 1809)

Holland, Thomas Agar. *The Colossal Statue of William Wallace: A Poem. By an Undergraduate* (Oxford, 1824)

Holt, J. C. *Robin Hood* (London, 1983)

Holt, Julia. *William Wallace* (Abingdon, 2000)

Hutcheson, Thomas S. *Bibliotecha Wallasiana. List of the various works relating to Sir William Wallace, from 1488 to 1858* (Glasgow, 1858)

[Hutcheson, Thomas Smith] Anon. *Life of Sir William Wallace; or Scotland Five Hundred Years Ago* (Glasgow, 1858) Appendix of *Bibliotheca Wallasiana*

Hutchison, H. S. P. *Six Plays from Scottish History for Amateur Acting* (Glasgow, *c.*1931)

Illustrated Souvenir of the National Wallace Monument, Stirling (Stirling, 1896)

Johnston, W. T. *Wallace and the Hall of Heroes* (Edinburgh, 1992)

Jones, D. A. *Wee Guide to William Wallace* (Edinburgh, 1997)

Justice to Scotland. Report of the Great Public Meeting of the National Association for the Vindication of Scottish Rights, held in the City Hall, Glasgow, December 15 1853

Kamm, Antony and Jennifer Campbell. *Wallace, Bruce and the War of Independence* (Edinburgh, 1996)

Keen, M. *The Outlaws of Medieval Legend* (London, 1961)

Keith, A. *Several Incidents in the Life of Sir William Wallace, with an account of Lanark, the theatre of his exploits, and a description of the romantic scenery in the neighbourhood* (Lanark, 1844)

Kidd, C. 'The Strange Death of Scottish History revisited. Constructions of the Past in Scotland, *c.* 1790–1914', *Scottish Historical Review*, Vol. LXXVI, 201 April (1997)

——. 'Sentiment, race and revival. Scottish identities in the aftermath of

Enlightenment', in *A Union of Multiple Identities. The British Isles, c.1750–c.1850*, eds. L. Brockliss and D. Eastwood (Manchester, 1997)

King, A. 'Englishmen, Scots and Marchers: National and Local Identities in Thomas Gray's *Scalacronica*', *Northern History*, Vol. XXXVI, No. 2 (2000)

King, Elspeth. *Introducing William Wallace: the life and legacy of Scotland's liberator* (Fort William, 1997)

Knightley, C. *Folk Heroes of Britain* (London, 1982)

Lamb, Thomas. *The Life and Death of Sir William Wallace, the hero of Scotland. A Historical Drama, in five acts* (Carluke, 1866; 1867)

The life and adventures of Sir William Wallace, General and Governor of Scotland . . . containing, a particular account of his most remarkable battles with King Edward (Longshanks); and his mournful fate at London, . . . With an account of the Battle of Bannockburn, which was fought June 24th, 1314 (Glasgow, 1801)

The Life and Heroic Achievement of Sir William Wallace, the Scottish Patriot, and the life of Robert Bruce, King of Scotland: from the original verse (Jedburgh, 1845)

Life and Surprising Adventures of that Renowned Hero, Sir William Wallace [Chapbook] (Edinburgh, n.d.)

The Life and surprising adventures of that renowned hero, Sir William Wallace (Otley, c.1860)

Life in the Times of Wallace and Bruce. Dundee College of Education (Dundee, 1979)

The life of the celebrated Scottish patriot Sir Wm. Wallace. Containing an account of his wonderful exploits, and his battles with the English, &c. [Chapbook] (Glasgow, 1852)

Look at the National Wallace Monument. Loch Lomond, Stirling and Trossachs Tourist Board (Doncaster, c. 1994)

Loudon, Crawfuird C. *In Pursuit of William Wallace* (Darvel, c. 1999)

Low, Alexander. *Scottish Heroes: In the Days of Wallace and Bruce* (London, 1856)

McArthur, C. 'Braveheart and the Scottish Aesthetic Dementia', in *Screening the Past. Film and the Representation of History*, ed. T. Barta (Westport, 1998)

——. 'Scotland and the Braveheart Effect', *Journal of the Study of British Cultures*, Vol. 5, No. 1 (1998)

McDiarmid, M. P. *Hary's Wallace (Vita Nobilissimi Defensoris Scotie Wilelmi Wallace Militis)*, 2 vols. (Edinburgh, 1968–69)

——. 'The Date of the *Wallace*', *Scottish Historical Review*, Vol. xxiv (1955)

Macdougall, N. A. T. 'The sources: a reappraisal of the legend', in *Scottish Society in the Fifteenth Century*, ed. J. M. Brown (London, 1977)

McGowan, A. 'Searching for William the Welshman', *The Double Treasure*, No. 22 (1999)

Mackay, J. *William Wallace: Brave Heart* (Edinburgh, 1995; 1996)

McKerlie, P. H. *Sir William Wallace: the Hero of Scotland. Contains Fresh Information about the Traitorous Opposition he had to encounter in his struggle for Scottish Independence* (Glasgow, 1900)

Maclean, Lachlan. *Eachdraidhean-beatha nan Albannach iomraiteach ud Uilleam Vallas, Iain Knox agus Rob Ruadh* (Struibhle, 1912)

McNamee, C. 'Willliam Wallace's invasion of Northern England, 1297'. *Northern History*, Vol. 26 (1990), 40–58

McNie, A. *Clan Wallace* (Jedburgh, 1986)

Macrae, D. *The Story of William Wallace, Scotland's National Hero* (Glasgow: Scottish Patriotic Association, 1905)

McSeveney, Margaret and Elizabeth Roberts. *Wallace's Women. A play in two acts.* Stirling Smith Art Gallery and Museum

Mair, J. *A History of Greater Britain as well England as Scotland compiled from the ancient authorities by John Major* (1521), ed. and trans. A. Constable (Edinburgh: Scottish History Society, 1892) Vol. X

Maxwell, H. E. *The Early Chronicles Relating to Scotland* (Glasgow, 1912)

May it Please your Majesty. The Petition of the undersigned, your Majesty's loyal subjects, inhabiting that part of your Majesty's United Kingdom called Scotland (c. 1854)

Meeting of the Custodians' Committee [National Wallace Monument], Stirling, 12 February 1906

Meeting of the Custodians' Committee [National Wallace Monument], 14 December 1936

Memorial of the Council of the National Association, to the Right Honourable the Lords Commissioners of her Majesty's Treasury, 27 September 1854

The Metrical History of Sir William Wallace, Knight of Ellerslie, by Henry, commonly called Blind Harry: carefully transcribed from the ms. copy of that work in the Advocates' Library, under the eye of the Earl of Buchan. And now printed for the first time, according to the ancient and true orthography. With Notes and Dissertations. In Three Volumes (Perth, 1790)

Millar, Alexander Hastie. *The Story of William Wallace* (Glasgow, 1889)

Miller, J. F. *Blind Harry's Wallace*. Glasgow Bibliographical Society (Glasgow, 1914)

——. 'Some additions to the Bibliography of *Blind Harry's Wallace*'. Read 19 March 1917). *Records of the Glasgow Bibliographical Society*, Vol. VI (Glasgow, 1920)

Moir, J. *Sir William Wallace: a critical study of his biographer Blind Harry* (Aberdeen, 1888)

——. ed. *The Actis and Deidis of the Illustere And Vailyeand Campioun Schir William Wallace, Knight of Ellerslie by Henry the Minstrel, commonly known as Blind Harry* (Edinburgh, 1885–89)

Morrison, Dorothy. *The Wars of Independence* (London, 1996)

Morton, Graeme. *William Wallace: Man and Myth* (Stroud, 2001)

——. 'The Most Efficacious Patriot: the heritage of William Wallace in nineteenth-century Scotland'. *Scottish Historical Review*, Vol. LXXVII, 2. No. 204 (1998)

——. Review: 'Sir William Wallace and other tall stories (unlikely mostly)', *Scottish Affairs*, No. 14 (Spring 1996)

Murison, A. F. *Sir William Wallace: Guardian of Scotland* (Edinburgh, 1898; New York, 2003)

National Wallace Monument. Official Papers and Newspaper Extracts relating to the Wallace Monument Movement kept by Wm. Burns

National Wallace Monument. Stirling: Minute Book kept by William Burns. Minutes of the meeting held at Glasgow 1 May 1856

Neilson, G. 'On Blind Harry's, *Wallace*' in *Essays and Studies* (by members of the English Association), Vol. I (Oxford, 1910)

'A New Work'. Answer to the Pamphlet, 'Wallace on the Forth', proving the stratagem at Stirling Bridge and that the Bridge was at Kildean, etc. Also the history of the famous Battle of Stirling Bridge, to which is added two letters written by Sir William Wallace himself, and Wallace's charter to Scrymgeour of Dundee (Dunfermline, 1841; Stirling, 1861)

Ohlgren, Thomas H., ed., *Medieval Outlaws: ten tales in modern English* (Stroud, c.1998)

Paterson, J. *Wallace and His Times* (Edinburgh: William Paterson, 1858)

———. *Wallace, the Hero of Scotland.* 3rd edn (Edinburgh, 1881)

Porter, J. *The Scottish Chiefs and the Heroism of Sir William Wallace* (Wakefield, c.1880)

Power, William. *Official Guide to the National Wallace Monument* (Stirling Town Council, n.d.)

Prestwich, M. C. *Edward I* (New Haven and London, 1988)

———. 'England and Scotland during the Wars of Independence', *Scottish Historical Review*, Vol. LXV (1986)

———. *War, Politics and Finance under Edward I* (London, 1972)

Prospects of the Scottish Home Rule Association (Edinburgh, 1892)

Red Lion, *Scotland and 'The Times'. To the editors of the 'Edinburgh Evening Post' and the 'Scottish Record'* (1853)

Reese, Peter. *Wallace: A Biography* (Edinburgh, 1996)

Ritchie, William Kidd. *Scotland in the Time of Wallace and Bruce* (London, 1970; 1971; 1974)

Rogers, Charles. *The Book of Wallace in Two Volumes* (Edinburgh, 1889)

———. *Stirling: The Battle Ground of Civil and Religious Liberty* (London and Stirling, 1857)

Rosebery, Lord. *In Memory of Sir William Wallace: Address by Lord Rosebery* (Stirling, 1897)

———. *Wallace, Burns, Stevenson: Appreciations by Lord Rosebery* (Stirling, 1905)

Ross, D. R. *In Wallace's Footsteps: A Guide to Places Associated with the Life of William Wallace* (Glasgow, n.d.)

———. *On the Trail of William Wallace* (Edinburgh, 1999)

Sawers, P. R. *Footsteps of Sir William Wallace. Battle of Stirling: Or, Wallace on the Forth* (Glasgow, 1856)

'Scheme of the Acting Committee'. National Monument to Sir William Wallace on the Abbey Craig near Stirling (n.d. [*c.* 1856])

Schofield, W. H. *Mythical Bards and the Life of Sir William Wallace* (Cambridge, Mass., 1920)

Scotichronicon, by Walter Bower, ed. D. E. R. Watt (Aberdeen, 1991–98), 9 vols. [Wallace material is in Vol. 6]

Scotichronicon, Jobannis de Fordun Chronica gentis Scotorum, ed. W. E. Skene (Edinburgh, 1871), Vol. 1

Scotland During the Wars of Independence: a teacher's resource book (Central Regional Council, 1984)

Scotland in the time of Wallace and Bruce: a teaching pack for P6-S1 pupils (Aberdeen, 1996)

Scotland in 1298: Documents relating to the campaign of Edward the First in that year, and especially to the Battle of Falkirk, ed. H. Gough (Paisley, 1888)

Scotland Yet! An Address Delivered by the Revd James Barr, B.D., at the Wallace Monument, at Elderslie, on 27 August 1921; and now reprinted from the 'Forward' of September 3, 1921 (Glasgow, 1921)

Scott, Tom. *Tales of Sir William Wallace, guardian of Scotland, freely adapted from The Wallas of Blind Hary* (Edinburgh, *c.*1981)

Scott, Sir Walter. *Tales of a Grandfather* (Edinburgh, 1828)

The Scottish Hero Wallace, and his period (Edinburgh, 1847?)

Scottish Historical Pageant to be held at Craigmillar Castle (13–16 July 1927, in aid of the Queen Victoria Jubilee Institute for Nurses (Scottish Branch), Official Souvenir Programme

Seal, G. *The Outlaw Legend. A cultural tradition in Britain, America and Australia* (Cambridge, 1996)

Shade of Wallace, The: A poem (Glasgow, 1807)

Shearer's Illustrated Souvenir of the National Wallace Monument, Stirling (Stirling, 1896)

Sibbald, J. *Chronicle of Scottish Poetry from the Thirteenth Century to the Union of the Crowns, to which is added a glossary*, 4 vols. (London, 1802)

Siddons, Henry. *William Wallace; or, The Highland Hero. A tale founded on historical fact*, 2 vols. (London, 1791)

Some Records of the Origin and Progress of the National Wallace Monument Movement, initiated at Glasgow in March 1856 (printed for private circulation, 1880)

Speidel, Theodor. *Wallace, der schottische Held. Inaugural dissertation* (Bayreuth, 1911)

Spence, James Lewis Thomas Chalmers. *The Story of William Wallace* (London, 1919)

Stevenson, J., ed., *Documents Illustrative of Sir William Wallace, his Life and Times*, 2 vols. (Edinburgh, 1841; 1870)

Story of Wallace (Scottish Patriotic Association, n.d.)

Sub-committee appointed by a General Committee of Subscribers at Edinburgh, for carrying into execution the design for erecting a National Monument in Scotland in Commemoration of the Triumphs of the Late War by Sea and Land (Edinburgh, 1822)

Subscription Schedule for the National Monument of Sir William Wallace on the Abbey Craig, Near Stirling (n.d.)

Taylor, J. *Pictorial History of Scotland* (London, 1859)

Telfer, Glenn. *William Wallace: A Scots Life* (Glendaruel, 1995; 1996; 1998)

Traditions, etc. respecting Sir William Wallace; collected chiefly from publications of recent date/by a former subscriber for a Wallace monument. [Major-General Yuille] (Edinburgh, 1856)

The Tragedy of the Valiant Knight Sir William Wallace to which is prefixed a brief Historical Account of the Knight, and his Exploits for the Delivery of Scotland, and added a more particular Account of the way which he was betrayed into the hands of the English (Glasgow, 1815?)

Tranter, Nigel. *The Wallace* (London, 1975)

Traquair, P. *Freedom's Sword* (London, 1998; 2000)

Tytler, P. E. *Lives of the Scottish Worthies* (London, 1831), Vol. 1

Waddie, Charles. *Wallace or The Battle of Stirling Bridge: An Historical Play in Five Acts* (Edinburgh, 1890)

Walker, Thomas. *Sir William Wallace, his life and deeds . . . in modern prose* (Glasgow, 1910)

Wallace and Bruce, a poem (n.d. [c.1825])

Wallace Commemoration Day, Saturday, 26 August, 1933, Held at Wallace Monument, Elderslie. Official Souvenir Programme

'Wallace Statue Appeal by the Saltire Society, Edinburgh'. Designed and published by Clydesdale District Council (c. 1992)

Wallace, or, the Vale of Ellerslie with Other Poems (Glasgow, 1802)

Wallace, the Hero of Scotland, a drama, in three Acts: Adapted to Hodgeson's Theatrical Characters and Scenes in the Same (London, 1822)

Wallace, the Hero of Scotland; or Battle of Dumbarton, An Historical Romance in which the love of liberty and Conjugal Affections are exemplified in the characters of Sir William Wallace and Lady Wallace, with the unparalleled Bravery of the former against a band of Ruffians in the rescue of the Earl of Mar, and his revenge on the governor of Lanark for the Murder of Lady Wallace (London, n.d. [c. 1825])

Wallace; or the life and acts of Sir William Wallace, of Ellerslie. By Henry the Minstrel. Published from a manuscript dated MCCCLXXXVIII, ed. J. Jamieson (new edn, Glasgow, 1820, 1869)

Wallace, Randall. *Braveheart* (London, 1995)

Watney, John. *William Wallace. Braveheart* (Andover, c.1997)

Watson, Fiona. 'The Enigmatic Lion. Scotland, Kinship and National Identity in the Wars of Independence', in *Image and Identity*, eds. Dauvit Broun, Richard J. Finlay and Michael Lynch (Edinburgh, 1998)

——. *Under the Hammer: Edward I and Scotland, 1286–1307* (East Linton, 1998)

Watson, J. S. *Sir William Wallace, the Scottish Hero: A narrative of his Life and Actions, chiefly as recorded in the Metrical History of Henry the Minstrel on the authority of*

John Blair, Wallace's Chaplain, and Thomas Gray, Priest of Liberton (London, 1861)

William Wallace: National Hero of Scotland. Scottish Secretariat (Glasgow, 1955?)

William Wallace: National Hero of Scotland, Special Commemorative Publication to Mark the 650th Anniversary of his Martyrdom (Glasgow, 1955)

William Wallace Album, Sir, Wallace Monument Stirling, Bridge of Allan, Dunblane, Doune, Callander, The Trossachs, and Loch Katrine (Stirling, n.d. [*c*.1904])

Wyntoun, Andrew of, *The Orygynale Cronykil of Scotland*, ed. David Laing, 3 vols. (Edinburgh, 1872) [Wallace material in Vol. 2]

Young, A. *Robert the Bruce's Rivals: The Comyns, 1212–1314* (East Linton, 1997)

Young, Alan and Michael J. Stead. *In the Footsteps of William Wallace* (Stroud, 2002)

Young, D. C. C. *William Wallace and this War*. Speech at the Elderslie Commemoration (1943)

Yule, General Patrick. *A Former Subscriber for a Wallace Monument, Traditions, etc., respecting Sir William Wallace. Collected Chiefly from Publications of Recent Date* (Edinburgh, 1856)

VIDEORECORDING

Braveheart (Twentieth Century Fox, 1995), motion picture. Directed by Mel Gibson

The Three Lives of William Wallace (Saltire Films, 2005). Directed by Ross Harper

William Wallace: The True Story (Cromwell Films, 1998). Directed by Jock Ferguson

WORLD WIDE WALLACE

http://ctc.simplenet.com/braveheart

http://historymedren.about.com/homeword/history,edrem/library.movies

http://mccoist.hypermart.net/wallace.html

http://world-interactive.com/armory/Indexes/scottish_sword_index.htm

http://www.bbc.co.uk/history/scottishhistory/independence/features.independence.wallace.html

http://www.biggar-net.co.uk/wallace700

http://www.braveheart.co.uk

http://www.clan.com/history/menu.html

http://www.clannada.org/docs/wallace.htm

http://www.drcelt.com/celtictreasure.sirwilwal.html

http://duncans-of-scotland.com/independence.html

http://www.freedom-scotland.demon.co.uk

http://www.highlanderweb.co.uk/wallace/thetruth.html

http://www.impressions.uk.com/castles/castle_8.html

http://www.macbraveheart.freeserve.co.uk/about.htm

http://www.nms.ac.uk/mos
http://www.scotlandspast.org/wallaceID1.asp
http://scotsmart.com/info/histfigures/wallace.html
http://www.scottishradiance.com/wallrev.htm
http://silcom.com/~manatee.mackay_wallace.html
http://www.rchams.gov.uk
http://snp.org.uk

Abbreviations

PRIMARY

Alison, *Autobiography* — Archibald Alison, *Some Account of My Life and Writings: An Autobiography* (Edinburgh, 1883)

APS — *The Acts of the Parliaments of Scotland*, eds. T. Thomson and C. Innes, 12 vols. (Edinburgh, 1814–75)

Barbour, *Bruce* — John Barbour, *The Bruce*, ed. A. A. M. Duncan (Edinburgh, 1997)

Bellenden, *Chronicles* — John Bellenden (trans.), *The Chronicles of Scotland compiled by Hector Boece*, eds. E. C. Batho and H. Winifred Husbands (Scottish Text Society, 1938–41)

CDS — *Calendar of Documents relating to Scotland*, ed. J. Bain, 5 vols. (Edinburgh, 1881–1986)

Chron. Bower — Walter Bower, *Scotichronicon*, ed. D. E. R. Watt, 9 vols. (Aberdeen and Edinburgh, 1989–98)

Chron. Fordun — John of Fordun, *Chronica Gentis Scotorum*, ed. W. F. Skene (Edinburgh, 1871–2)

Chron. Guisborough — *The Chronicle of Walter of Guisborough*, ed. H. Rothwell (Royal Hist. Soc., Camden 3rd series, 1957)

Chron. Lanercost — *Chronicon de Lanercost*, ed. Joseph Stevenson (Maitland Club, 1839)

Chron. Rishanger — *Willelmi Rishanger . . . Chronica et Annales regnantibus Henrico Tertio et Edwardo Primo*, ed. H. T. Riley (Rolls Series, 1865)

Chron. Wyntoun — *The Original Chronicle of Andrew of Wyntoun*, ed. F. J. Amours (Scottish Text Society, 1903–14)

Chron. Wyntoun (Laing) — Andrew of Wyntoun, *The Orygynale Cronykil of Scotland*, ed. D. Laing (Edinburgh, 1872–79)

Hamilton, *Wallace* — William Hamilton of Gilbertfield, *Blind Harry's Wallace*, introduced by Elspeth King (Edinburgh, 1998)

Hary, *Wallace* — Blind Hary, *Wallace*, ed. Matthew P. McDiarmid (Scottish Text Society, 1968–69)

Mair, *History* — John Mair, *A History of Greater Britain* (Scottish History Society, 1892)

Palgrave, *Docs. Hist. Scot.* — *Documents and Records Illustrating the History of Scotland*, ed. F. Palgrave (London, 1837)

PRO — Public Record Office (now the National Archives)

RMS — *Registrum Magni Sigilli*

Rogers, *Autobiography* — Charles Rogers, *Leaves from My Autobiography* (London, 1876)

Rogers, *Wallace* — Charles Rogers, *The Book of Wallace* (Edinburgh, 1889)

Scalacronica — *Scalacronica, by Sir Thomas Gray of Heton Knight* (Maitland Club, 1836)

Stevenson, *Documents* — *Documents Illustrative of the History of Scotland from the death of King Alexander the Third to the accession of Robert the Bruce, 1286–1306*, ed. Joseph Stevenson (Edinburgh, 1870)

Stevenson, *Wallace Docs.*   *Documents Illustrative of Sir William Wallace, His Life and Times*, ed. Joseph Stevenson (Maitland Club, 1841)

SECONDARY

Ash, 'Wallace and Bruce'   Marinell Ash, 'William Wallace and Robert the Bruce: the life and death of a national myth', in Raphael Samuel and Paul Thompson, eds., *The Myths We Live By* (London, 1990)

Barrow, *Bruce*   Geoffrey Barrow, *Robert Bruce and the Community of the Realm of Scotland* (London, 1965; rev. ed., Edinburgh 1976, 1988)

Cowan, *Freedom*   Edward J. Cowan, *'For Freedom Alone': The Declaration of Arbroath, 1320* (East Linton, 2003)

Fisher, *Wallace*   Andrew Fisher, *William Wallace* (Edinburgh, 1986; 2nd edn 2002)

Fraser, 'A Swan from a Raven'   James E. Fraser, '"A Swan from a Raven": William Wallace, Brucean propaganda, and *Gesta Annalia* II', *SHR*, lxxxi (2002)

Grant, 'Scottish Peerage'   Alexander Grant, 'The Development of the Scottish Peerage', *SHR*, lvii (1978)

Hanham, *Scottish Nationalism*   H. J. Hanham, *Scottish Nationalism* (London, 1969)

Morton, *Unionist Nationalism*   Graeme Morton, *Unionist Nationalism: Governing Urban Scotland, 1830–1860* (East Linton, 1999)

Morton, *Wallace*   Graeme Morton, *William Wallace: Man and Myth* (Stroud, 2001)

Nicholson, *Later Middle Ages*   Ranald Nicholson, *Scotland: The Later Middle Ages* (Edinburgh, 1974)

Prestwich, *Documents*   M. C. Prestwich, *Documents Illustrating the Crisis of 1297–8 in England*, ed. M. C. Prestwich (Royal Hist. Soc., Camden 4th ser., 24, 1980)

Prestwich, *Edward I*   M. C. Prestwich, *Edward I* (London, 1988)

SHR   *Scottish Historical Review*

Watson, *Hammer*   Fiona Watson, *Under the Hammer: Edward I and Scotland, 1286–1307* (East Linton, 1998)

Watson, 'Sir William Wallace, etc'   J. S. Watson, *Sir William Wallace, the Scottish Hero: A narrative of his Life and Actions* (London, 1861)

Notes

Abbreviations are listed on pages 206–7

CHAPTER 1 (COWAN)

1 Some of what follows is drawn from Cowan, 'The Wallace Factor in Scottish History', in Robin Jackson and Sydney Wood (eds.), *Images of Scotland, The Journal of Scottish Education*, Occasional Paper Number One', 5–17, and Cowan, *Freedom*, 20–9, 72–6.

2 Stevenson, *Wallace Docs.*, 33.

3 On which see Dauvit Broun, 'A new look at *Gesta Annalia* attributed to John of Fordun' in Barbara E. Crawford (ed.), *Church, Chronicle and Learning in Medieval and Early Renaissance Scotland: Essays presented to Donald Watt* (Edinburgh, 1999), *passim*. In their respective contributions below Professor Duncan cites this text as 'Fordun', while Dr Grant prefers *Gesta Annalia* II.

4 For a recent assessment of these battles see Peter Armstrong, *Stirling Bridge and Falkirk 1297–98*, illustrated by Angus McBride (Oxford, 2003).

5 *Chron. Fordun*, ii, 321–32.

6 David Ross, pers. comm. See now David R. Ross, *For Freedom: The Last Days of William Wallace* (Edinburgh, 2005).

7 *Chron. Wynton* (Laing), ii, 339–49.

8 *Chron. Bower*, Vol. 6, 83.

9 *Chron. Bower*, Vol. 6, 93.

10 Hary, *Wallace*, vi.

11 Mair, *History*, 176–95.

12 George Buchanan, *The History of Scotland*, 4 vols., trans. James Aikman (Glasgow, 1827), Vol. 1, 401–14.

13 See the Preface to his edition of *The Wallace, The Bannatyne Miscellany*, Vol. 3, Bannatyne Club (Edinburgh, 1855).

14 William Robertson, *The History of Scotland*, 3 vols. (1759: London, 1809), Vol. 1, 212.

15 David Hume, *The History of England*, 8 vols. (London, 1823), Vol. 1, 312.

16 John Hill Burton, *The History of Scotland from Agricola's Invasion to the Extinction of the Last Jacobite Insurrection*, new edition, 8 vols. (Edinburgh, 1876), Vol. 2, 180–1.

17 G. M. Brunsden, 'Aspects of Scotland's Social, Political and Cultural Scene in the Late Seventeenth and Eighteenth Centuries, as Mirrored in the Wallace and Bruce Traditions', in *The Polar Twins*, ed. Edward J. Cowan and Douglas Gifford (Edinburgh, 1999), 88–9. On this topic see also J. F. Miller, 'Blind Harry's "Wallace"', Glasgow Bibliographical Society (Glasgow, 1914), *passim*.

18 J, Moir (ed.), *The Actis and Deidis of the Illustere and Vailyeand Campioun Schir William Wallace*, Scottish Text Society (Edinburgh, 1889) xiii.

19 James Hogg, *Memoirs of the Author's Life & Familiar Anecdotes of Sir Walter Scott*, (ed.) Douglas S. Mack (Edinburgh, 1972), 8.

20 Blind Harry, *The Wallace*, ed. Anne McKim, Canongate Classics (Edinburgh, 2003), 175.

21 Hamilton, *Wallace*, 103.

22 Walter Scott, *Tales of a Grandfather Being Stories Taken from Scottish History*, First Series, 3 vols. (London and Glasgow, 1923), Vol. 1, 61–2.

23 *History of Sir William Wallace the Renowned Scottish Champion* (Glasgow), Printed for the Booksellers. Glasgow University Library Bh.13–*c*.13.

24 Hogg, *Memoirs*, 130.

25 F. Groome, *Ordnance Gazetteer of Scotland*, 3 vols. (Edinburgh, 1886), Vol. 1, 377; Robert Burns, *The Complete Letters of Robert Burns*, ed. James A. Mackay (Alloway, 1987), 131.

26 Charles Rogers, *The National Wallace Monument. The Site of the Design* (Edinburgh, 1860), 14.

27 Lord Rosebery, *Wallace, Burns, Stevenson* (Stirling, 1912), 12.

28 George Eyre-Todd (ed.), *The Glasgow Poets Their Lives and Times*, 2nd edn (Paisley, 1906), 190–1.

29 John D. Carrick, *Life of Sir William Wallace of Elderslie* (Glasgow, 1827), 5th edn n.d., iii.

30 David Dalrymple, Lord Hailes, *Annals of Scotland From the Accession of Malcolme III to the Accession of the House of Stewart to which are added Several Valuable Tracts relative to the history and antiquities of Scotland, A New Edition*, 3 vols. (Edinburgh, 1797), Vol. 1, 269, 311.

31 James Paterson, *Wallace The Hero of Scotland* (Glasgow, 1881), xii, xvi, xviii.

32 [Thomas Smith Hutcheson], *Life of Sir William Wallace; or Scotland Five Hundred Years Ago* (Glasgow, 1858), vii.

33 William Burns, *The Scottish War of Independence*, 2 vols. (Glasgow, 1874), Vol. 1, 1–2.

34 Miss Holford, *Wallace; or, The Fight of Falkirk; A Metrical Romance*, 2nd edn (London, 1810), 16–17.

35 Lachlan Macquarie, *Lachlan Macquarie Governor of New South Wales Journals of his Tours in New South Wales and Van Diemen's Land 1810–1822* (Sydney, 1956), 67.

36 'A Sporting Nation: Donald Dinnie' by Gordon Dinnie, www.bbc.co.uk.

37 Lesley Duncan and Elspeth King (eds.), *The Wallace Muse: Poems and Artworks inspired by the Life and Legend of William Wallace* (Edinburgh, 2005), 67.

38 Robyn Annear, *Nothing But Gold: The Diggers of 1852* (Melbourne, 1999), 294–301.

39 Eyre-Todd (ed.), *Glasgow Poets*, 437–8. For a selection of the other poets mentioned see *The Wallace Muse*.

40 Edward J. Cowan, *Scottish History and Scottish Folk, Inaugural Lecture, Chair of Scottish History and Literature, University of Glasgow, 15 March 1995* (University of Glasgow, 1998), 3ff.

41 Elspeth King, *Introducing William Wallace: The Life and Legacy of Scotland's Liberator*, Stirling Smith Art Gallery and Museum (Stirling, 1997).

42 Alasdair Cameron, 'Scottish Drama in the Nineteenth Century' in *The History of Scottish Literature*, Vol. 3, *The Nineteenth Century*, ed. Douglas Gifford (Aberdeen, 1988), 437.

43 Charles Waddie, *Wallace or The Battle of Stirling Bridge: An Historical Play in Five Acts* (Edinburgh, 1890), 64.

44 Sydney Goodsir Smith, *Wallace: A Triumph in Five Acts* (Edinburgh, 1960), 169–70.

45 Alexander Brunton, *A New Edition of The Life and Heroic Actions of Sir William Wallace, Knight of Elderslie, in Three Parts* (Glasgow, 1881), 147–50. See also 91–138, 151–203.

46 Lin Anderson, *Braveheart: From Hollywood to Holyrood* (Edinburgh, 2005).

47 This is the version of Wallace's speech as rendered by Buchanan, *History of Scotland*, trans. Aikman, Vol. 1, 406–7.

48 Sallust, *The Jugurthine War: The Conspiracy of Cataline*, trans. S. A. Sanford (London, 1963), 99–100, 117–20.

CHAPTER 2 (WATSON)

1 There is, of course, a limit to the detail that can be set down here. The only really credible biography of Wallace is by Andrew Fisher.

2 I am not denying that Wallace was, technically, of noble blood. But I suspect his status was nearer the salt than the high table, and it is certainly the case that he has been turned into a 'common' man, not least by Mel Gibson in *Braveheart*.

3 It may well be, for example, that the battle of Loudon Hill described by Hary in fact incorporates recollections of the one fought by Bruce in 1307; see Hamilton, *Wallace*, 23–9.

4 Interestingly, John Mair, who published his history in 1521, notes that: 'This William was one of a family of only inferior nobility in the district of Kyle, in which the surname is common', Mair, *History*, 195. Despite associating his family with Elderslie, which was in Renfrewshire, Hary also has one of his characters, Corspatrick (supposedly the Earl of Dunbar), describe Wallace as 'King of Kyle', Hary, *Wallace*, 111.

5 *CDS*, 191.

6 Stevenson, *Documents*, 31–2.

7 *Chron. Guisborough*, 294; Prestwich, *Documents*, 73. I am ignoring the fact that an uprising took place in the northwest Highlands at least as early as March 1297.

8 *Chron. Wyntoun* (Laing), ii, 342; *CDS*, ii, no. 1497, p. 418; Hary, *Wallace*, 24–5.

9 *Chron. Guisborough*, 295–6; Stevenson, *Documents*, ii, 192.

10 *Chron. Guisborough*, 294. Hary certainly describes Wallace taking and burning Kinclaven after coming to Perth, Hary, *Wallace*, 37–8.

11 *Rotuli Scotiae in Turri Londinensi et in Domo Capitulari Westmonasteriensi Asservati* (*Rot. Scot.*), i, ed. D. Macpherson *et al.* (London, 1814–19), 42; *The Scots Peerage*, ed. Sir J. Balfour Paul (Edinburgh, 1904–14), iv, 10; *Liber Quotidianus Controtulatoris Garderobiae, 1299–1300*, ed. J. Topham *et al.* (London, 1787), 101.

12 *Rot. Scot.*, i, 40; Prestwich, *Edward I*, 418–19; *Rerum Britannicarum Medii Aevi Scriptores, Memorandum de Parliamento, 1305*, ed. F. W. Maitland (London, 1893), no. 280, no. 302; *Calendar of Close Rolls, 1296–1302*, ed. H. C. Maxwell-Lyte (London, 1906), 108; *CDS*, ii, pp. 198, 210; *Rot. Scot.*, i, 32; *CDS*, ii, no. 894. Edward I thanked a number of loyal Scots for their help against this rebellion on 13 June 1297. These men were all from Dumfriesshire, clearly implying that the far southwest was the theatre of war.

13 *Chron. Guisborough*, 299.

14 *Rot. Scot.*, i, 41; Stevenson, *Documents*, ii, 175, 210; *CDS*, ii, no. 922; Stevenson, *Documents*, ii, 233; *CDS*, ii, no. 1737; *Rot. Scot.*, i, 42; Stevenson, *Documents*, ii, 217–18; *CDS*, ii, no. 971.

15 Hary, *Wallace*, 105; *Memo. de Parl.*, no. 356.

16 *Chron. Wyntoun* (Laing), ii, 343–4.

17 Stevenson, *Documents*, ii, 201–2.

18 Edward was still on the Continent, fighting, rather ineffectually, against France.

19 *Rot. Scot.*, i, 49–50.

20 Stevenson, *Documents*, ii, 232.

21 Murray's wounds at Stirling Bridge challenge any view that he subsequently played an active role in the affairs of state.

22 Prestwich, *Edward I*, 479; Public Record Office, London (PRO) Exchequer, Queen's Remembrancer, Various Accounts, E101/6/35, mm.7, 9; E101/354/31/2.

23 *Chron. Guisborough*, 304–7; Barrow, *Bruce*, 93.

24 *Chron. Guisborough*, 313–15; Prestwich, *Edward I*, 479.

25 It is to be doubted whether Edward I would have taken such a defeat lying down. It is possible, however, that the damage done to his reputation within the context of the already volatile political situation in England might have made it difficult for him to continue with his Scottish wars.

26 *Docs. Hist. Scot.*, Palgrave, i, 332, 339.

27 Stevenson, *Documents*.

28 *Parliamentary Writs and Writs of Military Summons*, ed. F. Palgrave (Record Commission, 1827–33), i, 312–16.

29 Only three days before the two sides did actually meet at Falkirk.

30 *Scotland in 1298: Documents relating to the campaign of Edward the First in that year, and espe-cially to the Battle of Falkirk*, ed. H. Gough (Paisley, 1888), 129.

31 *Chron. Guisborough*, 326.

32 *Chron. Lanercost*, 191; *Chron. Guisborough*, 325–8; J. E. Morris, *The Welsh Wars of Edward I* (Oxford, 1901), 66.

33 *Chron. Wyntoun* (Laing), 348.

34 *Chron. Rishanger*, 188; *CDS*, iv, Appendix 1, no. 7; *Chron. Guisborough*, 328–9; *Lib. Quot.*, 101.

35 PRO, King's Remembrancer's Memoranda Rolls, E159/72, m.12.

36 Sir Malcolm Wallace's presence in Bruce's retinue perhaps lends credence to the view that it was the future king who had bestowed the honour of knighthood on Sir William and his elder brother.

37 *CDS*, ii, no. 1949.

38 The obvious deduction to be made is that Wallace did not have the permission of Sir John Comyn, the Guardian whose supporter made all the fuss, but he must, therefore, have had the permission of the other Guardian, Bruce. It is to be wondered, if the event was accurately reported, what the Comyns were afraid of.

39 Fisher, *Wallace*, 96; Barrow, *Bruce*, 168.

40 Stevenson, *Documents*, 163.

41 Barrow, *Bruce*, 95, 119. For a fuller discussion of these issues, see Watson, *Hammer*, chs. 5, 6.

42 Sir John was a key follower of Comyn and indeed was singled out by King Edward, together with the Guardian, for having 'been more concerned to harm and travail the king and his people and [having] done worse than the others'. Palgrave, *Docs. Hist. Scot.*, i, 296–8.

43 PRO, E159/76, m.18.

44 PRO, E101/11/21, mm.55–59; *CDS*, i, no. 1390.

45 Stevenson, *Documents*, ii, 492–4.

46 *CDS*, ii, nos. 1437, 1465; Stevenson, *Documents*, ii, 467–70.

47 *CDS*, iv, p. 475. The lands of Happrew did, in fact, belong to Fraser.

48 H. G. Richards and G. Sayles, 'The Scottish Parliaments of Edward I', *SHR*, xxv, 311.

49 *CDS*, ii, no. 1424.

50 Bruce's youngest brother was currently a member of the Prince of Wales' house-hold, PRO, E101/364/13, m.96; *CDS*, ii, no. 1516.

51 *CDS*, ii, no. 1564.

52 Palgrave, *Docs. Hist. Scot.*, i, 276.

53 Watson, *Hammer*, 187.

54 See Fiona Watson, 'Settling the Stalemate: Edward I's peace in Scotland, 1303–1305', in M. Prestwich, R. Britnell, R. Frame (eds.), *Thirteenth Century England VI* (Woodbridge, 1997).

55 Palgrave, *Docs. Hist. Scot.*, i, 283–5; PRO, E159/79, m.30.

56 *CDS*, iv, no. 477.

57 We should note that one John of Musselburgh made Wallace and Fraser's where-abouts known to government forces immediately prior to Happrew, receiving 10s. for his pains. He was certainly not a noble, *CDS*, iv, 475.

58 Barrow, *Bruce*, 136–7.

59 For a fuller discussion of the whole horrific and vexed issue of Wallace's execution, see Watson, *Hammer*, 211–14, as well as Fisher, *Wallace*, ch. 10.

CHAPTER 3 (DUNCAN)

1 A valuable recent short account with full references is Morton, *Wallace*: 'Scotland is

again hunting the snark, the true history of Wallace, although, to be fair, this time there are real sitings to go on', p. 32. For a shorter treatment, E. J. Cowan, 'The Wallace Factor in Scottish History', *Images of Scotland*, ed. R. Jackson and S. Wood (Dundee, 1997), 5–17; also for an argument that Robert I's support had a hand in moulding the repute of Wallace, Fraser, 'A Swan from a Raven'.

2 The date of Murray's death is not recorded.

3 It must be said that the canon's safe-conduct is not copied in full in the chronicle, where the text opens: *Andreas etc.* But this presumes repetition of the opening of the previous letter of protection. The safe-conduct's date is also omitted and could have been later than that of the protection. Fraser has Murray incapacitated and Wallace in command of this invasion, but also has the letters 'appear to name Murray as the leader of the invasion', 'creating the impression that Murray was understood to have been . . . in command', 'A Swan from a Raven', 3, 8, 7. An impression, an understanding, now or then? There is a convincing account of the 1297 invasion stressing the indiscipline of the Scots, the economic motives for widespread plundering and the poor strategic grasp of the Scottish command, by C. J. McNamee, 'William Wallace's Invasion of Northern England in 1297', *Northern History*, xxvi (1990), 40–58. He discusses the 1298 Stainmoor campaign on pp. 54–5.

4 *Chron. Guisborough*, 305.

5 *Chron. Guisborough*, 277 confirmed by *Chron. Lanercost*, 174–5; the latter says nothing of destruction at Hexham in 1297. Discussion in M. Strickland, 'A Law of Arms or a Law of Treason? Conduct of War in Edward I's Campaigns in Scotland, 1296–1307', *Violence in Medieval Society*, ed. R.W. Kaeuper (Woodbridge, 2000), 44–7.

6 J. Anderson, *Diplomata Scotiae*, no. XLIII, reproduced in *APS*, i, 452–3 and in National Manuscripts of Scotland, i, p. xiv, and here (plate 6). Text only in *Wallace Docs.*, 161–2. Anderson's practice was to engrave seals after, but not attached to, the document. His engraving of the Franco-Scottish treaty of 1295 is followed by a fragment of King John's seal, that of the Wallace letter by a complete seal of John on cords. The best evidence is that the matrix of this seal had been destroyed, so the engraving misleads here. The Scrymgeour letter itself claims to carry the 'common seal of the kingdom', which must surely have been, or been like, the (lion rampant) obverse of the seal used on the Lübeck letter discussed below. In Wallace's titles Anderson clearly shows *ductor exercitus*; the reading of *Wallace Docs.*, 161, *ductor exercituum*, is an error.

7 When Wallace rebelled, he called the exiled to him 'and was made *quasi princeps*' of them, *Chron. Guisborough*, 294; those condemned to exile by the English chose Wallace, *eligentes in principem*, Nicholas Trivet: Annales [*Annals Trivet*], ed. T. Hog, Rolls Series (London, 1845), 356. Trivet was summarising Guisborough.

8 *Chron. Fordun*, i, 328. The hostility here may be somewhat exaggerated, but English sources comment on the gulf between Wallace and the nobility; cf. the assessment in Fraser, 'A Swan from a Raven'.

9 Trivet and Rishanger added Murray and Wallace to Guisborough's list of the Scottish commanders at Irvine, an error, but one that shows their growing reputations about that time: *Annals Trivet*, 357; *Chron. Rishanger*, 172. Murray's only occurrence in Guisborough is in the Hexham writs; he is not in the index of *Chron. Guisborough*.

10 *Chron. Lanercost*, 190. The claim (twice) by Fraser, 'A Swan from a Raven', 9, 16, that Gray, in his *Scalachronica*, says 'explicitly that [Wallace] was not the leader' at Stirling Bridge, is incorrect. The source of the error is Maxwell's translation: 'Wallace, to whom the Scots adhered, immediately after this discomfiture, followed . . . Warenne . . .' (*Scalacronica*, 19). In the printed French (*Scalacronica*, 124), the first comma is

there but not the second one; even if the MS has two punctuation marks, they will not bear the weight of the proposed interpretation. Gray clearly regarded Wallace as commander of the Scots at Stirling.

11 *Chron. Fordun*, i, 329. *Cecidit vulneratus*, which does not mean that he was wounded and died later.

12 *CDS*, ii, no. 1178.

13 The word used for leader changed from *dux* to *ductor*, but I doubt if this is significant.

14 *Chron. Guisborough*, 307–8 for the attacks by Clifford on Annandale. *Chron. Bower*, vi, 89–93, 239. Fisher, *Wallace*, 66–70, and Reese, *Wallace*, 64–70, make no mention of the 1298 Stainmoor episode.

15 Rather than *portando vexillum exercitus Scocie*.

16 Mathew of Westminster, *Flores Historiarum*, 3 vols, Rolls Series (London, 1890), iii, 98; *Wallace Documents*, 17. I have preserved the ambiguity of the Latin as to whether Sir William or his unnamed son carried the banner. The description of King John suggests a Scottish source.

17 This is his description in the Scrymgeour charter.

18 Palgrave, *Docs. Hist. Scot.*, 347. The banner was presumably lost, perhaps destroyed, at the battle of Methven.

19 P. Contamine, *Guerre, état et societé à la fin du Moyen Âge* (Paris, 1972), 671–3.

20 *Regesta Regum Scottorum, v, The Acts of Robert I*, ed. A. A. M. Duncan (Edinburgh, 1988), nos. 131, 251, 323.

21 *Chron. Bower*, vi, 83–4, new passage on 236. Bower assumes that Wallace was Guardian from the time of Stirling Bridge. The opening words of the new passage are *Non tam eleccione quam . . . divina provisione . . . custos regni deputatus est*. It is possible that the recognition of Guardianship was given at St Andrews.

22 *Chron. Guisborough*, 314–15; *Chron. Lanercost*, 190.

23 *Chron. Rishanger*, 384.

24 G. F. C. Sartorius, *Geschichte des Hansischen Bundes* (Göttingen, 1802–08), i, 352.

25 G. F. Sartorius, *Urkundliche Geschichte des Ursprungs der deutschen Hanse, herausgegeben von J. M. Lappenberg* (Hamburg, 1830). The letter is in Vol. ii, no. LXXXVIII, pp. 188–9, the corrections on p. 736.

26 'Our Scottish Antiquarian friends will be gratified to hear that Dr Lappenberg of Hamburg in his researches among the ancient records of that city has discovered a letter of date of 1287 [*sic*] addressed by Robert Wallace [*sic*] and Andrew Murray to Hamburg and Lubeck. Many English records are also among the number of his discoveries . . .' *Foreign Quarterly Review*, iv (1829), 685.

27 *Life of Wallace*, ii, 192. In the 1840 (unchanged text) edition, the Appendix with text is on pp. 112–14. The *Life* itself is a rehash of Hary's *Wallace*.

28 *Wallace Docs.*, no. XV, p. 159 and n. The lithograph is frontispiece and the account of it is on pp. xxxii–xxxiii.

29 *Urkundenbuch der Stadt Lübeck*, i (Lübeck, 1843), no. DCLXVIII, pp. 599–600. I refer to this edition below, n. 36.

30 For a readable account of the event, Perilla Kinchin and Juliet Kinchin, *Glasgow's Great Exhibitions, 1888. 1901. 1911. 1938. 1988* (Bicester, no date), 95–125; it mentions on p. 100, 'the letters [sic] of Sir William Wallace'. The late J. D. Mackie vividly recalled trying to lecture on Scotland and Sweden to an ever-moving throng of passers-by in the Palace of History. Unfortunately, the file of correspondence for this exhibition was stolen from the Mitchell Library in 1971.

31 *Scottish Exhibition of National History, Art and Industry, Glasgow (1911): Palace of History, Catalogue of Exhibits* (Glasgow, Edinburgh and London, 1911). The contents of this Palace were insured for £459,000 (George Eyre-Todd, *Leaves from the Life of a Scottish Man of Letters* (1934), 171–81 at 176). I am unsure whether the original hope was

for one chair of history and literature as is usually said; in 1911 the usual approach to literature was historical. The sponsors certainly asked the University for two chairs when handing over the money (£20,000), but unsuccessfully. See also Edward J. Cowan, *Scottish History and Scottish Folk*, Inaugural Lecture, Chair of Scottish History and Literature, University of Glasgow 15 March 1995 (Glasgow, 1998), 3–10.

32 See Plate 5. It is Archiv der Hansestadt Lübeck, Urkunden, Anglicana 12a. This unfortunate reference was probably given in the nineteenth century. For the controversy over the absence of the letter from the new Museum of Scotland, see, e.g., Morton, *Wallace*, 30–1. There is more to be said on this episode.

33 All the evidence discussed by James W. Dilley, 'German Merchants in Scotland, 1297–1327', *SHR*, xxvii (1948), 142–55, comes from the reign of Edward II. The letter is not discussed in D. Ditchburn, *Scotland and Europe*, i (East Linton, 2000).

34 National Archives, Kew, E101/684/5/6. The keeper of the Wardrobe and Reginald de Thonderle, a London merchant, repaid the money to Viricus Huske and Wilhelm Beyr, merchants of Lübeck acting on behalf of their associates, *tam citra mare quam ultra*, who made the loan. Some lenders were presumably based in London, but all would be German.

35 The full place date is *apud Hadsingtonam in Scocia*, where *in Scocia* was presumably included for recipients unfamiliar with rural Scottish towns. It was not an error, for the use of *Scocia* for Scotland north of the Forth was then obsolescent.

36 The edition in *Urkundenbuch der Stadt Lübeck*, i, 599–600 carries the remark (in German), 'Of the two seals, the first is no longer on the tag, the second, next to it, is well preserved', followed by a description of the existing seal. A seal that disintegrates will nonetheless leave a shadow of its former existence; there is no such shadow of a first seal on the tag of the Lübeck letter.

37 J. H. Stevenson and M. Wood, *Scottish Heraldic Seals*, i (Glasgow, 1940), 25.

38 The letters in italics would be abbreviated in the legend.

39 Its legend was SIGILLVM SCOCIE DEPVTATVM REGIMINI REGNI. The broken matrix was in the English treasury, but there would be numerous impressions in Scotland.

40 Mitchell Library, B 313539. See Plate 4. A slight scratch, made since I saw the casts in 1999, reveals the copper. The casts cannot be removed from their setting. The weight of casts and wood (about 170 ccs) is about 4 grams, of which I reckon less than half represents the wood.

41 He is in the 1908 *P. O. Directory* under Dentistry (not Dentists) at what is probably his parents' address. In 1909 he had moved to a tenement flat at 7 Lochburn Road (running eastwards off Maryhill Road by the canal) and remained there with his wife until 1929, but in 1930, when she is not mentioned, had moved to Jardine Street. He disappears after 1931. In the Voters' Roll 'Peter S. Rae' is 'Dental Mechanic' in 1912, but at some time thereafter he qualified (presumably by apprenticeship) as a dentist, his description in the 1920s; he is absent from the statutory register of practising dentists in 1926. We owe the Wallace cast entirely to his skill as a dental technician but do not know whether he was active in the 1911 exhibition, nor how he obtained access to the seal. Possibly he had little connection until commissioned to make the casts by someone of influence among the exhibition promoters.

42 Ashby McGowan, 'Searching for William the Welshman', *The Double Tressure*, no. 22 (1999), 62–73.

43 See the illustration in Matthew Strickland and Robert Hardy, *The Great Warbow: From Hastings to the Mary Rose* (Sutton, 2005), 161.

44 Stevenson and Wood, *Scottish Heraldic Seals*, i, 25, lists this among royal privy seals, from casts in Lyon Office. It appends a fairly long and misleading essay that offers,

among other information, the reading by the Inspector of Ancient Monuments (then James Richardson) of the legend on the reverse, as VSTI . . . VSA . . . W . . . where T is a misreading of F. It is said that the charge on the reverse, previously described as 'two hands shooting an arrow from a bow', is doubtful, that the device is unlike any known seal of the period but appears to be in the style of an earlier seal; and that possibly the device is a crossbow. The following paragraph in this account has more nonsense, but the letters read are almost correct: VSFI[LI]VSA[LANI]W[ALAIS]. There is a wholly inaccurate reading in A. Young and M. J. Stead, *In the Footsteps of William Wallace* (Stroud, 2002), 31.

45 There is no impression of his seal but his father's is described by W. R. Macdonald, *Scottish Armorial Seals*, no. 2052, and is illustrated in *CDS*, ii, plate I, no. 5.

46 *CDS*, ii, 193–6; *Inst. Pub.*, 61–113.

47 The towns were treated separately; *CDS*, ii, nos. 813–15, 819–20, as were some religious houses.

48 *CDS*, ii, 196–214, and nos. 746–820; *Inst. Pub.*, 115–74.

49 Dr McAndrew points out that the first seals on each string relate to the earlier names on the document, but that the rest are in no order; article cited below, 672.

50 *CDS*, ii, no. 826. *Anglice* an inquest *post mortem*.

51 The origin of the name and word is obscure: *Oxford English Dictionary*, under 'ragman'.

52 Adam mac Gillemuire (FILIVS GILMORI) on his seal (no. 1350) is fitz Grimbaud on RR: *CDS*, ii, 202; *Inst. Pub.*, 137.

53 Bruce A. McAndrew, 'The sigillography of the Ragman Roll', *Proceedings of the Society of Antiquaries of Scotland*, Vol. 129 (1999), 663–752.

54 These figures are approximate.

55 There is no other large collection of seals of one date. For a good collection (282 seals) covering a broad timespan, W. Greenwell and C. Hunter Blair, 'Durham Seals, V, Scottish Private Seals', *Archaeologia Aeliana*, third series, xii (1915), 287–332.

56 As did those who assessed the holdings of Elena la Zouche. One example: Henry le Ferur (a smith) from Tranent whose device was a hammer (no. 3225) and who sat on the assize of Edinburgh sheriff court to retour Elena's holdings in that sheriffdom (*CDS*, ii, no. 824 (3)).

57 I do not think that all were crown tenants, for the obligation of a crown tenant was usually to send a suitor to the sheriff court, who could be one of his own tenants; personal presence would be demanded annually only at the three head courts.

58 For example, Elys the gate-keeper ('le porter' text, IANITOR seal) of Rutherglen, device a bird on a twig (*CDS*, ii, 201; seal no. 1308). I give the numbers as in McAndrew's list; from his 3000 remove the first figure 3 to find the number in Bain's Appendix III list.

59 National Archives, Kew, E39/102/18. I am indebted to Mr Adrian Ailes of the Archives for identifying this document from the account given in *CDS*, ii, 533–4, no. 3. The list of seals in *CDS* is inaccurate in some respects. Thus, nos. 42 and 43 are duplicates of no. 33 (not 37) (McAndrew disagrees and I have not been able to check), 51 of no. 22 (not 27). McAndrew nos. 1301–1368, but the last two figures do not exactly correspond to Bain's numbering on pp. 533–4.

60 In *CDS*, ii, it is Appendix I, no. 3 – whence its seals are numbered by McAndrew from 1301.

61 *CDS*, ii, 201–2; *Inst. Pub.*, 136–7.

62 For example, from the Edinburgh list, Alan of Liberton, *CDS*, ii, 199, 201, seals nos. 3362, 3377, but neither of these seals (both of Alan but with different devices) can have come from Text 13, and Alan had either two seals or a relative of the same name. Hugh Ridel, *CDS*, ii, 194, 198, 201; seal survives only on 13, no. 1310.

William de Drilaw, *CDS*, ii, 199, 201; identical seal survives from both documents, nos. 1325, 3396.

63 The Ayrshire names found elsewhere are John de Crawford, *CDS*, ii, 202, 214; seals nos. 1322, 1411 (with different devices); Thomas Winchester, *CDS*, ii, 194, 202; seal no. 1314. In addition, the last name in 13, Patrick le Archer (*CDS*, ii, 202) has a seal with device of a stringed horn and bow and arrow (correcting Bain and McAndrew), legend (S PATRICII ARCHER) in mirror image (no. 1336). McAndrew identifies a seal reading . . . CHER (no. 1321, omitted by Bain between his nos. 17 and 18 on *CDS*, ii, 533) with Patrick, but the charge (a trefoil) differs from Patrick's.

64 *CDS*, ii, 205–6; *Inst. Pub.*, 148–9. McAndrew identifies the seal ROG WALAYS (no. 3339) with Nicol le Waleys of RR; this seal is indeed preserved on a string with two others of names found among the 75 in RR with Adam and Nicholas Wallace. It is difficult to believe that Roger could be miscopied as Nicol. A Sir Alan Wallace witnessed a charter of the Bishop of the Isles in the 1230s, *Paisley Reg.*, 135–6. An Ayrshire contemporary was Adam Wallace, *ibid.*, 19, 24, 225.

65 The invaluable discussion by P. D. A. Harvey, 'Personal Seals in Thirteenth-Century England', *Church and Chronicle in the Middle Ages*, ed. I. Wood and G. A. Loud (London, 1991), 117–27, deals with this phenomenon in England (p. 125) but the whole article is a challenge to study non-armigerous seals in Scotland.

66 *CDS*, ii, 201–2, 205; *Inst. Pub.*, 137, 147. The seals of the St Andrews text do not seem to have survived as a group.

67 *Chron. Fordun*, i, 328; ii, 321.

68 Young and Stead, *Footsteps of William Wallace*, 33–4; *Chron. Guisborough*, 294, 296; *Chron. Lanercost*, 190; *Flores Historiarum*, iii, 123. *Lanercost* makes James Stewart call Wallace *ribaldus*, a menial, rascal, the description in the Royal MS chronicle (*Wallace Docs.*, 144). Interestingly, Gray's *Scalacronica* has no harsh words on Wallace.

69 *Chron. Rishanger*, 383–4, *Wallace Docs.*, 8–9: *sagittarius qui arcu et pharetra victum querebat; de infima progenie et exili ortus et educatus, cum audaciam suam in multis locis examinasset, ut mos est virorum fortium, petivit a Scotis licentiam ut Anglicanis posset obviare, necnon eorum exercitui arcu suo resistere* . . . It is uncertain whether 'the way of strong men' qualifies 'audacity' or 'leave'.

70 *CDS*, ii, 191.

71 *CDS*, ii, 202 at middle, p. 534, no. 32 and in McAndrew's list, no. 1336. I have not found anything comparable in R. Ellis, *Catalogue of Seals in the Public Record Office, Personal Seals*, save in Vol. ii, no. P942, the seal of Roger Archer, serjeant at arms, in 1350, displaying a shield of arms, including three arrow-heads.

72 For what follows I owe a great debt to R. Hardy, *Longbow: a social and military history* (Sparkford, 1992) and to discussions with my colleague, Dr Matthew Strickland, who kindly let me see *The Great Warbow*, cited above, note 43, before publication.

73 See the measured examples in J. D. G. Clark, 'Neolithic Bows . . . and the Prehistory of Archery in North-western Europe', *Proceedings of the Prehistoric Society*, new ser. 29 (1963), 50–98; from eighth-century Swabia, G. Rausing, *The Bow, some notes on its origin and development* (Lund, 1967), 60; a tenth-century bow from Hedeby (192 cm tall), E. Roesdahl, *The Vikings* (London, 1998), 143.

74 Hardy, *Longbow*, 150–1.

75 Hardy, *Longbow*, 217.

76 *Chron. Wyntoun*, v, 298, line 1990; 306, line 2085 (without manlyk); 307, line 2125.

77 Ultimately from Pseudo-Turpin. *Chron. Bower*, vi, 83, 234–5; ii, 173, 261–2.

78 Hary, *Wallace*, book 10, lines 1224–30.

79 Hary, *Wallace*, book 4, lines 548–51.

80 These statements about Cressingham's skin are made in chronicles and were not repeated in the charges of 1305.

81 This phrase is used in the letters appointing the justices; it is unusual.

82 They make no mention of 'treason' by that name.

83 *The Brut*, ed. Brie, I, 222, cited in J. G. Bellamy, *The Law of Treason in England in the Later Middle Ages* (Cambridge, 2004), 49.

84 Dr Paul Brand confirms this to me, noting that it would certainly not be in Latin and could 'just possibly' have been in English – but that Wallace stood a better chance of understanding the French than English. He had, it was alleged, 'spared none who used the English tongue' when invading England.

85 J. Bellamy, *The Law of Treason in England in the Later Middle Ages* (Cambridge, 1970), 26. Unlike the Wallace trial, there is no record evidence for that of David, and our source, a chronicler, may have misattributed penalties to offences.

86 Barrow, *Bruce*, 136–7; Bellamy, *Law of Treason*, 36–9; Fisher, *Wallace*, ch. 10; there is also a good account in C. Knightly, *Folk Heroes of Britain* (1982).

87 *Devaletur*, but *devaleo* does not occur in the dictionary; read *divelletur*, from *vellere*, to pluck, tear out.

88 J. G. Edwards, 'The treason of Thomas Turberville', *Studies in Medieval History presented to F. M. Powicke*, ed. R. W. Hunt *et al*, 296–309.

89 This verb has been dropped by the copyist of the text.

90 From Latin *mica*, small pieces, whence *micare*, to break into pieces, *Dictionary of Medieval Latin from British Sources*, i, 667. I am grateful to Dr David Howlett for confirming this definition.

91 In *Wallace Documents*, 191, the word is wrongly printed as *frustratim*.

92 *Chron. Fordun*, i, 328.

93 *Chron. Wyntoun*, v, 318–19; an alternative of the second line reads 'Great tales, I heard say, are made'.

94 mother.

95 In the exchange (*Chron. Wyntoun*, v, 298–303) I have updated the Scots somewhat to make it more readily intelligible. The sword was a *double entendre* (not in DOST) for the penis; see Hary, *Wallace*, book 6, line 143. The woman is described as Wallace's *leman*; in Hary, *Wallace*, she is his wife.

96 Curiously, Hary has Wallace kill the young Heselrig but makes no mention of the sheriff.

97 *Chron. Wyntoun*, v, 304–5. I have modernised the text here; the alternative reading is 'I shall now quit it'.

98 Hary, *Wallace*, book 6; at line 156 he writes of 200 men, although it is not clear to me whether these are Wallace's or English.

99 E. L. G. Stones (ed.), *Anglo-Scottish Relations, 1174–1328* (Oxford, 1970), no. 33.

100 *defuncti corpus . . . membratim vel in frustra immaniter concidentes.*

101 *Les Registres de Boniface VIII*, ed. G. Digard *et al*, ii, col. 576–7, no. 3409. For a full discussion, see Elizabeth A. R. Brown, 'Death and the Human Body in the later Middle Ages: The Legislation of Boniface VIII on the division of the corpse', *Viator* xii (1981), 221–70, reprinted in her *The Monarchy of Capetian France and Royal Ceremonial* (Aldershot, 1991), no. VI.

102 The practice was much less usual in England than on the Continent.

103 That Edward I ordered similar exequies for himself, his bones to lead the army into Scotland, is a much later fiction: Prestwich, *Edward I*, 557.

104 J. H. Denton, *Robert Winchelsey and the Crown, 1294–1313* (Cambridge, 1980), 219–39.

105 Morton, *Wallace*, 53–5.

106 Bellamy, *Law of Treason*, 33–9; Barrow, *Bruce*, 178–9; Fisher, *Wallace*, ch. 10.

107 Fenchurch.

108 This work (*attach*' in the patent roll) has many meanings, and while it could possibly be the record of Wallace's arrest, it could also mean 'object seized as exhibit'. I suggest that here it means the documents taken with Wallace at his arrest.

109 This verb is missing in the Latin text.
110 *congregationes.*
111 *concorditer et animose*, a phrase that seems out of place.
112 Smithfield Elms.
113 Perth.

CHAPTER 4 (PRESTWICH)

1 *Chronicles of Edward I and Edward II*, ed. W. Stubbs, i (Rolls Series, 1882), 140.
2 Prestwich, *Documents*, 104; Stevenson, *Documents*, 207.
3 Stevenson, *Documents*, ii, 192–4, 198–200; Barrow, *Bruce*, 119–20.
4 J. E. Morris, *The Welsh Wars of Edward I* (Oxford, 1901), 160, 247.
5 *Chron. Guisborough*, 294.
6 Stevenson, *Documents*, ii, 222–4.
7 Barrow, *Bruce*, 123.
8 *Chron. Guisborough*, 299–303. Some chronicles simply ignored the battle, such as the *Annales Angliae et Scotiae*, in *Chron. Rishanger*, 383–4; and that from Hagnaby, British Library Vespasian B. xi, f 41v.
9 *Chron. Guisborough*, 302. Marmaduke Thweng held estates close to Guisborough Priory: *Chron. Guisborough*, xxviii. See also M. C. Prestwich, 'An Everyday Story of Knightly Folk', *Thirteenth Century England* IX, ed. M. C. Prestwich, R. H. Britnell, R. F. Frame (Woodbridge, 2003), 152, 157.
10 *Chron. Rishanger*, 179–80.
11 *Scalacronica*, 124.
12 *Chron. Bower*, 87.
13 J. Beverley Smith, *Llywelyn ap Gruffudd, Prince of Wales* (Cardiff, 1998), 563. Another similarity that might be noted is that between William Latimer, who swam on his horse to safety when the English were attacked while crossing from Anglesey in 1282, and the unnamed knight who saved himself in similar fashion at Stirling Bridge: Walter of Guisborough, 219–20, 302.
14 *Chron. Guisborough*, 300–1.
15 N. B. Lewis, 'The English Forces in Flanders', 310–18.
16 Bartholomaei de Cotton, *Historia Anglicana*, ed. H. R. Luard (Rolls Ser., 1859), 337.
17 *Chron. Guisborough*, 303. For Cressingham's corrupt methods as steward to Queen Eleanor, see J. C. Parsons, *Eleanor of Castile* (New York, 1995), 108.
18 *Langtoft*, ed. Thiolier, 388.
19 W. P. Hedley, *Northumberland Families* (Newcastle upon Tyne, 1968), i, 146; Barrow, *Bruce*, 130 n. A poem on the Scottish war regretted the deaths of Vescy, Morley, Somerville and Bertram, but of these, only Somerville died at Stirling Bridge: *Political Songs*, ed. T. Wright (Camden Soc., 1839), 173.
20 K. DeVries, *Infantry Warfare in the Early Fourteenth Century* (Woodbridge, 1996), discusses these and other battles of the period.
21 *Chron. Guisborough*, 302–3.
22 Prestwich, *Edward I*, 385.
23 *Chron. Guisborough*, 219.
24 Smith, *Llywelyn ap Gruffudd*, 537–42.
25 Peter of Langtoft, *Edition critique et commenté de Pierre de Langtoft: le règne d'Edouard Ier*, vol. 3 (Paris, 1989), 336.
26 *Political Songs*, 171.
27 *Chron. Bower*, vi, 89.
28 The events of the period 1294–98, here briefly summarised, are discussed in Prestwich, *Edward I*, 376–435.
29 Prestwich, *Documents*, 100, 104–5.

30 Prestwich, *Documents*, 117.

31 Prestwich, *Documents*, 137–8.

32 *Parliamentary Writs*, i, 56–64.

33 *Calendar of Close Rolls, 1296–1302*, 129.

34 The National Archives (formerly Public Record Office), SC 6/1087/17.

35 Prestwich, *Documents*, 149.

36 *The Chronicle of Bury St Edmunds, 1212–1301*, ed. A. Gransden (London, 1964), 143–4; Prestwich, *Documents*, 32–3.

37 *Calendar of Patent Rolls, 1292–1301*, 391.

38 *CDS*, ii, no. 946.

39 Prestwich, *Documents*, 151.

40 M. C. Prestwich, 'Edward I and Adolf of Nassau', *Thirteenth Century England III*, ed. P. Coss and S. D. Lloyd (Woodbridge, 1991), 132–3. The bad news that Adolf was not coming, and had insufficient troops with him, came in a letter sent to Edward from the Rhineland on 15 October: Prestwich, *Documents*, 161.

41 Prestwich, *Documents*, 110–12, 158–60.

42 *Calendar of Patent Rolls, 1292–1301*, 312–4; Prestwich, *Edward I*, 478–9.

43 *Chron. Guisborough*, 315.

44 The Scottish raid is fully discussed by C. McNamee, 'William Wallace's Invasion of Northern England in 1297', *Northern History* (1990), 40–58.

CHAPTER 5 (BROADIE)

1 An important Scottish source of biographical information about Scotus is Mair, *History*, 206–7. Mair confirms that 'when he was no more than a boy', Scotus was taken to Oxford by two Franciscan friars after he had received a grounding in Latin grammar. At that time there was no university in Scotland. He might otherwise have continued his studies in his native country.

2 A. Broadie, *Why Scottish Philosophy Matters* (Edinburgh, 2000), 34.

3 Scotus, at that time teaching in Paris, took the side of the pope and as a result had to go into exile. John Duns Scotus, *John Duns Scotus' Political and Economic Philosophy* (St Bonaventure, NY, 2001), ed. Allan B. Wolter, viii–ix (hereinafter Scotus).

4 For the texts of these declarations, see A. A. M. Duncan, 'The Declarations of the Clergy, 1309–10', in *The Declaration of Arbroath: History, Significance, Setting*, ed. Geoffrey Barrow, Society of Antiquaries of Scotland (Edinburgh, 2003), 44–5, and Cowan, *Freedom*, 144–7 (translation also by Duncan).

5 The chief source for my exposition of Scotus on the will is *Scotus on the Will and Morality*, trans. and with an introduction by Allan B. Wolter (Washington DC, 1986). In my exposition here I also make use of some ideas developed in A. Broadie, *The Shadow of Scotus: Philosophy and Faith in Pre-Reformation Scotland* (Edinburgh, 1995), chs. 2–3. See also A. Broadie, 'Scotus on the unity of the virtues', in *Studies in Christian Ethics*, 12 (1999), 70–83.

6 *Scotus*, 28–103.

7 *Scotus*, 29.

8 *Corpus Iuris Canonici*, ed. Emil Friedberg (Leipzig, 1879), I, col. 742.

9 *Scotus*, 29.

10 *Scotus*, 33.

11 *Scotus*, 33.

12 *Scotus*, 33–5.

13 Scotus does not mention forms of transference of authority where the ruler is a group, but the implication seems to be that a ruling group would be succeeded by another that would be elected as the earlier had been elected.

14 For example, the Declaration of Arbroath is written in the name of 'the whole community of the realm of Scotland'. Cowan, *Freedom*, 144.

15 In fact it gives the date 24 February 1309, which is 1310 by modern reckoning.

16 Duncan, 'Declarations', 45.

17 Cowan, *Freedom*, 145–6. The 'us' are the numerous barons who sealed the declaration. No clergy sealed the document, although it was probably written by Abbot Bernard of Arbroath, who was also the chancellor of King Robert, an interesting circumstance given that the document spells out the circumstances under which the signatories would oust the king.

18 For discussion of this aspect of will, see A. Broadie, 'Duns Scotus on sinful thought', in *Scottish Journal of Theology*, 49 (1996), 291–310, reprinted in 'Duns Scotus on sinful thought', in *Classical and Medieval Literature Criticism*, 59 (2003).

19 Broadie, *Why Scottish Philosophy Matters*, 34.

20 I first raised the question of the relationship between John Duns Scotus and William Wallace in a BBC Scotland Radio programme, 'The brilliant dunce', directed by Jack Regan, in 1993 on the occasion of Scotus's beatification. Since then I have maintained an active interest in the question and more recently have benefited greatly both from conversations on the topic with Fr. Bill Russell and also from his generosity in showing me his as-yet-unpublished writings in the field, which afford considerable support for the position adopted here. I am most grateful to him.

CHAPTER 6 (GRANT)

1 This chapter has grown out of papers given since 1996 at Warwick, Stirling and Lancaster. My thanks to all who offered constructive comments and criticisms, especially Ted Cowan, Keith Stringer and Angus Winchester.

2 Ash, 'Wallace and Bruce' (quotations at pp. 83–4); Morton, *Wallace*, ch. 6 (quotation at p. 94).

3 For example, Barrow, *Bruce*, 71, 81; Fisher, *Wallace*, 6, 11; Nicholson, *Later Middle Ages*, 52; Michael Lynch, 'Wallace, William', in Michael Lynch (ed.), *The Oxford Companion to Scottish History* (Oxford, 2001), 634; Morton, *Wallace*, 19, and 125–30 for regular nationalist celebrations of Wallace's birth at Elderslie. Ellerslie in Ayrshire has been unconvincingly claimed as Wallace's birthplace in James Mackay, *William Wallace: Brave Heart* (Edinburgh, 1995), ch. 1.

4 Chris Given-Wilson, *The English Nobility in the Later Middle Ages* (London, 1987), chs. 2–3; Peter Coss, *The Origins of the English Gentry* (Cambridge, 2003), ch. 10.

5 Although precise definitions varied. See Georges Duby, *The Chivalrous Society* (London, 1977), chs. 3, 5, 9, 13; Maurice Keen, *Chivalry* (New Haven, 1984); Philippe Contamine, 'The European nobility', in Christopher Allmand (ed.), *The New Cambridge Medieval History*, Vol. VII: *c. 1415–1500* (Cambridge, 1998); Michael Jones (ed.), *Gentry and Lesser Nobility in Later Medieval Europe* (Gloucester, 1986), chs. 4–6, 8, 10.

6 Keith M. Brown, *Noble Society in Scotland: Wealth, Family and Culture from Reformation to Revolution* (Edinburgh, 2000), 1–21; Jenny Wormald, 'Lords and lairds in fifteenth-century Scotland: nobles and gentry', in Jones, *Gentry and Lesser Nobility*.

7 Thomas Innes, *Scots Heraldry: A Practical Handbook . . .* (2nd edn, Edinburgh, 1956), ch. 7.

8 Nicholson, *Later Middle Ages*, 115–16, 375–6, 423; Roland Tanner, *The Late Medieval Scottish Parliament: Politics and the Three Estates, 1424–1488* (East Linton, 2001), 48–9, 96–7, 199, 267–72; Grant, 'Scottish Peerage', *SHR*, lvii (1978).

9 *Paisley Reg.*, 57.

10 Although academic studies usually say Wallace was of knightly stock, they do not

count him as 'noble'; and such anachronistic concepts as 'middle class' and 'bourgeois' have been used (Barrow, *Bruce*, 92; Morton, *Wallace*, 15).

11 *Chron. Rishanger*, 383–4; also Duncan, 'William son of Alan', above.

12 *Chron. Lanercost*, 193.

13 *Chron. Fordun*, i, 328.

14 *Ibid.*; *Chron. Bower*, vi, 83. Throughout, quotations from *Gesta Annalia* II have been checked with the text incorporated in Watt's edition of *Scotichronicon*, the translation of which I follow, although sometimes with emendation. Since *parentes* does not mean 'parents' in the modern sense, I have translated it as 'kindred'.

15 *Chron. Wyntoun*, v, 298.

16 *Chron. Bower*, vi, 82–3.

17 *Chron. Fordun*, i, 328 (my trans.; the text's *latibulis* is a plural form of *latibulum*, 'hiding-place').

18 *Chron. Bower*, vi, 298, 312, 314–17.

19 He was not styled *miles* in the Hamburg/Lübeck letters of October 1297, but was so styled in the Scrymgeour charter of March 1298: Stevenson, *Wallace Docs.*, 159; *APS*, i, 453.

20 *Chron. Bower*, vi, 235–6.

21 *Ibid.*, vi, 234–5.

22 Hary, *Wallace*, i, 2, 13.

23 Assuming, that is, that Hary was referring to the Sir Richard Wallace who is recorded in the late thirteenth century: see below. Crawford was lord of Loudon: *Scots Peerage*, v, 490; *Regesta Regum Scottorum*, v, no. 128.

24 See McDiarmid's analysis in Hary, *Wallace*, i, pp. lxvii–lxxxviii, ciii–civ.

25 Barbour, *Bruce*, 152–3; Hary, *Wallace*, ii, 138–45.

26 For Crawford as sheriff of Ayr, see e.g. *CDS*, ii, no. 739.

27 Craigie was acquired in the late fourteenth century, when Sir John Wallace of Riccarton married a daughter of Sir John Lindsay of Craigie: *Registrum Magni Sigilli* [*RMS*], i, no. 363; App. II, no. 1850; *Paisley Reg.*, 79. Hary, *Wallace*, i, pp. li–liv; ii, 122.

28 *RMS*, i, no. 363; William Fraser, *Memoirs of the Maxwells of Pollok* (Edinburgh, 1863), i, no. 10.

29 In *c.*1272 and 1260–1283: *Paisley Reg.*, 60, 233. For Wallace possession of Riccarton in the thirteenth century, G. W. S. Barrow, *The Kingdom of the Scots* (London, 1973), 350.

30 *CDS*, iii, no. 1236; Hary, *Wallace*, i, 159–60; ii, 209. For the real Rokeby, Robin Frame, 'Thomas Rokeby, sheriff of Yorkshire, the custodian of David II', in David Rollason and Michael Prestwich (eds.), *The Battle of Neville's Cross, 1346* (Stamford, 1998).

31 Hary, *Wallace*, i, 17, 19; ii, 145; *Paisley Reg.*, 21; *RMS*, i, no. 365; ii, nos. 90, 836.

32 William Fraser, *Memorials of the Montgomeries Earls of Eglinton* (Edinburgh, 1859), ii, no. 23; George Crawfurd, *A Genealogical History of the Royal and Illustrious Family of the Stewarts . . .* (Edinburgh, 1710), 126. Crawfurd states that John Wallace of Elderslie resigned Auchenbothie to his younger son Thomas (citing a lost charter) and that Thomas's family acquired the land of Johnstone by marriage. Since Auchenbothie-Wallace belonged to Robert Wallace of Johnstone in 1491 (*RMS*, ii, no. 2010), Crawfurd can presumably be trusted. But if the Elderslie Wallaces possessed Auchenbothie, then there can be absolutely no doubt that Hary's 'Elrisle' is Elderslie in Renfrewshire; the Ayrshire Ellerslie can be utterly dismissed. McDiarmid's comment about Auchenbothie (Hary, *Wallace*, ii, 126) is mistaken.

33 *Paisley Reg.*, 151, 370; *Exchequer Rolls of Scotland*, ix, 659; *RMS*, ii, no. 2527.

34 *Scots Peerage*, iii, 171. He was an adherent of the seventh and eighth earls of Douglas: Michael Brown, *The Black Douglases* (East Linton, 1998), 23, 279.

35 That is, after its forfeiture and the ninth earl's defection to England. See Michael Brown, '"Rejoice to hear of Douglas": the house of Douglas and the presentation of magnate power in late medieval Scotland', *SHR*, lxxvii (1997).

36 *Facsimiles of the National Manuscripts of Scotland* (London, 1867–71), ii, no. 8.

37 *Chron. Lanercost*, 207 (which calls John Wallace *dominus*, i.e. 'Sir'); Prestwich, *Edward I*, 510; National Archives, London, Public Record Office, E101/370/16, fo. 9v.

38 Duncan, 'William son of Alan', ch. 3 above.

39 P. R. Coss, 'Knights, esquires and the origins of social gradation', *Trans. Roy. Hist. Soc.*, 6th ser., v (1995), 173–7. This refers to England, but there is no reason to think Scottish practice was different.

40 Alexander Grant, 'The province of Ross and the kingdom of Alba', in Edward J. Cowan and R. Andrew McDonald (eds.), *Alba: Celtic Scotland in the Middle Ages* (East Linton, 2000), 123.

41 *Nat. Mss. Scot.*, ii, no. 8; trans. Barrow, *Bruce*, 107.

42 A relatively small piece of land in Lanarkshire (12 merks-worth in Pettinain) was held of the crown for the service of two archers *c*.1259: *APS*, i, 98. For contemporary English gentry seals depicting arrows, see Coss, *Origins of English Gentry*, 233–5.

43 Duncan, 'William son of Alan', ch. 3 above.

44 K. J. Stringer, 'Earldoms and "provincial lordships" 1124 to 1286', in Peter G. B. McNeill and Hector L. MacQueen (eds.), *Atlas of Scottish History to 1707* (Edinburgh, 1996), 183–6.

45 *Chron. Guisborough*, 328; *Chron. Rishanger*, 188.

46 *Scots Peerage*, ii, 437; iii, 142; *RMS*, i, no. 365; ii, nos. 90, 836. Another Carrick-Wallace link is in the marriage of the previously widowed countess, Alianora, to a Richard Wallace.

47 Auchincruive (NS3823) is close to the northeast bank of the River Ayr, three miles from the centre of Ayr. Just across the river lies the parish of Sundrum, which was acquired by Robert Wallace of Auchincruive (Sir Duncan's father) *c*.1342: *RMS*, i, App. II, no. 788.

48 Hary, *Wallace*, i, 17, 25.

49 Keen, *Chivalry*, 141–8.

50 Morton, *Wallace*, chs. 6, 7.

51 Richard Finlay, 'Historians: 1800–1900', in Lynch, *Oxford Companion*, 307; also Richard Finlay, 'Myths, heroes and anniversaries in modern Scotland', *Scottish Affairs*, xviii (1997).

52 Morton, *Wallace*, 114–17; Graeme Morton, 'The most efficacious patriot: the heritage of William Wallace in nineteenth-century Scotland', *SHR*, lxxvii (1998).

53 Morton, *Wallace*, 59, 104, citing Carlyle's review of Scott's *Tales of a Grandfather* (1828). The passage was quoted from a nationalist standpoint in *William Wallace: National Hero of Scotland. Special Commemorative Publication to Mark the 650th Anniversary of his Martyrdom* (Perth, 1955); and from a socialist standpoint in Thomas Johnston, *A History of the Working Classes in Scotland* (Glasgow, 1923), 32: see Morton, *Wallace*, 169 n. 48, 178 n. 44.

54 Patrick Fraser Tytler, *History of Scotland*, Vol. I: *1289–1329* (2nd edn, Edinburgh, 1841), 109, 137–8.

55 Stevenson, *Wallace Docs.*, pp. xv–xvi. He made similar remarks in 1870: Stevenson, *Documents*, i, pp. lii–liii.

56 For example, John Hill Burton, *The History of Scotland* (Edinburgh, 1867–70), chs. 20–2; or P. Hume Brown, *History of Scotland* (1899–1909), ch. 3.

57 Barrow, *Robert Bruce*, 80.

58 Michael Brown, *The Wars of Scotland, 1214–1371* (Edinburgh, 2004), chs. 8–10.

59 *CDS*, ii, pp. 193–214.

60 Hary, *Wallace*, i, 41–2, 117, 130, 135, 138, 156, 171, 249–50; ii, 71–2, 102, 111, and (McDiarmid's comments) 155–6.

61 *Ibid.*, ii, 47–53.

62 Earl of Lennox: *ibid.*, i, 52–3, 158–60, 175, 192, 215; ii, 42, 58. Stewart of Bute: *ibid.*, ii, 44–7. The surnames of Wallace's followers include Boyd, Campbell, Gordon, Hay, Keith, Montgomery, Ramsay and Seton (Cetoune): *ibid.*, ii, index. The Douglases are also praised: *ibid.*, ii, 27.

63 *Chron. Fordun*, i, 330; *Chron. Bower*, vi, 97.

64 *Chron. Wyntoun*, v, 316.

65 *Chron. Bower*, vi, 92–5.

66 Mair, *History*, 196.

67 Bellenden, *Chronicles*, ii, 256.

68 Sally Mapstone, 'The *Scotichronicon*'s first readers', in Barbara E. Crawford (ed.), *Church, Chronicle and Learning in Medieval and Early Renaissance Scotland: Essays presented to Donald Watt* (Edinburgh, 1999), 38–9.

69 *Chron. Fordun*, i, 330; *Chron. Bower*, vi, 95.

70 *Chron. Wyntoun*, v, 314–16; *Chron. Bower*, vi, 94; Mair, *History*, 199–200; Bellenden, *Chronicles*, ii, 256.

71 Barrow, *Bruce*, 102; Alan Young, *Robert the Bruce's Rivals: The Comyns, 1212–1314* (East Linton, 1997), ch. 1 and p. 168; Fraser, 'A Swan from a Raven', 18; Fiona Watson, 'The demonisation of King John', in Edward J. Cowan and Richard J. Finlay (eds.), *Scottish History: The Power of the Past* (Edinburgh, 2002).

72 *Chron. Fordun*, i, 325–6; *Chron. Bower*, vi, 75.

73 *Chron. Fordun*, i, 330; *Chron. Bower*, vi, 97.

74 Watt, in *Chron. Bower*, vi, 242; Fraser, 'A Swan from a Raven', 17.

75 The passage on Bruce begins *Communiter autem dicitur*. Skene translated *autem* as 'But'; Watt omitted it altogether. I prefer 'Moreover', which gives a stronger link to the preceding sentences.

76 I am unconvinced by Fraser's efforts ('A Swan from a Raven', 18–19) to reconcile this episode with his general argument that *Gesta Annalia* II's account derives from Bruce propaganda – with which I differ.

77 Except Barbour, who is not relevant because *The Bruce* simply omits the years 1297–1305.

78 *Chron. Bower*, vi, 94–7.

79 Hary: McDiarmid's comment, in *Wallace*, i, pp. xcix–c, and Mapstone, '*Scotichronicon*'s first readers', 41–2. Boece: Nicola Royan, '*Scotichronicon* rewritten? Hector Boece's debt to Bower in the *Scotorum Historia*', in Crawford, *Church, Chronicle*, 63. Mair (most critical of all, portraying Bruce as suspicious that Wallace was seeking the crown): *ibid.*, 69, n. 4, and Mair, *History*, 201–2.

80 For example, Barrow, *Bruce*, 101–3; Nicholson, *Later Middle Ages*, 57–8; Fisher, *Wallace*, 82; Young, *Robert the Bruce's Rivals*, 168; Watson, *Hammer*, 67; Brown, *Wars of Scotland*, 187. Watt, *Chron. Bower*, vi, 242–3, seems ambivalent. Only Cowan (*Freedom*, 23–4, 72–6) and Fraser ('A Swan from a Raven', 18–19) provide satisfactory discussion.

81 *Chron. Guisborough*, 325–8; *Chron. Rishanger*, 186–8, 385–7, 415; *Chron. Lanercost*, 191–2. Note that Guisborough does record that the earls of Angus and Dunbar were in Edward's army.

82 *Chron. Guisborough*, 328; *Chron. Rishanger*, 188.

83 Barrow, *Bruce*, 104–5. Even the faction-focused discussions in Brown, *Wars of Scotland*, 189, and Michael Penman, *David II, 1329–71* (East Linton, 2004), 16, demonstrate Bruce's acceptability to the bulk of the politically significant classes.

84 Stephen Boardman, 'Chronicle propaganda in late medieval Scotland: Robert the Steward, John of Fordun and the "Anonymous Chronicle"', *SHR*, lxxvi (1997).

85 Dauvit Broun, 'A new look at *Gesta Annalia* attributed to John of Fordun', in Crawford, *Church, Chronicle,* esp. 15–19.
86 *Chron. Fordun,* i, 310; *Chron. Bower,* v, 423.
87 *Chron. Fordun,* i, 311–12; *Chron. Bower,* vi, 5.
88 *Chron. Fordun,* i, 327–8; *Chron. Bower,* vi, 80; *Chron. Guisborough,* 264; *Chron. Lanercost,* 161–2. The *Gesta* also misdates the Scottish earls' invasion of England to after Dunbar and King John's removal!
89 For example, *Chron. Bower,* vi, 233–4; Barrow, *Bruce,* 338 n. 47. Watson, 'Demonisation of King John', 36, seems to blame this distortion on Bruce propaganda; I would differ.
90 *Chron. Fordun,* i, 325. This appears to be taken seriously by Brown, *Wars of Scotland,* 176.
91 *Chron. Guisborough,* 273.
92 *Ibid.,* 277–9; Stevenson, *Documents,* ii, 26–7; *CDS,* ii, nos. 742, 930.
93 *Chron. Guisborough,* 278.
94 For example, Stevenson, *Documents,* ii, 62–3, 66, 108, 185; *CDS,* ii, no. 897.
95 The *Gesta*'s emphasis on defeats being caused by flight might stem from the fact that Robert the Steward and the earl of March abandoned David II at Neville's Cross (*Chron. Fordun,* i, 367), which David never forgave (Penman, *David II,* 4–5, and *passim*).
96 Fraser, 'A Swan from a Raven', 6–10. Murray is mentioned only as dying at Stirling Bridge: *Chron. Fordun,* i, 329. For Murray's revolt, E. M. Barron, *The Scottish War of Independence* (2nd edn, Inverness, 1934), chs. 3–7, has still not been superseded.
97 *Chron. Fordun,* i, 328; *Chron. Bower,* vi, 83–5.
98 *Chron. Fordun,* i, 331–6.
99 *Ibid.,* i, 333; trans. *Chron. Bower,* vi, 291.
100 *Chron. Fordun,* i, 333–5, 346–7. For the scale of the battle of Roslin, see Watson, *Hammer,* 170–1.
101 The *Gesta* does not mention Bruce's participation in joint guardianship after 1298: John Comyn is presented as the only guardian.
102 *Chron. Fordun,* i, 337–53.
103 *Chron. Bower,* vi, 296–7 (trans. slightly emended); and vi, 312–13 (mournful death of John Comyn), 316–17 (Robert Bruce 'discovered to be of royal stock', which seems distinctly sarcastic), 342–3 (defeat of the earl of Buchan). See also the pro-Balliol 'Scottish poem' in *Liber Extravagans* [a supplement to *Scotichronicon*], ed. Dauvit Broun, in *Chron. Bower,* ix, 54–9, 66–84, 107–19.
104 As argued by Fraser, 'A Swan from a Raven', 19.
105 *Chron. Wyntoun,* v, 318.
106 *CDS,* ii, nos. 1432, 1465; iv, p. 474; as suggested by Fraser, 'A Swan from a Raven', 19. We do not know whether Bruce was enthusiastic or unenthusiastic about this, but he presumably had no choice.
107 Norman H. Reid, 'Crown and community under Robert I', in Alexander Grant and Keith J. Stringer (eds.), *Medieval Scotland: Crown, Lordship and Community* (Edinburgh, 1993), 203–7.
108 Its account of the Great Cause (*Chron. Fordun,* i, 313–18) strikes me as far too neutral to be unambiguously pro-Bruce.
109 Penman, *David II,* chs. 4–7, 9. This may have been especially relevant in 1363–64, the likely date of *Gesta Annalia* II, when the issue of an English succession was at its height: *ibid.,* 318. Penman, however, argues that the *Gesta* deliberately omitted the story about the redeeming Wallace–Bruce meeting at Falkirk because of 'mounting disgust at David II's [pro-English] diplomatic agenda' (*ibid.,* 323); I cannot agree.
110 Indeed, her first husband was the son of a man executed for plotting to kill Robert I in 1320.

111 'A question about the succession, 1364', ed. A. A. M. Duncan, in *Scottish History Society Miscellany*, xii (Scot. Hist. Soc., 1994), 54–7.

112 *Chron. Fordun*, i, 337–40. The account is broadly similar to Barbour's, although Duncan notes significant differences: see Barbour, *Bruce*, 68–80.

113 *Chron. Fordun*, i, 381; *Chron. Bower*, vii, 325; Penman, *David II*, chs. 8–10; A. A. M. Duncan, 'The "Laws of Malcolm MacKenneth"', in Grant and Stringer, *Medieval Scotland*.

114 *Chron. Wyntoun*, v, 300–4.

115 See M. Keen, *The Outlaws of Medieval Legend* (London, 1977), 65; Stephen Knight, *Robin Hood: A Complete Study of the English Outlaw* (Oxford, 1994), 39.

116 *Chron. Bower*, v, 354–5.

117 *Chron. Wyntoun*, v, 136–7 (Wyntoun's date made Robin a slightly older contemporary of Wallace).

118 R. B. Dobson and John Taylor, *Rymes of Robin Hood* (London, 1976), 18.

119 *Chron. Bower*, v, 354–5, 470. Admittedly, the Latin words for 'raised' differ: *Gesta Annalia II* uses *levavit* (*Chron. Fordun*, i, 328) whereas Bower uses *erexit*; also, Bower suppressed the *Gesta* statement about Wallace. Nevertheless, that shows he was conscious of the *Gesta*'s phrase, so it is reasonable to assume an echo in the Robin Hood passage.

120 Knight, *Robin Hood*, 39. Knight attaches considerable significance to Wyntoun, Bower and Mair in the creation of the Robin Hood image. He stresses that Mair was responsible for relocating Robin Hood to Richard I's reign, where he has stayed ever since; Mair did so, Knight argues, because he applied Bower's mention of 'the prince' to Prince John (*ibid.*, 32–9; Mair, *History*, 156–7). Wallace and Robin Hood came closer in the sixteenth century through Maid Marian. She is a late addition, not specifically associated with Robin Hood until 1509 (Dobson and Taylor, *Rymes of Robin Hood*, 3, 39–42; Knight, *Robin Hood*, 269). Shortly afterwards, the traditional first name of Wallace's wife, Marion, appears (although Hary was the first to name her, he gave her only a surname, Braidfute: *Wallace*, i, 91). And not only did Wallace and Robin Hood come together, they surely also begot another fictional freedom-fighting outlaw, William Tell, who is not recorded until the 1470s.

121 Dobson and Taylor, *Rymes of Robin Hood*, 43–5.

122 See Barbara A. Hanawalt, 'Ballads and bandits: fourteenth-century outlaws and the Robin Hood poems', in Stephen Knight (ed.), *Robin Hood: Anthology of Scholarship and Criticism* (Woodbridge, 1999).

123 *Chron. Guisborough*, 294, 296, 300; *Chron. Lanercost*, 190; *The Chronicle of Pierre de Langtoft*, ed. T. Wright (Rolls Series, 1868), ii, 362; *Chron. Rishanger*, 170, 226; *Flores Historiarum*, ed. H. R. Luard (Rolls Series, 1890), iii, 123. *Latro* can be translated as robber, thief, bandit or brigand. Only Thomas Grey's *Scalacronica* does not describe Wallace as a robber or brigand – but, being a lay member of a Northumbrian gentry family, Grey was perhaps more relaxed about this.

124 Fraser, 'A Swan from a Raven', 6–7. *Princeps latronum*, however, is not only 'chief of brigands' but also 'prince of thieves' – as in the 1991 Robin Hood film!

125 'A plea roll of Edward I's army in Scotland, 1296', ed. C. J. Neville, in *Scottish History Society Miscellany*, xi (Scot. Hist. Soc., 1990), no. 136; summarised in *CDS*, ii, p. 191.

126 For example, Wallace, William le, 'a thief', is indexed separately from Sir William (the hero) in *CDS*, ii, p. 707. Barrow, *Bruce*, ignores the story; Fisher, *Wallace*, 10, does not, but seems ambivalent about it.

127 R. Jouet, *La Résistance à l'occupation anglaise en Basse-Normandie (1418–1450)* (Caen, 1969); Nicholas Wright, *Knights and Peasants: The Hundred Years War in the French Countryside* (Woodbridge, 1998), ch. 4; Mark R. Evans, 'Brigandage and resistance in

Lancastrian Normandy: a study of the remission evidence', *Reading Medieval Studies*, xviii (1992). French historians see brigands as resistance fighters; English historians disagree.

128 Stevenson, *Documents*, ii, 28; Peter G. B. McNeill, 'Edward I in Scotland', in McNeill and MacQueen, *Atlas of Scottish History*, 87.

129 Real-life bandits mostly stole food, drink and clothing: Hanawalt, 'Ballads and bandits', 277.

130 Barbara A. Hanawalt, 'Fur-collar crime: the pattern of crime among the fourteenth-century English nobility', *Journal of Social History*, viii (1975). See also her *Crime and Conflict in English Communities, 1300–1348* (Cambridge, Mass., 1979); and her 'Ballads and bandits'.

131 John Bellamy, *Crime and Public Order in England in the Later Middle Ages* (London, 1973), esp. ch. 3 (quotation at p. 72).

132 E. L. G. Stones, 'The Folvilles of Ashby-Folville, Leicestershire, and their associates in crime', *Trans. Roy. Hist. Soc.*, 5th ser., vii (1957); J. G. Bellamy, 'The Coterel gang: an anatomy of a band of fourteenth-century criminals', *English Hist. Rev.*, lxxix (1964).

133 As is obvious from accounts of lawlessness in the Anglo-Scottish Borders: see e.g. Cynthia J. Neville, *Violence, Custom and Law: The Anglo-Scottish Border Lands in the Later Middle Ages* (Edinburgh, 1998).

134 *Chron. Fordun*, i, 310, 319–20.

135 Stevenson, *Documents*, i, 83–5, 155; *APS*, i, 448–9.

136 Brown, *Black Douglases*, 14–28.

137 *Ibid.*, 35–40; also M. H. Brown, 'The development of Scottish Border lordship, 1332–58', *Historical Research*, lxx (1997).

138 *Chron. Fordun*, i, 328.

139 My understanding of Falkirk is largely based on John Keegan, *The Face of Battle* (2nd edn, London, 1991), esp. 71–3, 296–8, 308–11.

140 *Chron. Guisborough*, 327–8 (circular formation); *Chron. Rishanger*, 187 (fence); Barrow, *Bruce*, 101–3 (combination of the two accounts – 'round each schiltrom wooden stakes had been driven into the ground and roped together').

141 *Chron. Lanercost*, 190, certainly indicates that.

142 Barrow, *Bruce*, 84–5; Brown, *Wars of Scotland*, 183.

143 *Chron. Guisborough*, 299; Stevenson, *Documents*, ii, 202.

144 Barrow, *Bruce*, 83.

145 *CDS*, ii, no. 1689. The jury included Sir David Graham, who was no doubt biased against Wallace; but taken as a whole, it appears to represent a fair cross-section of Tayside landowners, and they all presumably agreed in sympathising with Meigle.

146 Keen, *Chivalry*, chs. 8–9.

147 That said, one piece of chivalrous behaviour on Wallace's part should be noted. After Stirling Bridge, William de Ros was captured in Stirling Castle, and Wallace spared his life because he was the brother of Sir Robert de Ros of Wark, who had joined the Scots in 1296; however, Ros was not released but was imprisoned in irons in Dunbarton Castle until it surrendered to Edward I after Falkirk: *CDS*, iv, no. 1835. My thanks to Keith Stringer for reminding me of this.

148 Barrow, *Bruce*, 126–9, 136; Fisher, *Wallace*, 107–19.

149 Menteith was not alone. In 1296 Edward I appointed Englishmen to run Scotland, but in 1304–05 he used native Scots to run their own country. That is surely why, at least for a time, the conquest of 1304 looked much more permanent. See e.g. Watson, *Hammer*, chs. 2, 7.

150 Barrow, *Bruce*, 183, 186, 284, 286; *Regesta Regum Scottorum*, v, no. 239; *RMS*, i, App. II, no. 568; *APS*, i, 474.

151 Except in writing by Bower and Hary. In contrast, shrines were erected in Switzerland to William Tell, even although he was a mythical character.

152 As suggested by Cowan, *Freedom*, 75–6.

CHAPTER 7 (RIDDY)

1 The manuscript is Edinburgh, National Library of Scotland, MS 19.2.2 (ii), copied by John Ramsay.

2 Mair, *History* (Paris, 1521). Mair was born in 1469.

3 This is argued by McDiarmid in his edition, by R. James Goldstein, *The Matter of Scotland: Historical Narrative in Medieval Scotland* (Lincoln, NE, 1993), and by Sally Mapstone in her forthcoming study of Scottish kingship. Dr Mapstone generously allowed me to read the chapter on *The Wallace* in typescript.

4 John Cartwright (ed.), *The Buik of King Alexander*, Scottish Text Society, 5th series, 2 vols. (Aberdeen, 1985–89).

5 See my 'Empire and Civil War: Contexts for *Le Morte Darthur*', in A. S. G. Edwards and E. Archibald (eds.), *A Companion to Malory* (Woodbridge, 1996), 55–73.

6 Thomas Basin, *Histoire de Charles VII*, ed. and trans. Charles Samarin, 2 vols. (Paris, 1964), i, 106–13.

7 Hugh Miller, *My Schools and Schoolmasters or The Story of My Education* (Edinburgh, 1858), 41.

8 Ash, 'Wallace and Bruce', 84. For the *Braveheart* effect: the Hamilton of Gilbertfield version is again in print (William Hamilton, *Blind Harry's Wallace*, ed. Elspeth King [Edinburgh, 1999]), and a new edition of Hary's poem has been published in full (Anne McKim, ed., *The Wallace* [Edinburgh, 2003]), and in selected form (Anne McKim, ed., *The Wallace: Selections* [Kalamazoo, 2003]).

9 Letter from Burns to John Moore, August 1787, Edinburgh, National Library of Scotland, MS 15952: 'the story of Wallace poured a Scottish prejudice in my veins which will boil along there till the flood-gates of life shut in eternal rest'. See http://www.nls.uk/burns/mainsite/burns/cowie.htm and http://www.gutenberg.net/etext06/8burn10.txt.

10 Norman MacCaig, 'Celtic Cross', in *Collected Poems* (London, 1991).

11 See my 'Hardyng's Chronicle and the Wars of the Roses', *Arthurian Literature XII* (1993), pp. 91–108.

12 London, British Library, MS Harley 661, fol. 184.

13 Benedict Anderson, *Imagined Communities*, rev. edn (London and New York, 1991).

CHAPTER 8 (KING)

1 *Self-government for Scotland. R. B. Cunninghame Graham on Sir William Wallace*. Wallace Day programme, Elderslie. August 1920.

2 The choice of date for the polling day was accidental, the main aim of the administration being to select a Thursday.

3 *Scotland on Sunday* (letters), 10 December 1998.

4 *Courier*. Letters column, 4 December 1998.

5 *Scotland on Sunday* (letters), 21 March 1999. See also Ted Cowan, 'The Museum of Scotland', *History Today*, 49 (2), 1999, 24–5.

6 The subject grew from the publication of three books – Donald Horne, *The Great Museum: The Re-presentation of History* (London/New South Wales, 1984), Patrick Wright, *On Living in an Old Country. The National Past in Contemporary Britain* (London, 1985) and Robert Hewison, *The Heritage Industry: Britain in a Climate of Decline* (London, 1987). These spawned the publication of a number of Scottish books and articles on the same theme.

7 See George Rosie, 'Museumry and the Heritage Industry', in *The Manufacture of*

Scottish History, ed. Ian Donnachie and Christopher Whatley (Edinburgh, 1992) 157–67. The writer believes that museums are a decorative social frill: 'A bit like a well heeled family decorating the living room by putting old snapshots of the family in to silver frames'.

8 Lecture by Professor Michael Lynch, Glasgow Royal Concert Hall, 20 May 2004.

9 Morton, *Wallace*, 188–96.

10 T. M. Devine, 'Whither Scottish History', *SHR*, lxxiii (1994), 1.

11 Tim Edensor, 'National Identity and the Politics of Memory: Remembering Bruce and Wallace in symbolic space', *Environment and Planning D: Society and Space*, xxix (1997), 182–3.

12 *Stirling Natural History and Archaeology Society Transactions*, 1923–24, 141.

13 *Two Men in a Trench* series, Optomen Television for Channel 4, 13 April 2004.

14 *Stirling Observer*, 26 June 1887.

15 Hary, *Wallace*, i, cvi.

16 For a full discussion, see Hamilton, *Wallace*, xi–xxix.

17 *The Wallace, Blind Harry*, ed. Anne McKim (Edinburgh, 2003).

18 For a full rehearsal of the perceived faults of Blind Hary, see Morton's *Wallace*, 43–8.

19 Hary, *Wallace*, ii, 121.

20 D. E. R. Watt, *Fasti Ecclesiae Scoticanae Medii Aevi ad Annum 1638* (St Andrews, 1969), 96.

21 Barrow, *Bruce*, 340–1, 348, 375.

22 *Chron. Wyntoun*, v, 212–14. See also Edward J. Cowan, 'Identity, Freedom and the Declaration of Arbroath', in Dauvit Broun, R. J. Finlay and Michael Lynch (eds.), *Image and Identity – the making and re-making of Scotland through the ages* (Edinburgh, 1998), 44, citing the reconstruction of this speech using material found in Spain.

23 James Primrose, *Medieval Glasgow* (Glasgow, 1913), 51.

24 Primrose, *Medieval Glasgow*, 55–6.

25 See *Palace of History. Catalogue of Exhibits, Scottish Exhibition of National History, Art and Industry* (Glasgow, 1911). The cast made by the architect, Peter McGregor Chalmers, for the 1911 Scottish Exhibition was worked on by a professional sculptor in 1989 to restore the face, hands, feet, supporting angels and the colouring, using an English model of the same date. It was part of the Early Glasgow display at the People's Palace, 1989–95. See Elspeth King and Michael Donnelly, 'Bricks without straw: putting a face on Early Glasgow', in *A Glasgow Collection. Essays in Honour of Joe Fisher* (Glasgow, 1990), 74–83.

26 Elspeth King, 'Collecting for Cultural Identity', *Museums Journal* (1990), 25–8, and *The People's Palace and Glasgow Green* (Edinburgh, 1985, 1995 reprint), 118.

27 Illustrated in a watercolour drawing of Provand's Lordship by William 'Crimea' Simpson RI, FRGS (1823–99) in the collection of Glasgow Museums. The painting itself is a rare survivor, painted as a public house sign for the Wallace Tavern. Glasgow Museums inherited the work from the Provand's Lordship Society in 1979, but it has remained in store.

28 Bust of Blind Hary, plaster 1996, Stirling Smith Art Gallery and Museum collections.

29 W. Kenny, *The Annals of Aberdeen*, 2 vols. (Aberdeen, 1818), I, 19.

30 T. W. Ogilvie, *The Book of St. Fittich* (Aberdeen, 1901), 61–2.

31 The Lübeck letter was borrowed for the 1911 Scottish Exhibition and various facsimiles were made. An oak-framed facsimile owned by Rob McMillan, secretary of the Gaelic League, was loaned to the Stirling Smith Museum 1998–2002.

32 *Herald*, 26 February 1999, p. 8.

33 J. M. Allan (and others), *Stirling Girls. Towards a women's history of Stirling* (Stirling, 2003), 23.

34 James L. Hemstead, 'The Wallace Sword', in *Burns Chronicle* (2003), 15–18, offers a useful summary of sources and opinions on the Wallace sword.

35 J. Thomson, *History of Dundee* (Dundee, 1847), 26.

36 On display in Greenhill House, the Covenanters' Museum, in Biggar. I am grateful to Brian Lambie of Biggar Museum Trust for access to all the information on Wallace and the material culture of Biggar that he has sought out and curated over the last fifty years.

37 Information sheet issued by Mohammed Al Fayed, present owner of Balnagowan Castle and the Wallace Chair.

38 William Hunter, *Biggar and the House of Fleming* (Biggar, 1861), 74–6.

39 Brian Hayward, *Galoshins, The Scottish Folk Play* (Edinburgh, 1992), 8. The play was performed by Biggar Primary schoolchildren as part of the Wallace conference at the Stirling Smith, 1997, through the auspices of Brian Lambie.

40 James Fergusson, *William Wallace, Guardian of Scotland* (Stirling, 1938 and 1948), vii.

41 Ronald G. Cant, 'David Steuart Erskine, 11th Earl of Buchan: Founder of the Society of Antiquaries of Scotland', in A. S. Bell (ed.), *The Scottish Antiquarian Tradition* (Edinburgh, 1980), 1–20.

42 Hary, *Wallace*, i, 252, from line 775.

43 Hary, *Wallace*, ii, 245.

44 For a description of the 1661 scheme, see David McGibbon and Thomas Ross, *The Castellated and Domestic Architecture of Scotland* (Edinburgh, 1887–92; 1971 facsimile reprint), ii, 62–6.

45 James Paterson, *Wallace and His Times* (Edinburgh, 1858), Preface.

46 Photographic record of Niddrie Marischal House by Colin McWilliam for the Royal Commission on the Ancient and Historical Monuments of Scotland (RCAHMS) Archives. February 1954 Ref ED/4458 frame 22.

47 Reg. no. 19,858, purchased 1996.

48 Elspeth King and Michael Donnelly, *The People's Palace History Paintings: A Short Guide* (Glasgow Museums, 1990), 25.

49 George MacGregor (ed.), *The Collected Writings of Dougal Graham* (Glasgow, 1883), ii, 247.

50 Bonhams, *The Scottish Sale. Made in Scotland*, catalogue August 2004, 116. Burns's copy of Blind Hary's *Wallace*.

51 Colin D. I. G. Forrester, 'Finding the site of the Wallace Oak in Torwood', *The Scottish American*, v (1987); 'The Wallace Oak, Torwood and Roy's Military Survey', *Forth Valley Naturalist and Historian* (1998), 63–70.

52 John G. Harrison, 'The Torwood and the Wallace Oak: Some Early Records', *Forth Valley Naturalist and Historian* (1999), 93–6.

53 Lindsay Corbett, 'The Wallace Oak: Torwood. A supplement to Forrester' [FNH 21], *Forth Valley Naturalist and Historian* (1999), 79–91.

54 Angus Smith, 'Wallacebank Wood Wildlife Reserve 1986/99', *Forth Valley Naturalist and Historian* (1999), 45–53.

55 Dundee's Tree of Liberty planted in 1792 was lost to motorway development in the 1970s.

56 *Palace of History*, II, 691.

57 *Palace of History*, II, 690.

58 Printed in John D. Carrick, *Life of Sir William Wallace* (Edinburgh, 1830). Also illustrated in Elspeth King, *Introducing William Wallace* (Fort William, 1997), 21.

59 Jane D. Hogg, 'The Burning of the Douglas Room, Stirling Castle 18 November 1855', *Transactions of the Stirling Field Club*, xvi (1893–94), 77–8.

60 Janet Fyfe (ed.), *Autobiography of John McAdam (1806–1883)* (Edinburgh, 1980), 79–81, 173–6, 178.

61 David Trachtenberg and Thomas Keith, *Mauchline Ware: A Collector's Guide* (Suffolk, 2002), 252.

62 Allan Donnelly, 'Sir Walter Scott's contribution to Mauchline Ware', *Mauchline Ware Collectors' Club Journal* No. 31 (1996).

63 William Hodges, 'Census of books in Mauchline Ware Boards', *Mauchline Ware Collectors' Club Journal* No. 44 (2000).

64 Trachtenberg and Keith, *Mauchline Ware*, 226–73.

65 See example in *Home and Antiques Magazine*, June 2004, 142.

66 Birmingham Art Gallery and Museum Catalogue, *Birmingham Gold and Silver, 1773–1993* (Birmingham, 1993).

67 See www.scran.ac.uk.

68 Evelyn Wright (ed.), *A Scottish Country Doctor. Recalled by his son Thomas Wyld Pairman* (East Linton, 2003), 47.

69 J. and M. Norgate and Felix Hudson, *Dunfermline Clockmakers* (Dunfermline, 1982), 36.

70 See www.scran.ac.uk.

71 Scott was also the childhood friend of Jane Porter (1776–1850). She published her novel on Wallace, *The Scottish Chiefs*, in 1810, some years before *Waverley*, and made the story of Wallace her own. *The Scottish Chiefs* was an all-time bestseller. Translated into French and Russian, it was also highly popular in the USA where, in 1844, authors, publishers and booksellers made her a special presentation.

72 James Hogg, *Domestic Manners of Sir Walter Scott* (Stirling, 1909), 111.

73 Rob Gibson, *Andrew de Moray's North Rising* (Evanton, 1997).

74 Catalogue, *Brave Art. An exhibition of contemporary art celebrating the 699th Anniversary of the Battle of Stirling Bridge* (Stirling, 1996).

75 Elspeth King, 'Scotland's Liberator: The life and legacy of William Wallace 1297–1997', *Forth Valley Naturalist and Historian*, Vol. xx, 93–9.

76 *Official Souvenir Programme, Sir William Wallace National Commemoration Day, Elderslie, Saturday 22 August 1936.*

CHAPTER 9 (KIDD)

1 Morton, *Unionist Nationalism*; Morton, *Wallace*; R. Finlay, 'Myths, Heroes and Anniversaries in Modern Scotland', *Scottish Affairs*, xviii (1997), 108–26; C. Kidd, 'Sentiment, Race and Revival: Scottish Identities in the Aftermath of Enlightenment', in L. Brockliss and D. Eastwood (eds.), *A Union of Multiple Identities: The British Isles, c. 1750–c. 1850* (Manchester, 1997), 118–21.

2 For the ideological context surrounding the campaign, see N. Phillipson, *The Scottish Whigs and the Reform of the Court of Session 1785–1830*, Stair Society (Edinburgh, 1990).

3 *The Shade of Wallace: A Poem* (Glasgow, 1807), 9.

4 C. Kidd, *Subverting Scotland's Past: Scottish Whig Historians and the Creation of an Anglo-British Identity, 1689–c. 1830* (Cambridge, 1993), 164.

5 K. Robbins, *Nineteenth-Century Britain: Integration and Diversity* (1988: Oxford, 1995), 11.

6 M. Pittock, 'Scott and the British Tourist', in G. Carruthers and A. Rawes (eds.), *English Romanticism and the Celtic World* (Cambridge, 2003), 163.

7 K. Trumpener, *Bardic Nationalism: The Romantic Novel and the British Empire* (Princeton, 1997); G. Carruthers and A. Rawes, 'Introduction: romancing the Celt', in G. Carruthers and A. Rawes (eds.), *English Romanticism and the Celtic World* (Cambridge, 2003). See also L. Davis, *Acts of Union: Scotland and the Literary Negotiation of the British Nation, 1707–1830* (Palo Alto, 1998).

8 I. Ferris, *The Romantic National Tale and the Question of Ireland* (Cambridge, 2002).

9 There is a new edition: Christian Isabel Johnstone, *Clan-Albin: A National Tale*, ed. Andrew Monnickendam (Glasgow, 2003).

10 Walter Scott, 'General Preface to Waverley Novels', in D. Hewitt (ed.), *Scott on Himself: A Selection of the Autobiographical Writings of Sir Walter Scott* (Edinburgh, 1981), 249.

11 Kidd, *Subverting Scotland's Past*; J. Brims, 'The Scottish Jacobins, Scottish Nationalism and the British Union', in R. A. Mason (ed.), *Scotland and England, 1286–1815* (Edinburgh, 1987).

12 See for example, D. Forbes, *Hume's Philosophical Politics* (Cambridge, 1975).

13 J. Sutherland, *The Life of Walter Scott* (Oxford, 1995), 230.

14 J. W. Burrow, *A Liberal Descent: Victorian Historians and the English Past* (Cambridge, 1981), 172 fn.

15 R. Mitchell, *Picturing the Past: English History in Text and Image, 1830–1870* (Oxford, 2000), 87.

16 Cf. Sutherland, *Scott*, p. 123, which notes that Scott's novels were for southern export, with 700 of the first 1,000 copies of *Waverley* going to England. J. O. Hayden, 'Introduction', in Hayden (ed.), *Scott: The Critical Heritage* (London, 1970), 3, relates the contemporary reckoning that this first impression sold out in five weeks. Six editions appeared by the end of the year. Thereafter, sales accelerated, with *Old Mortality* selling 4,000 copies in the first six weeks and *Rob Roy* 10,000 in the first fortnight.

17 [Sarah Green], *Scotch Novel Reading; or, Modern Quackery. A Novel Really Founded on Facts* (3 vols., London, 1824), I, 4–5, 9, 11, 13–15, 43; III, 238, 244.

18 Robert Southey, *Complete Poetical Works* (London, 1845), 128.

19 John Stoddart, *Remarks on Local Scenery and Manners in Scotland during the years 1799 and 1800* (2 vols., London, 1801), I, 164–5.

20 M. Reed (ed.), *The Thirteen-Book Prelude by William Wordsworth* (2 vols., Ithaca and London, 1991), I, 112. See King, 'The Material Culture', ch. 8 above.

21 Margaret Holford, *Wallace; or the Fight of Falkirk: A Metrical Romance* (1809: 2nd edn, London, 1810), 'Dedication', p. vi.

22 A. Hook, 'Jane Porter, Sir Walter Scott, and the Historical Novel', *Clio*, v (1976), 181–92, at 185.

23 Jane Porter, *The Scottish Chiefs* (London, 1810), 'Preface'.

24 *Blackwood's Edinburgh Magazine* (December 1818), 336.

25 Felicia Hemans, *Poems* (Edinburgh and London, 1849), 63 fn; *Blackwood's Edinburgh Magazine* (September 1819), 686; *Edinburgh Monthly Review*, ii (November 1819), 575.

26 'Advertisement by the Author', Hemans, *Poems*, 63 fn.

27 W. D. Brewer, 'Felicia Hemans, Byronic cosmopolitanism and the ancient Welsh bards', in Carruthers and Rawes (eds.), *English Romanticism and the Celtic World*.

28 Hemans, *Poems*, 476–7.

29 Felicia Hemans to Matthew Nicholson, 17 July 1811, in *Felicia Hemans: Selected Poems, Letters, Reception Materials*, ed. S. J. Wolfson (Princeton and Oxford, 2000), 476.

30 Reproduced in Hemans, *Poems*, 63 fn; James Hogg, 'Wallace', in Hogg, *The Poetical Works of the Ettrick Shepherd* (5 vols., Glasgow and London, 1855?), IV, 280–91.

31 Reproduced in Hemans, *Poems*, 63 fn.

32 *Edinburgh Monthly Review*, ii (November 1819), 575.

33 *Scots Magazine*, lxxxiv (November 1819), 448–9.

34 James Ballantine (ed.), *The Hundredth Birthday of Robert Burns* (Edinburgh and London, 1859), 445.

35 Cf. remarks at the Exeter celebrations of the centenary in Ballantine (ed.), *Hundredth Birthday of Burns*, 451.

36 Joanna Baillie, *Poetical Works* (London, 1851), 708.

37 William Burns, *Scotland and her Calumniators* (Glasgow, 1858), 18.

38 Quoted in R. J. Morris and G. Morton, 'The remaking of Scotland: a nation with-

in a nation, 1850–1920', in M. Lynch (ed.), *Scotland 1850–1979: Society, Politics and the Union* (Historical Association Committee for Scotland and the Historical Association, 1993), 16–17.

39 Quoted in R. G. Hall, 'Creating a People's History: Political Identity and History in Chartism, 1832–1848', in O. Ashton, R. Fyson and S. Roberts (eds.), *The Chartist Legacy* (Rendlesham, 1999), 241–2.

40 For the origins of the Norman Yoke thesis, see C. Hill, 'The Norman Yoke', in Hill, *Puritanism and Revolution* (1958: Harmondsworth, 1986), 58–125.

41 C. Kidd, 'Race and the Scottish Nation, 1750–1900' (lecture delivered at the Royal Society of Edinburgh, January 2003).

42 S. Barczewski, *Myth and National Identity in Nineteenth-Century Britain: the Legends of King Arthur and Robin Hood* (Oxford, 2000).

43 Richard Lodge, *The Study of History in a Scottish University* (Glasgow, 1894), 11, 14–15.

44 G. A. Henty, *In Freedom's Cause: A Story of Wallace and Bruce* (London, 1885), esp. 21, 36, 224.

45 John Richard Green, *A Short History of the English People* (London, 1882 edn), 185.

46 George Macaulay Trevelyan, *History of England* (London, 1926), 218. For Trevelyan's career, see D. Cannadine, *G. M. Trevelyan: A Life in History* (London, 1992).

47 I should like to thank Dorothy McMillan and Andrew Hook for comments on a draft of this essay.

CHAPTER 10 (COLEMAN)

1 My thanks must go to Colin Kidd and Alex Tyrrell for their support in the writing of this piece.

2 The analysis in this chapter is inspired by, and is intended to elaborate upon, the analysis of the Wallace cult articulated by Graeme Morton, specifically in Graeme Morton, 'The Most Efficacious Patriot: the Heritage of William Wallace in Nineteenth-Century Scotland', *SHR*, lxxvii (1998); A. Morton, *Unionist-Nationalism*.

3 For a historical geographer's view of the changing meanings of Wallace, Bruce and their monuments, see T. Edensor, 'National Identity and the Politics of Memory: Remembering Bruce and Wallace in Symbolic Space', *Environment and Planning D*, 1997, Vol. 29.

4 T. Nairn, *The Break Up of Britain* (London, 1977); see also T. Nairn, 'Scotland and Europe', *New Left Review*, 83, Jan-Feb 1974, 57–82.

5 M. Ash, *The Strange Death of Scottish History* (Edinburgh, 1980).

6 Morton, *Unionist-Nationalism*.

7 Morton's thesis has recently been applied to the development of Scottish art in the nineteenth century in J. Morrison, *Painting the Nation: Identity and Nationalism in Scottish Painting, 1800–1920* (Edinburgh, 2003).

8 E. Hobsbawm, 'Mass Producing Nations: Europe, 1870–1914', in E. Hobsbawm and T. Ranger (eds.), *The Invention of Tradition* (Cambridge, 1983).

9 P. Nora, Introduction, in P. Nora (ed.), *Realms of Memory* (New York, 1998), I, 15.

10 Rogers, *Wallace*.

11 For an enlightening autobiographical sketch of Charles Rogers, see J. M. Allan, 'Who Was Charles Rogers?', *Forth Valley Naturalist and Historian*, xiii (1990).

12 Hobsbawm, 'Mass Producing Nations', 270, 274.

13 E. Renan, 'What Is a Nation?', reprinted in H. K. Babha (ed.), *Nation and Narration* (London, 1990), 20.

14 B. Anderson, *Imagined Communities: Reflections on the Origins and Spread of Nationalism* (London, 1991).

15 G. L. Mosse, *The Nationalisation of the Masses: Political Symbolism and Mass Movements in Germany from the Napoleonic Wars Through the Third Reich* (New York, 1975), 58–61;

Hobsbawm, 'Mass Producing Nations'; R. Gildea, 'The Past in French History' (New Haven, 1994); K. Pomian, 'Franks and Gauls', in Nora, *Realms of Memory*, III.

16 For a compendium of the uses and abuses of the Wallace image, see Morton, *Wallace*, chs. 5, 6, 7.

17 Ash, 'Wallace and Bruce', 83–5; R. Finlay, 'Heroes, Myths and Anniversaries in Modern Scotland', *Scottish Affairs*, no. 18, Winter 1997, 114–18. Ash's reading of the Wallace cult is a good example of the reductionist view of cultural nationalism as a legitimate expression of national consciousness.

18 'Inauguration of a Flagstaff at the Field of Bannockburn', *North British Daily Mail*, 27 June 1870.

19 'Wallace Celebration, The Banquet in the Public Hall, Address by Lord Rosebery', *Glasgow Herald*, 14 September 1897.

20 *The Wallace Monument, Barnweill, Ayrshire* (Glasgow, 1859), 8.

21 Rogers, *Wallace*, 282. For an outline of Dodds' views on the constitutional nature of Scottish history, albeit one with a radically different historical focus, see J. Dodds, *The Fifty Years' Struggle of the Scottish Covenanters, 1638–88* (Edinburgh, 1860), particularly ch. 1.

22 J. Fyfe (ed.), *Autobiography of John McAdam: 1806–1883* (Edinburgh, 1980), 79.

23 C. Rogers, *The National Wallace Monument: the Site and the Design* (Edinburgh, 1860), 14.

24 'Laying of the Foundation-Stone of The Wallace Monument', and editorial piece, *Glasgow Herald*, 25 June 1861.

25 *The Times*, 4 December 1856, quoted in Hanham, *Scottish Nationalism*, 80.

26 Archibald Alison, *Some Account of My Life and Writings: An Autobiography*, 2 vols. (Edinburgh, 1883), II, 317.

27 Alison, *Autobiography*, II, 317.

28 Rogers, *Wallace*, 271.

29 Rogers, *Wallace*, 265–6.

30 'Wallace Celebration, The Banquet in the Public Hall, Address by Lord Rosebery', *Glasgow Herald*, 14 September 1897.

31 T. Carlyle, *Past and Present* (London, 1843), ch. 2.

32 'The Wallace Sword: Transference from Dumbarton to Stirling', *Glasgow Herald*, 17 November 1888.

33 Morton, *Unionist-Nationalism*, 176–84.

34 'Wallace and his Monument', *Tait's Edinburgh Magazine*, Vol. 23, August 1856, 459; C. Rogers, *Social Life in Scotland from Early to Recent Times* (Edinburgh, 1884), I, 138.

35 Hanham, *Scottish Nationalism*, 171–7; see also Morton, *Unionist-Nationalism*, ch. 6.

36 Alison, *Autobiography*, II, 315–17.

37 Hanham, *Scottish Nationalism*, 81–3.

38 An editorial piece in the *Edinburgh Evening Courant* criticised the Wallace Monument foundation-stone ceremony as being anti-English and backward-looking in sentiment and makes reference to the Scottish Rights movement in so doing (reprinted by the *Glasgow Herald*, 27 June 1861).

39 C. Rogers, *The Serpent's Track: A Narrative of Twenty-Two Years Persecution* (London, 1880), 5.

40 Morton, *Unionist Nationalism*, ch. 4: Morton, 'Efficacious Patriot', 244.

41 Alison, *Autobiography*, II, 30–1.

42 Rogers, *Serpent's Track*, 6, original emphasis.

43 Rogers, *Autobiography*, 133.

44 Rogers, *Serpent's Track*, 6; Rogers, *Autobiography*, 132–5. Alison also describes the meeting in his *Autobiography*, II, 316–17.

45 A. T. Story, *The Life and Work of Sir Joseph Noel Paton, RSA, LLD, Her Majesty's Limner*

for Scotland (London, 1895), 15; M. H. Noel-Paton and J. P. Campbell, *Noel Paton: 1821–1901* (Edinburgh, 1990), 32; Rogers, *Autobiography*, 150.
46 Quoted in Rogers, *Autobiography*, 151.
47 Rogers, *Autobiography*, 150, 152.
48 Quoted in Rogers, *Wallace*, 273.
49 Rogers, *Wallace*, 277–8; 'Unveiling of the Wallace Statue', *Stirling Journal*, 1 July 1887.
50 F. Walker, 'National Romanticism and the Architecture of the City', in G. Gordon (ed.), *Perspectives of the Scottish City* (Aberdeen, 1985), 137; Story, *Sir Joseph Noel Paton*, 15; *Scotsman*, 28 June 1870.
51 R. MacInnes, '"Rubblemania": Ethic and Aesthetic in Scottish Architecture', *Journal of Design History*, ix (1996), 137, 140–1; Walker, 'National Romanticism', 135–7.
52 For Rogers' perspective on these events, countering those reported in the contemporary press, see Rogers, *Autobiography*, ch. 6.
53 Morton, *Wallace*, 79. The phrase is Morton's.
54 Fyfe (ed.), *Autobiography of John McAdam*, 80, 174–6.
55 Between 1856 and 1861, while Rogers was coordinating the raising of subscriptions, £6,766 was raised; under the stewardship of William Burns and the McAdams, between 1861 and 1869, the sum was £6,123. 'The Wallace Monument at Stirling', *Glasgow Herald*, 13 September 1869. See also, Rogers, *Autobiography*, chs. 5–6.
56 *Glasgow Herald*, 13 September 1869.
57 It was originally intended that the portrait be presented to the Rev. Dr Rogers' wife but, as she was unwell, Rogers saw fit to be present in order to receive the honour in person.
58 Fyfe (ed.), *Autobiography of John McAdam*, 81.
59 'Unveiling of Burns Bust at Stirling', *Glasgow Herald*, 6 September 1886.
60 Hanham, *Scottish Nationalism*, 83.
61 'Wallace Monument at Stirling: Unveiling of the Statue of Wallace', *Glasgow Herald*, 25 June 1887.
62 'Unveiling of the Wallace Statue', *Stirling Journal*, 1 July 1887.
63 'Wallace Celebration: Anniversary of the Battle of Stirling Bridge', *Glasgow Herald*, 14 September 1897.
64 *The Times*, 14 September 1897.
65 Quoted in 'Press Opinions on Rosebery's Speech', *Evening Citizen*, 14 September 1897.
66 'Scottish Home Rulers and Wallace', *North British Daily Mail*, 13 September 1897.

CHAPTER 11 (CALDWELL)
1 Hary, *Wallace*, I, 156, 140, 214.
2 *Wallace Monument Reports*, 2 vols., National Museums of Scotland, particularly Vol. 2.
3 Charles Rogers, *The Book of Wallace* (Grampian Club, 1889), Vol. 2, 299–301.
4 *Acts of the Lords of Council in Public Affairs, 1501–1554*, ed. R. K. Hannay (Edinburgh, 1932), 5.
5 John Irving, *History of Dumbartonshire Castle, County and Burgh* (Dumbarton, 1917–24), 104.
6 Iain MacIvor, *Dumbarton Castle* (official guide) (Edinburgh, 1958), 7.
7 Dorothy Wordsworth, *Recollections of a Tour Made in Scotland*, ed. Carol Kyros Walker (Yale, 1997), 79.
8 *Treasurer's Accounts*, iii, 175.
9 David H. Caldwell, 'Royal Patronage of Arms and Armour Making in Fifteenth

and Sixteenth-Century Scotland', in *Scottish Weapons & Fortifications, 1100–1800*, ed. David H. Caldwell (Edinburgh, 1981), 82–3.

10 *Exchequer Rolls*, x, 182.
11 Samuel Rush Meyrick, *A Critical Inquiry into Antient Armour* (London, n.d. [1824]), Vol. 2, 177. There is an illustration of the hilt of the Chester sword in the *British Museum Guide to Mediaeval Antiquities* (1924), 230, fig. 148.
12 C. N. McIntyre North, *Book of the Club of True Highlanders* (London, 1880), II, pl. XLI.
13 John Wallace, *Scottish Swords and Dirks* (London, 1970), 11–12.
14 Charles E. Whitelaw, *Scottish Arms Makers* (London, 1977), 170.
15 I am grateful to Carol Archibald, General Manager of Stirling District Tourism Limited, and Eleanor Muir, Manager at the Wallace Monument, for allowing me the opportunity to study the Wallace Sword.

CHAPTER 12 (FINLAY)

1 Colin MacArthur, *Brigadoon, Braveheart and the Scots: Distortions of Scotland in Hollywood Cinema* (London, 2003).
2 See for example the correspondence in the *Herald*, 10–19 February 1997.
3 For a discussion of some of these issues, see Ted Cowan, 'The Wallace Factor in Scottish History', in R. Jackson and S. Wood (eds.), *Images of Scotland* (Dundee, 1997).
4 For a brief discussion of the role of heroes and myths in history, see Oliver Zimmer, *Nationalism in Europe, 1890–1940* (Basingstoke, 2003), 27–50.
5 See J. F. McMillan, *Twentieth Century France: Politics and Society, 1898–1991* (London, 1992), 92.
6 Morton, *Wallace*, 108–11.
7 *Ibid.*, 88.
8 Some of the key nineteenth-century texts are: J. D. Carrick, *The Life of Sir William Wallace* (London, 1894); D. Macrae, *The Story of William Wallace: Scotland's National Hero* (Glasgow, 1905); A. F. Murison, *Sir William Wallace: Famous Scots Series* (Edinburgh, 1898).
9 John MacIntosh, *Scotland from the Earliest Times to the Present Century* (*Stories of the Nations Series*) (London, 1890), 52.
10 Thomas Carlyle, *Past and Present*, Vol. I (London, 1843 edn), ch. ii.
11 Sir Herbert Maxwell, *The Making of Scotland: lectures on the War of Independence delivered at the University of Glasgow* (Glasgow, 1911).
12 Sir Henry Craik, *A Century of Scottish History* (Edinburgh, 1901); J. Colville, *By-ways of Scottish History* (Edinburgh, 1897).
13 Colin Kidd, 'The Strange Death of Scottish History Revisited: Constructions of the Past in Scotland *c.* 1790–1914', *SHR*, lxxvi (1997).
14 The Duke of Atholl *et al*, *A Scotsman's Heritage* (London, n.d.), 8.
15 John Buchan, *Memory Hold the Door* (London, 1940), 198.
16 See R. J. Finlay, 'National Identity in Crisis?: Politicians, Intellectuals and the 'End of Scotland', 1920–1939', *History*, 97, 256 (1994), 240–59.
17 A good example of Unionist negativity is the statement by Bob Boothby, MP for Aberdeenshire: 'prior to 1707, the Scots were a miserable pack of savages, living in incredible poverty, and playing no part in the development of civilisation'. *The Nation*, 9 March 1929.
18 National Library of Scotland, Scottish National Party (Miscellaneous Collections), Acc.7295.
19 See I. G. C. Hutchison, *Scottish Politics in the Twentieth Century* (Basingstoke, 2001), 72–9.
20 See J. Mitchell, *Strategies for Self-Government: The Campaign for a Scottish Parliament* (Edinburgh, 1996), 257–8.

21 A good example of this line of thinking is to be found in Esmond Wright, 'In Defence of the United Kingdom', in Neil MacCormick (ed.), *The Scottish Debate* (Oxford, 1970), 103–21.

22 *Scotsman*, 27 November 1993.

23 *Liberty*, March 1920, 28.

24 Thomas Johnston, *A History of the Scottish Working Class* (Glasgow, n.d.), 23.

25 James D. Young, *The Rousing of the Scottish Working Class* (London, 1979), 177.

26 *House of Commons Parliamentary Debates*, 5th series, Vol. 307, col. 127.

27 R. J. Finlay, *Independent and Free: Scottish Politics and the Origins of the Scottish National Party, 1918–1945* (Edinburgh, 1994), 1–24.

28 *Scottish Home Rule*, September 1925.

29 See R. J. Finlay, *A Partnership for Good: Scottish Politics and the Union Since 1880* (Edinburgh, 1997), 95–102, and D. Howell, *A Lost Left: Three Studies in Socialism and Nationalism* (Manchester, 1986), 229–65.

30 For example, see the transcript of a radio broadcast by James Maxton, Bridgeton MP for Glasgow, National Library of Scotland, A. A. MacEwen Collection, Acc. 6113.

31 *Scots Independent*, February 1929, 39.

32 *Scots Independent*, June 1930, 6.

33 *Ibid.*, September 1931, 163.

34 *Scottish Home Rule*, August 1923; *Scots Independent*, August 1931, 152.

35 *Ibid.*

36 *Ibid.*, September 1931, 171.

37 *Liberty*, June 1920, 59.

38 *Scots Independent*, August 1931, 151.

39 Quoted in *Scots Independent*, December 1929, 19.

40 *Ibid.*, August 1931, 151.

41 *Ibid.*, March 1934, 74.

42 *Ibid.*, August 1931, 153.

43 See Finlay, *Independent and Free*, 126–62.

44 Quoted in J. D. Young, 'Marxism and the Scottish National Question', *Journal of Contemporary History*, 1983.

45 *Scottish Scene*, 1935.

46 *Scottish Journey* (London, 1983 edn), 180.

47 Edwin Muir, *Scott and Scotland: The predicament of the Scottish Writer. Introduction by Allan Massie* (Edinburgh, 1982), 32, 45. On Gibbon and the Picts, see Colin Kidd, 'The Ideological Uses of the Picts, 1707–c. 1990', in E .J. Cowan and R. J. Finlay (eds.), *Scottish History: The Power of the Past* (Edinburgh, 2002), 181–2.

48 Finlay, *Independent and Free*, 225–43.

49 See for example the weight attached to Fletcher in Morrison Davidson, *Leaves from the Books of Scots: The Story of William Wallace, Robert the Bruce, Fletcher of Saltoun and other Patriots* (Scottish Secretariat, n.d.).

50 Hanham, *Scottish Nationalism*, 214.

51 See R. J. Finlay, 'Scotland and the Monarchy in the Twentieth Century', in W. L. Miller, *Anglo-Scottish Relations, 1900–2000: Proceedings of the British Academy* (Oxford, 2005).

52 A good example of the growth in republican-type ideals can be seen in the opening of the Scottish Parliament in 2004. Apart from the fact that there was a republican counter-celebration on Calton Hill that attracted a large number of the literati, much of the ceremony alluded to republican themes, such as the opening fanfare for the common man, the sentiments of Edwin Morgan's poem and the singing of Burns's *Auld Lang Syne*.

Index